NO LONGER PROPERTY OF
SEATTLE PUBLIC LIBRARY

CREATED BY **JOSS WHEDON**

GREG **PAK**   DAN **McDAID**   MARCELO **COSTA**

firefly™

THE UNIFICATION WAR PART THREE

Published by

BOOM!
STUDIOS

Designer
Scott Newman with **Marie Krupina**

Assistant Editor
Gavin Gronenthal

Editor
Chris Rosa

Executive Editor
Jeanine Schaefer

Special Thanks to **Sierra Hahn**, **Becca J Sadowski**,
Nicole Spiegel and **Carol Roeder**.

Ross Richie CEO & Founder
Joy Huffman CFO
Matt Gagnon Editor-in-Chief
Filip Sablik President, Publishing & Marketing
Stephen Christy President, Development
Lance Kreiter Vice President, Licensing & Merchandising
Bryce Carlson Vice President, Editorial & Creative Strategy
Kate Henning Director, Operations
Spencer Simpson Director, Sales
Scott Newman Manager, Production Design
Elyse Strandberg Manager, Finance
Sierra Hahn Executive Editor
Dafna Pleban Senior Editor
Shannon Watters Senior Editor
Eric Harburn Senior Editor
Sophie Philips-Roberts Associate Editor
Amanda LaFranco Associate Editor
Jonathan Manning Associate Editor
Gavin Gronenthal Assistant Editor
Gwen Waller Assistant Editor
Allyson Gronowitz Assistant Editor

Ramiro Portnoy Assistant Editor
Kenzie Rzonca Assistant Editor
Shelby Netschke Editorial Assistant
Michelle Ankley Design Lead
Marie Krupina Production Designer
Grace Park Production Designer
Chelsea Roberts Production Designer
Samantha Knapp Production Design Assistant
José Meza Consumer Sales Lead
Esther Kim Marketing Lead
Breanna Sarpy Marketing Coordinator
Amanda Lawson Marketing Assistant
Morgan Perry Retail Sales Lead
Megan Christopher Operations Coordinator
Rodrigo Hernandez Operations Coordinator
Zipporah Smith Operations Coordinator
Jason Lee Senior Accountant
Sabrina Lesin Accounting Assistant
Lauren Alexander Administrative Assistant

FIREFLY: THE UNIFICATION WAR Volume Three,
August 2021. Published by BOOM! Studios, a division of
Boom Entertainment, Inc. © 2021 20th Television. Originally
published in single magazine form as FIREFLY No. 9-12. ©
2019 20th Television. BOOM! Studios™ and the BOOM!
Studios logo are trademarks of Boom Entertainment, Inc.,
registered in various countries and categories. All characters,
events, and institutions depicted herein are fictional. Any
similarity between any of the names, characters, persons,
events, and/or institutions in this publication to actual names,
characters, and persons, whether living or dead, events, and/
or institutions is unintended and purely coincidental. BOOM!
Studios does not read or accept unsolicited submissions of
ideas, stories, or artwork.

BOOM! Studios, 5670 Wilshire Boulevard, Suite 400, Los
Angeles, CA 90036-5679. Printed in China. First Printing.

ISBN: 978-1-68415-694-8
eISBN: 978-1-64668-238-6

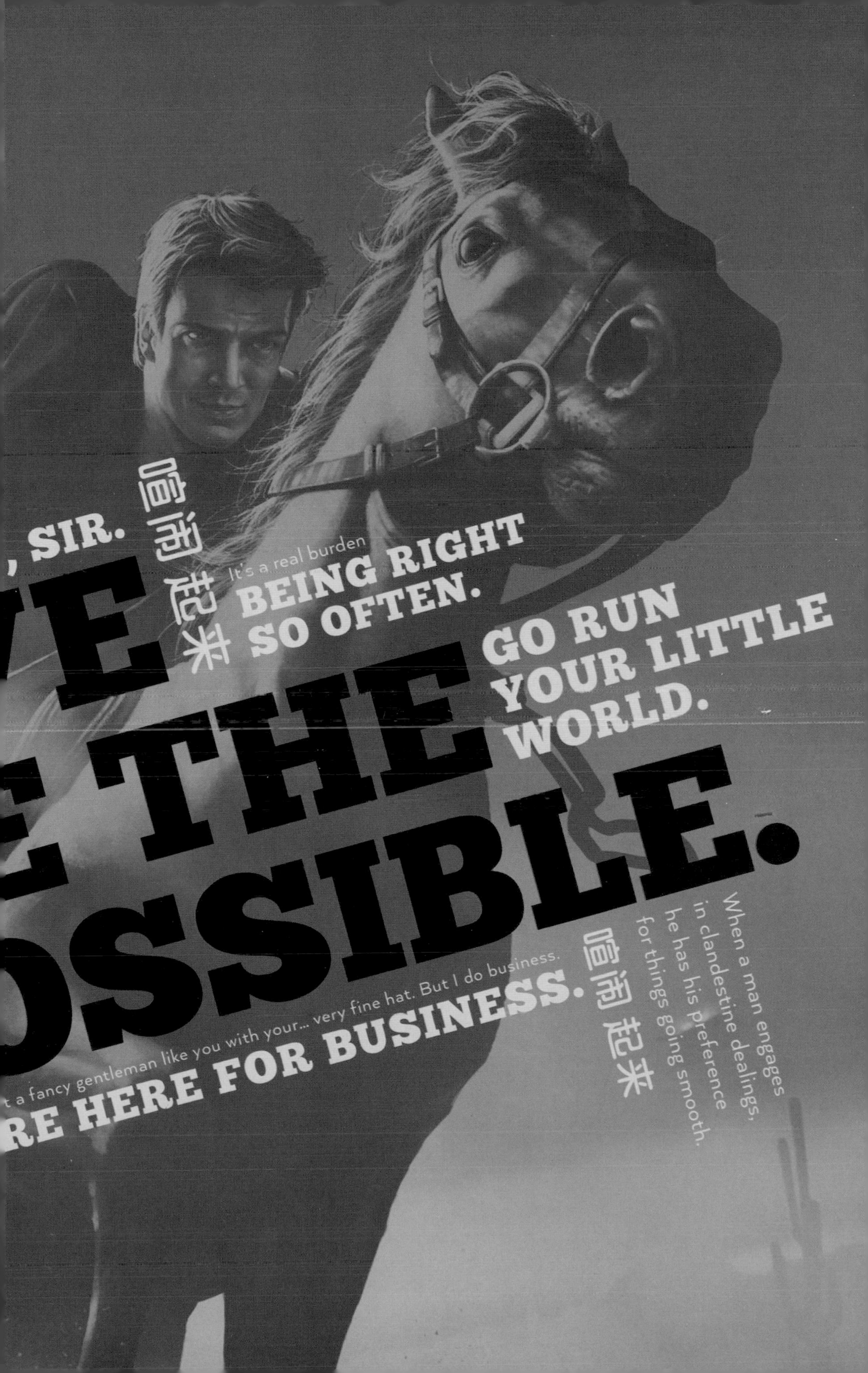

, SIR.
喧闹起来
It's a real burden
BEING RIGHT
SO OFTEN.
VE
E THE
OSSIBLE.
GO RUN
YOUR LITTLE
WORLD.
t a fancy gentleman like you with your... very fine hat. But I do business.
RE HERE FOR BUSINESS.
喧闹起来
When a man engages
in clandestine dealings,
he has his preference
for things going smooth.

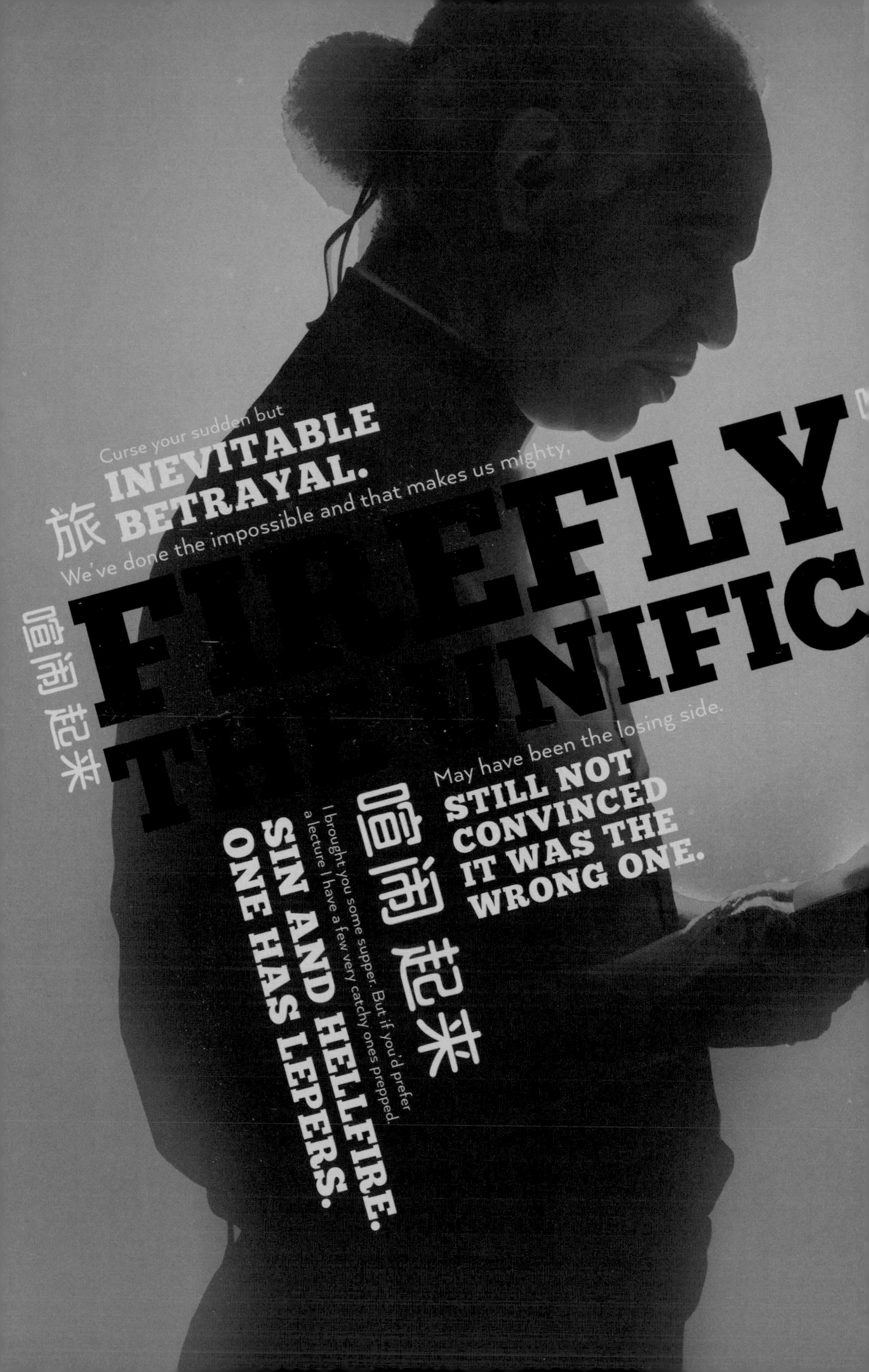
Curse your sudden but
INEVITABLE
BETRAYAL.
旅
We've done the impossible and that makes us mighty,
喧闹起来
May have been the losing side.
STILL NOT
CONVINCED
IT WAS THE
WRONG ONE.
喧闹起来
I brought you some supper. But if you'd prefer
a lecture I have a few very catchy ones prepped.
SIN AND HELLFIRE.
ONE HAS LEPERS.

闹 起来

OH, I GOT HEATHENS APLENTY RIGHT HERE.

ATION WAR

喧闹 起来

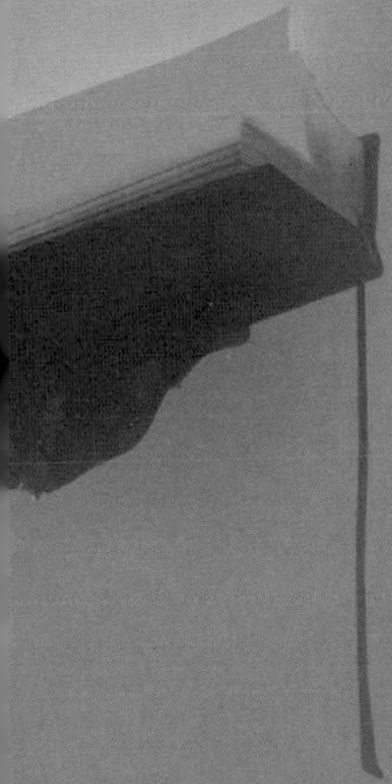

Created by

Joss Whedon

Written by

Greg Pak

Illustrated by

Dan McDaid

with Inks by **Vincenzo Federici**, Chapters Ten through Twelve

Colored by

Marcelo Costa

and **Joana LaFuente**, Chapter Ten

Lettered by

Jim Campbell

Cover by

Lee Garbett

CHAPTER NINE

喧闹 起来

旅

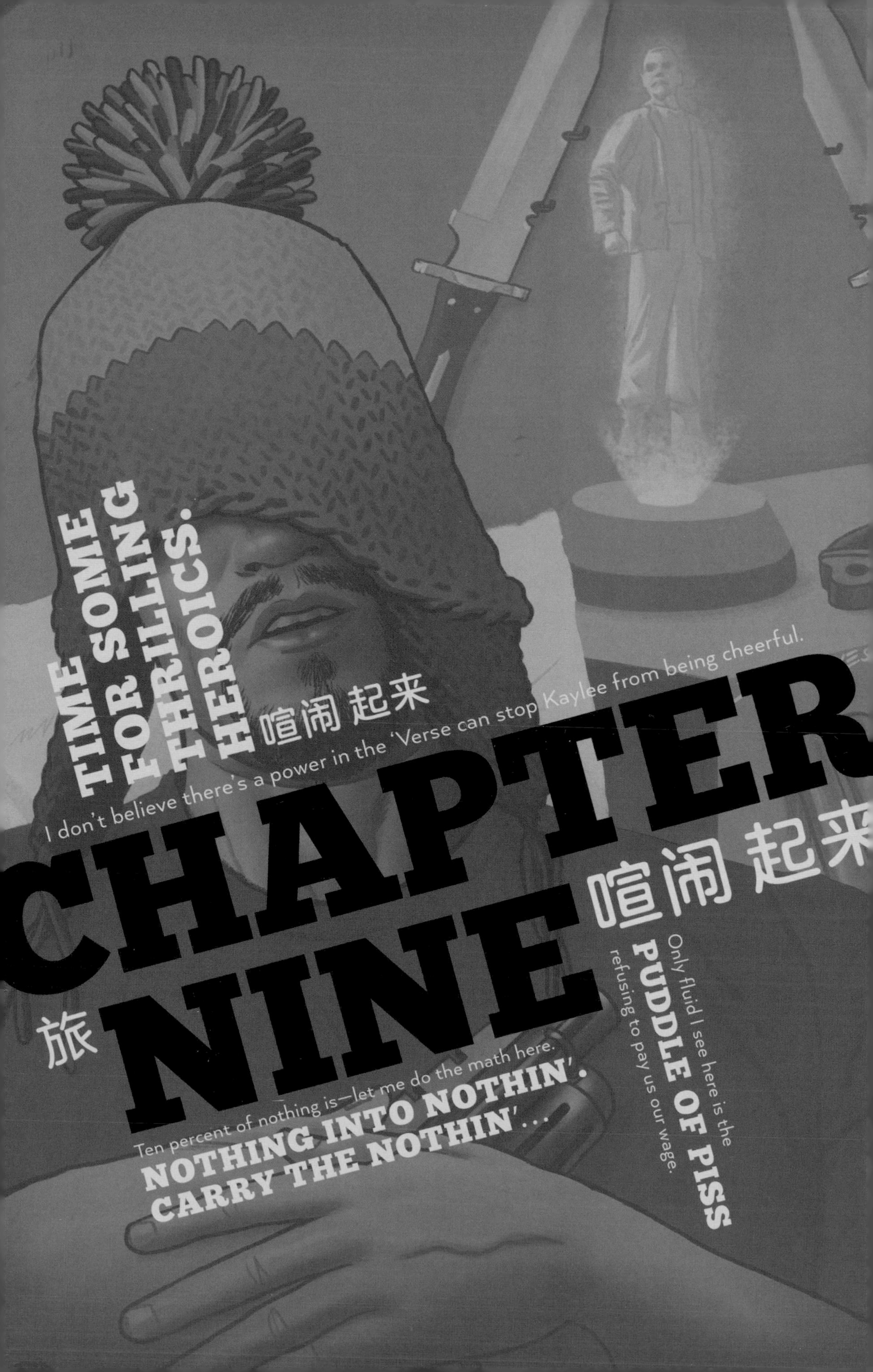

TIME FOR SOME THRILLING HEROICS.

喧闹 起来

I don't believe there's a power in the 'Verse can stop Kaylee from being cheerful.

Ten percent of nothing is—let me do the math here. **NOTHING INTO NOTHIN'. CARRY THE NOTHIN'...**

Only fluid I see here is the **PUDDLE OF PISS** refusing to pay us our wage.

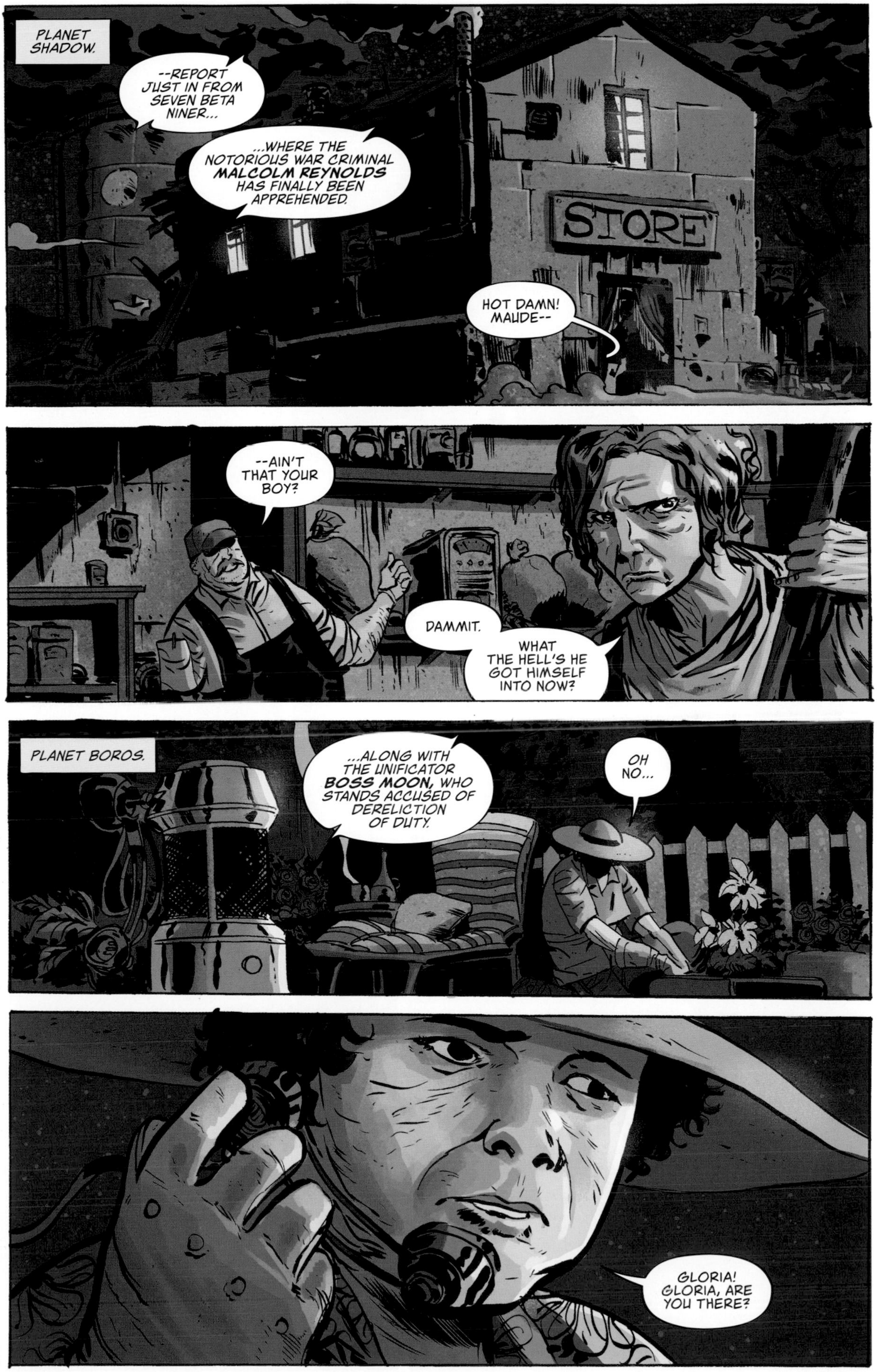

PLANET SHADOW.
--REPORT JUST IN FROM SEVEN BETA NINER...
...WHERE THE NOTORIOUS WAR CRIMINAL MALCOLM REYNOLDS HAS FINALLY BEEN APPREHENDED.
STORE
HOT DAMN! MAUDE--
--AIN'T THAT YOUR BOY?
DAMMIT.
WHAT THE HELL'S HE GOT HIMSELF INTO NOW?
PLANET BOROS.
...ALONG WITH THE UNIFICATOR BOSS MOON, WHO STANDS ACCUSED OF DERELICTION OF DUTY.
OH NO...
GLORIA! GLORIA, ARE YOU THERE?

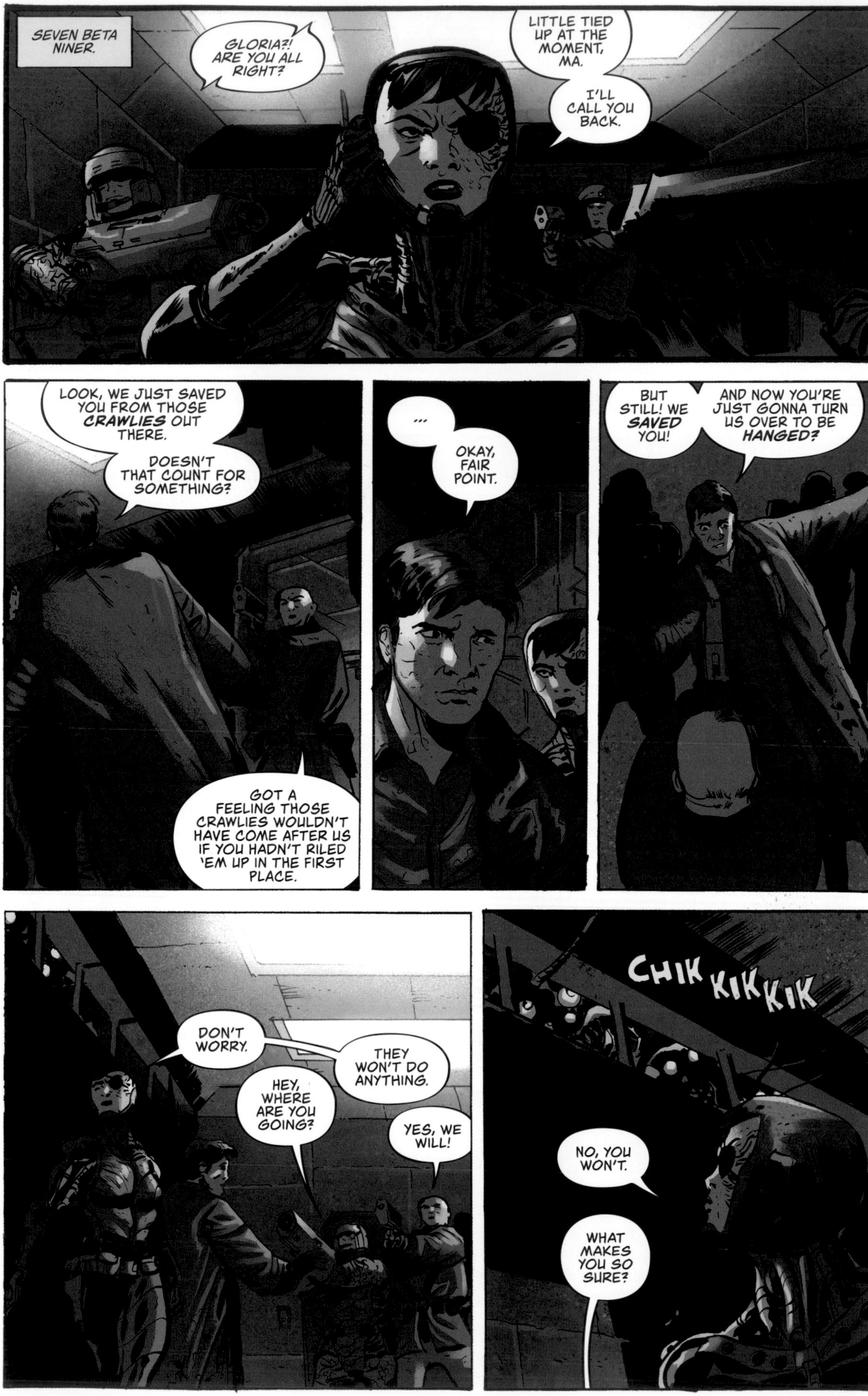
SEVEN BETA NINER.
GLORIA?! ARE YOU ALL RIGHT?
LITTLE TIED UP AT THE MOMENT, MA.
I'LL CALL YOU BACK.
LOOK, WE JUST SAVED YOU FROM THOSE CRAWLIES OUT THERE.
DOESN'T THAT COUNT FOR SOMETHING?
GOT A FEELING THOSE CRAWLIES WOULDN'T HAVE COME AFTER US IF YOU HADN'T RILED 'EM UP IN THE FIRST PLACE.
...
OKAY, FAIR POINT.
BUT STILL! WE SAVED YOU!
AND NOW YOU'RE JUST GONNA TURN US OVER TO BE HANGED?
DON'T WORRY.
THEY WON'T DO ANYTHING.
HEY, WHERE ARE YOU GOING?
YES, WE WILL!
CHIK KIK KIK
NO, YOU WON'T.
WHAT MAKES YOU SO SURE?

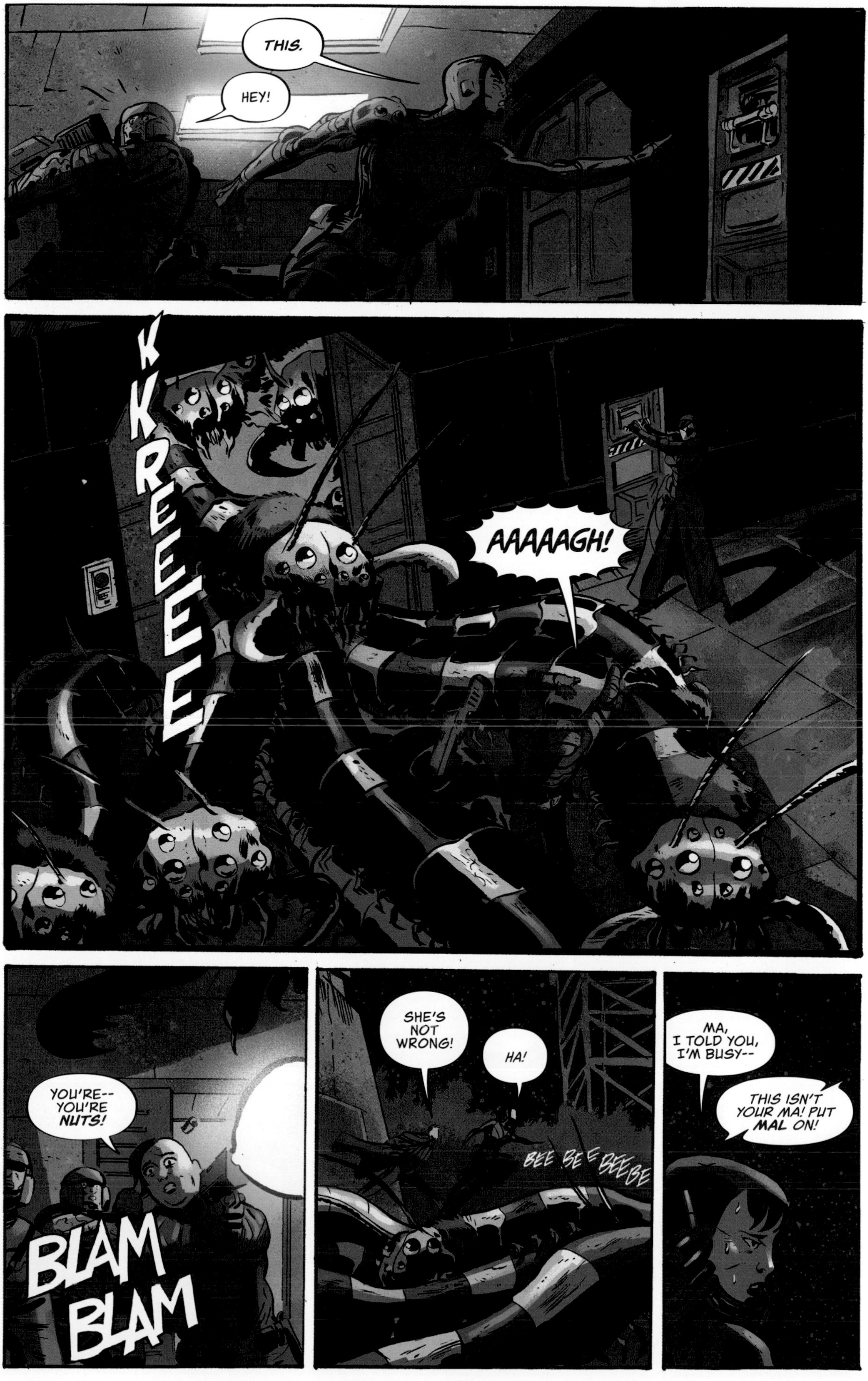
THIS.
HEY!
KKREEEEEE
AAAAAGH!
YOU'RE-- YOU'RE NUTS!
BLAM BLAM
SHE'S NOT WRONG!
HA!
BEE BEE BEE BE
MA, I TOLD YOU, I'M BUSY--
THIS ISN'T YOUR MA! PUT MAL ON!

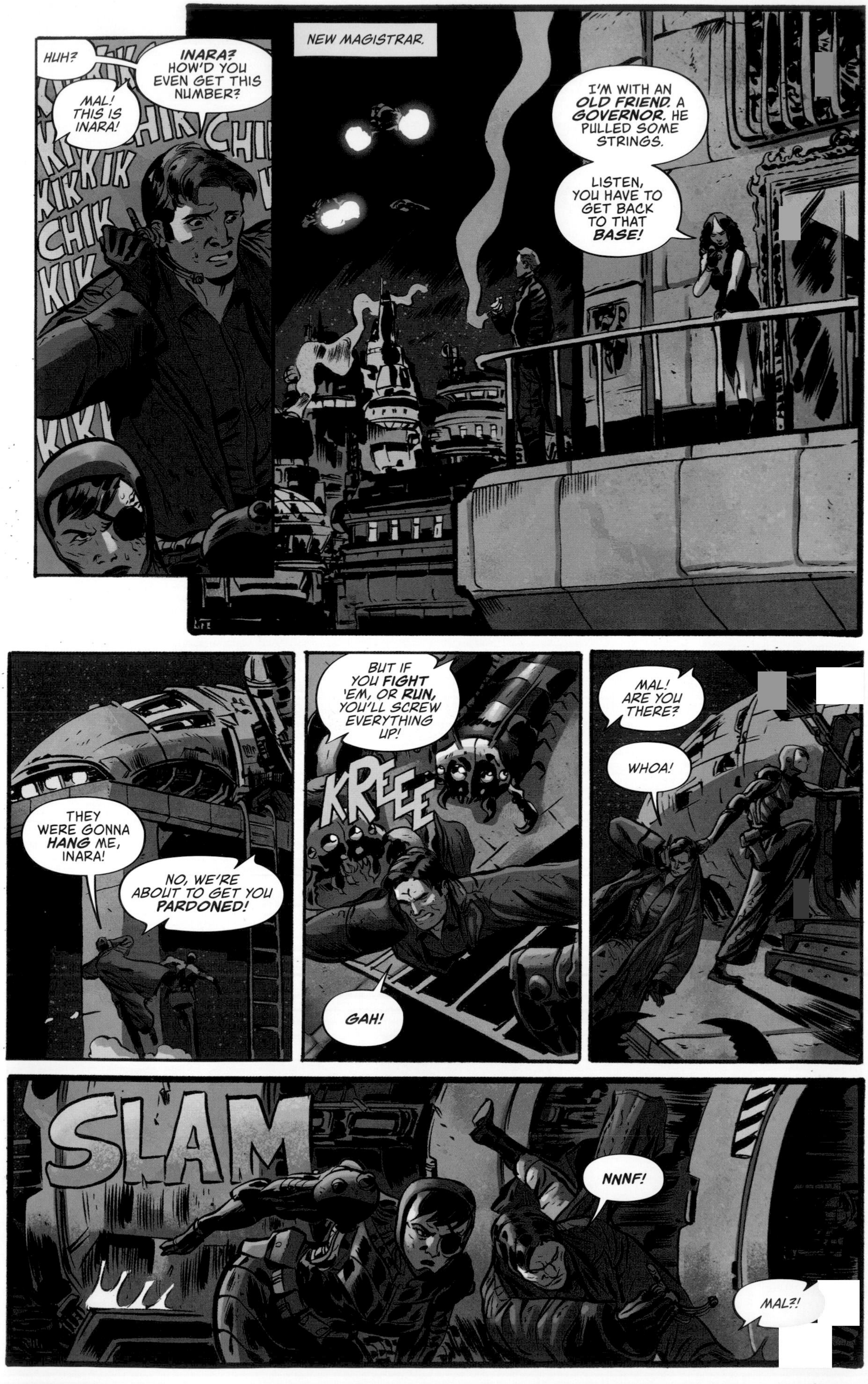

HUH?
MAL! THIS IS INARA!
INARA? HOW'D YOU EVEN GET THIS NUMBER?
KIKKIK CHIK CHIK KIKKIK CHIK KIK
NEW MAGISTRAR.
I'M WITH AN OLD FRIEND. A GOVERNOR. HE PULLED SOME STRINGS.
LISTEN, YOU HAVE TO GET BACK TO THAT BASE!
THEY WERE GONNA HANG ME, INARA!
NO, WE'RE ABOUT TO GET YOU PARDONED!
BUT IF YOU FIGHT 'EM, OR RUN, YOU'LL SCREW EVERYTHING UP!
KREEE
GAH!
MAL! ARE YOU THERE?
WHOA!
SLAM
NNNF!
MAL?!

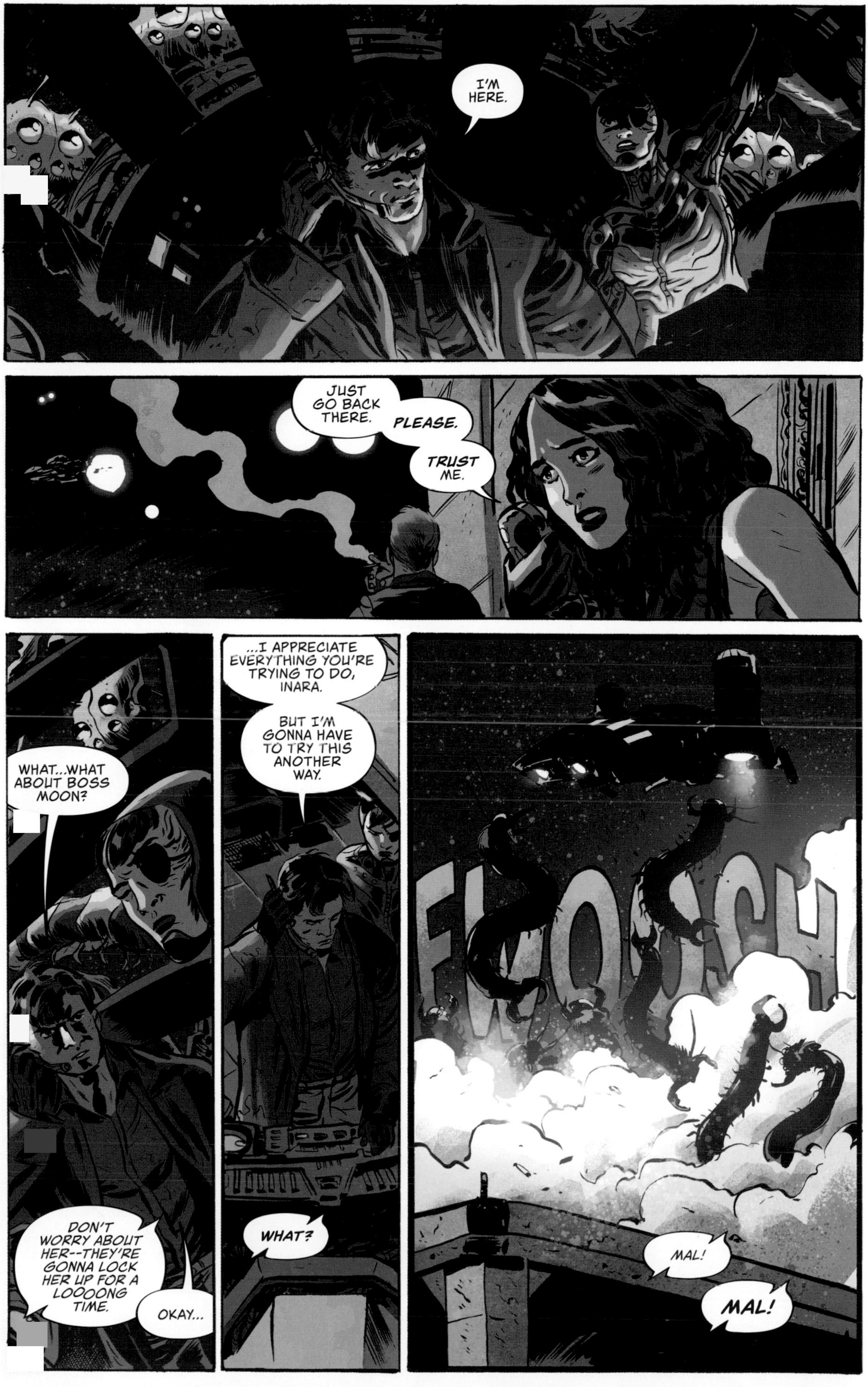
I'M HERE.
JUST GO BACK THERE.
PLEASE.
TRUST ME.
WHAT...WHAT ABOUT BOSS MOON?
DON'T WORRY ABOUT HER--THEY'RE GONNA LOCK HER UP FOR A LOOOONG TIME.
OKAY...
...I APPRECIATE EVERYTHING YOU'RE TRYING TO DO, INARA.
BUT I'M GONNA HAVE TO TRY THIS ANOTHER WAY.
WHAT?
MAL!
MAL!

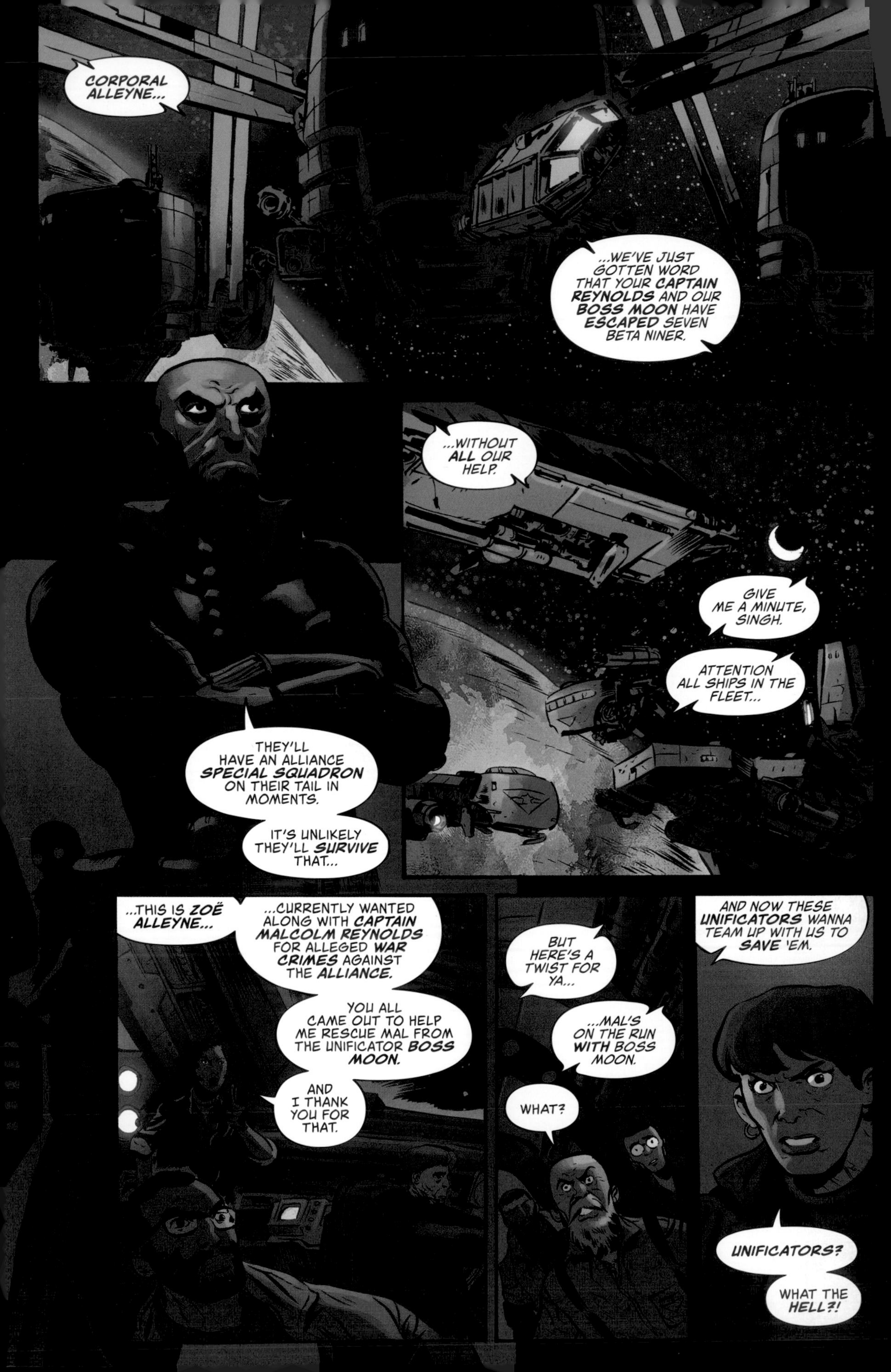
CORPORAL ALLEYNE...
...WE'VE JUST GOTTEN WORD THAT YOUR CAPTAIN REYNOLDS AND OUR BOSS MOON HAVE ESCAPED SEVEN BETA NINER.
...WITHOUT ALL OUR HELP.
GIVE ME A MINUTE, SINGH.
ATTENTION ALL SHIPS IN THE FLEET...
THEY'LL HAVE AN ALLIANCE SPECIAL SQUADRON ON THEIR TAIL IN MOMENTS.
IT'S UNLIKELY THEY'LL SURVIVE THAT...
...THIS IS ZOË ALLEYNE...
...CURRENTLY WANTED ALONG WITH CAPTAIN MALCOLM REYNOLDS FOR ALLEGED WAR CRIMES AGAINST THE ALLIANCE.
YOU ALL CAME OUT TO HELP ME RESCUE MAL FROM THE UNIFICATOR BOSS MOON.
AND I THANK YOU FOR THAT.
BUT HERE'S A TWIST FOR YA...
...MAL'S ON THE RUN WITH BOSS MOON.
WHAT?
AND NOW THESE UNIFICATORS WANNA TEAM UP WITH US TO SAVE 'EM.
UNIFICATORS?
WHAT THE HELL?!

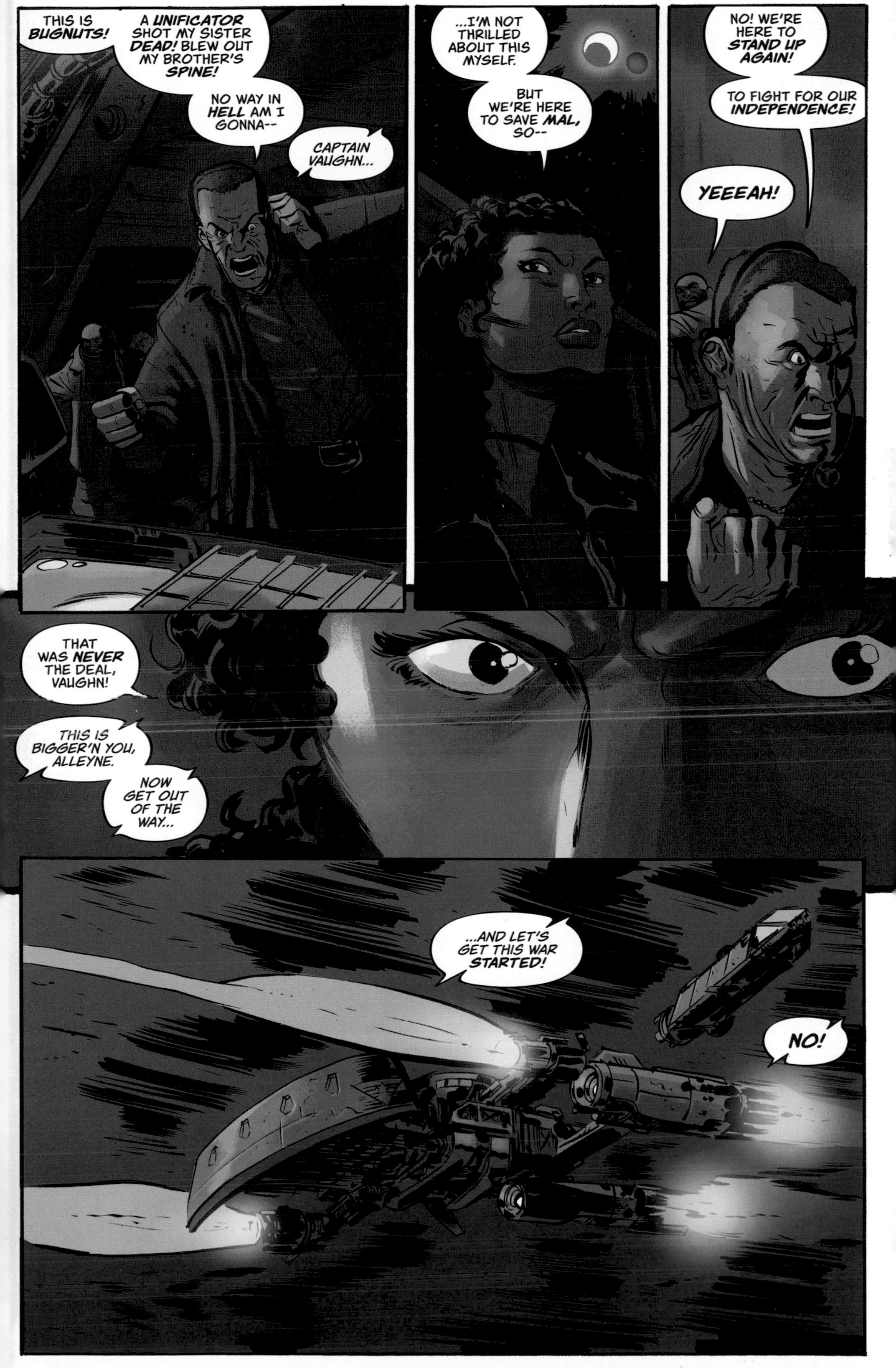
THIS IS BUGNUTS!
A UNIFICATOR SHOT MY SISTER DEAD! BLEW OUT MY BROTHER'S SPINE!
NO WAY IN HELL AM I GONNA--
CAPTAIN VAUGHN...
...I'M NOT THRILLED ABOUT THIS MYSELF.
BUT WE'RE HERE TO SAVE MAL, SO--
NO! WE'RE HERE TO STAND UP AGAIN!
TO FIGHT FOR OUR INDEPENDENCE!
YEEEAH!
THAT WAS NEVER THE DEAL, VAUGHN!
THIS IS BIGGER'N YOU, ALLEYNE.
NOW GET OUT OF THE WAY...
...AND LET'S GET THIS WAR STARTED!
NO!

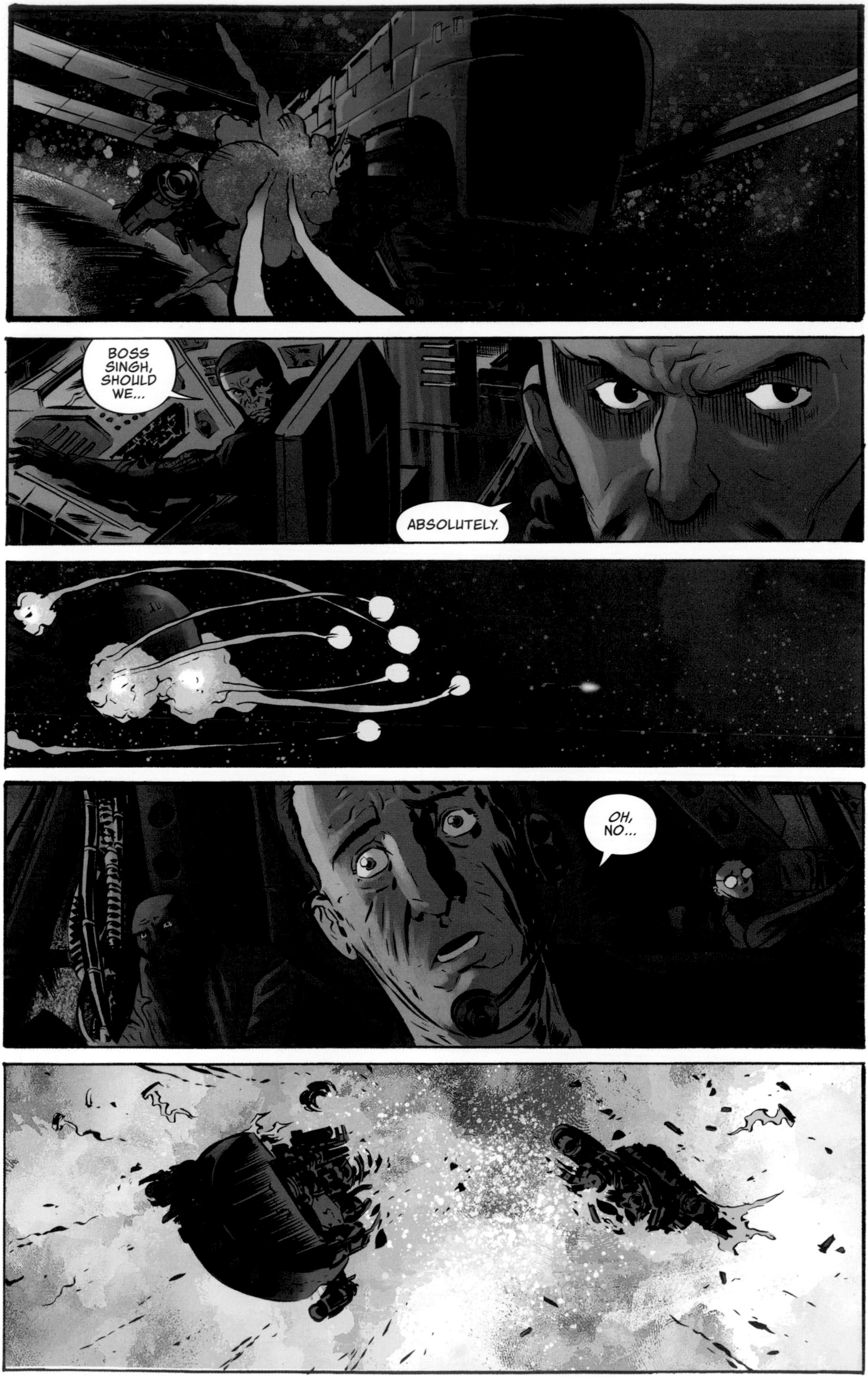
BOSS SINGH, SHOULD WE...
ABSOLUTELY.
OH, NO...

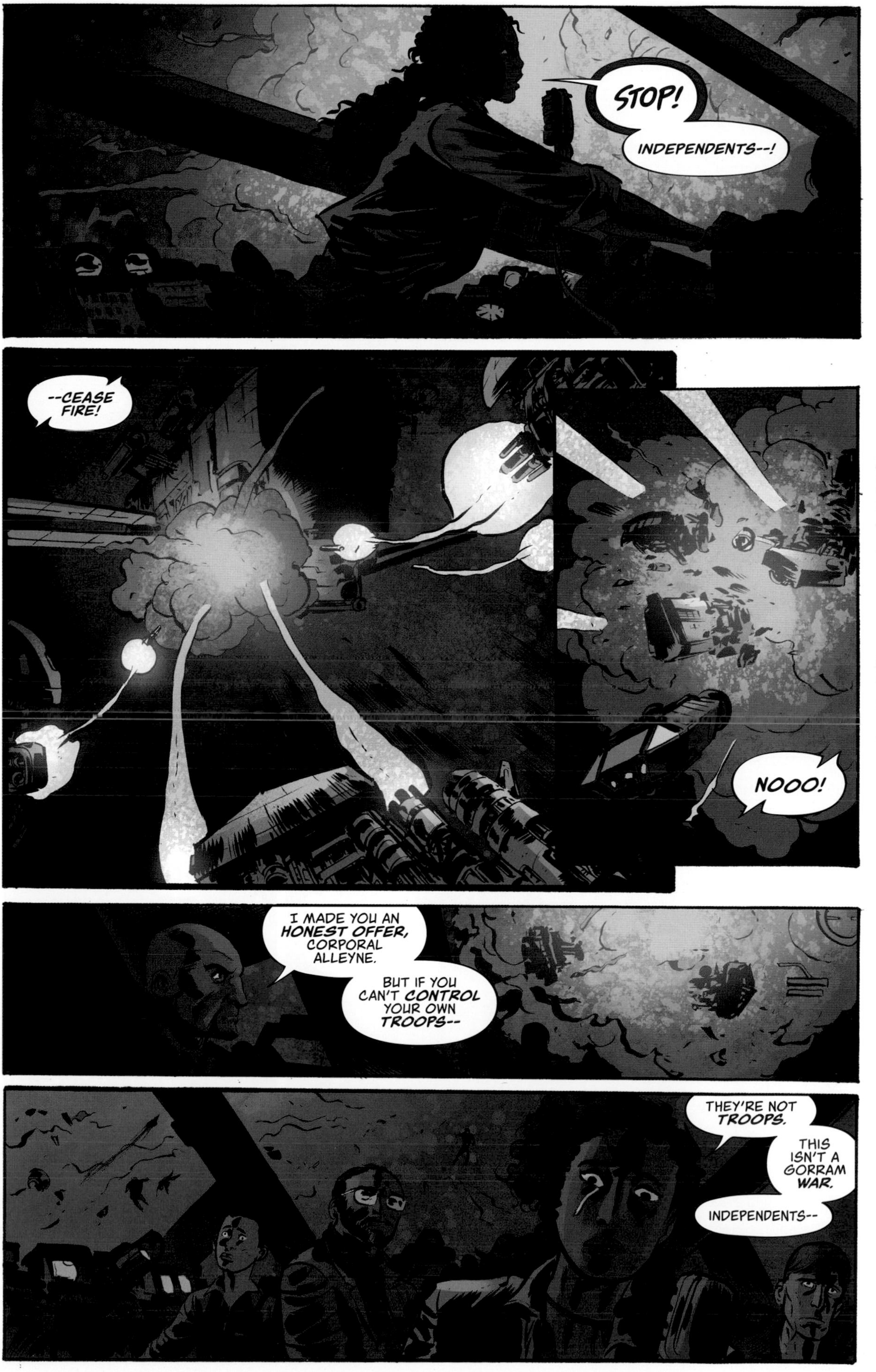
STOP!
INDEPENDENTS--!
--CEASE FIRE!
NOOO!
I MADE YOU AN HONEST OFFER, CORPORAL ALLEYNE.
BUT IF YOU CAN'T CONTROL YOUR OWN TROOPS--
THEY'RE NOT TROOPS.
THIS ISN'T A GORRAM WAR.
INDEPENDENTS--

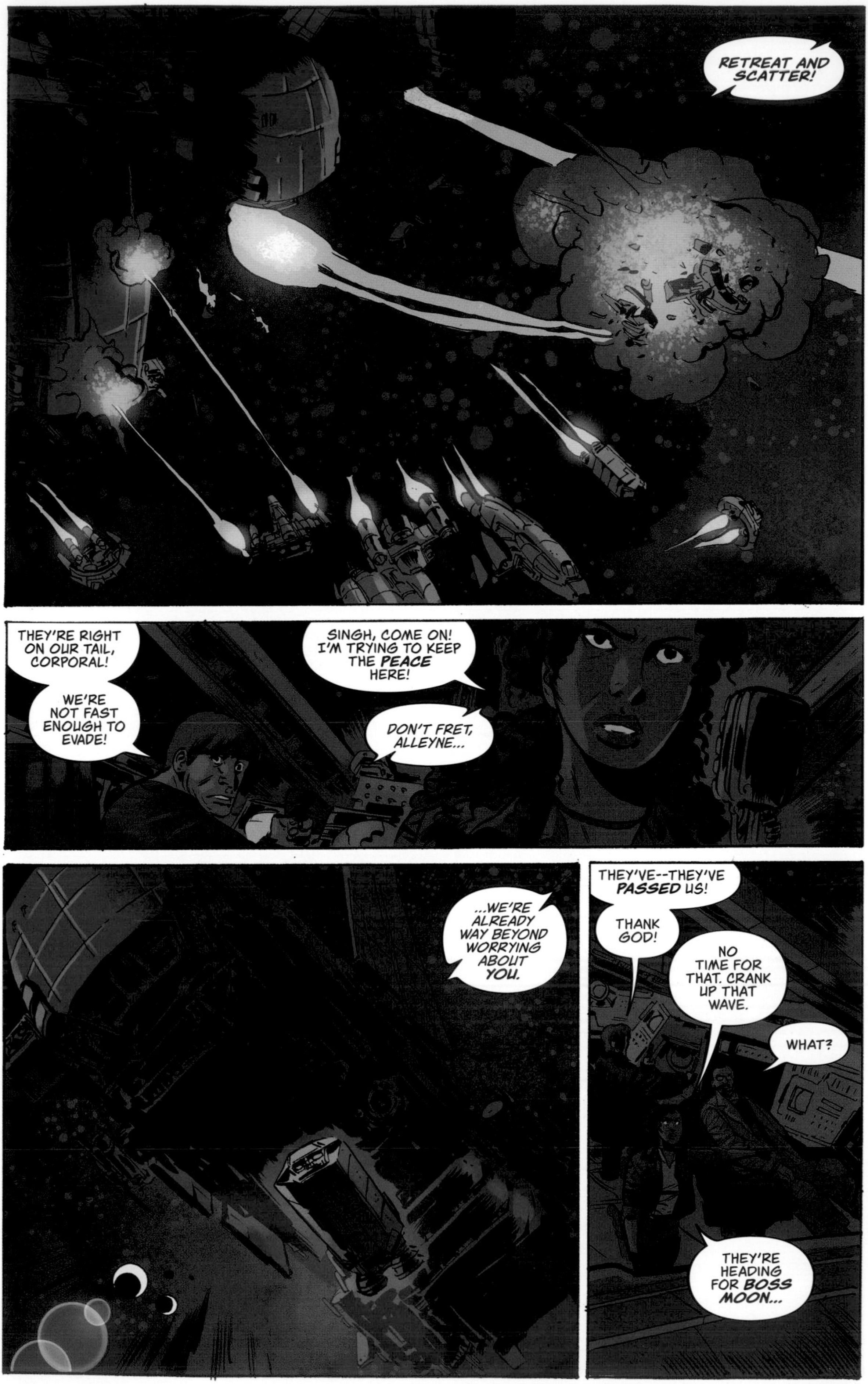
RETREAT AND SCATTER!
THEY'RE RIGHT ON OUR TAIL, CORPORAL!
WE'RE NOT FAST ENOUGH TO EVADE!
SINGH, COME ON! I'M TRYING TO KEEP THE PEACE HERE!
DON'T FRET, ALLEYNE...
...WE'RE ALREADY WAY BEYOND WORRYING ABOUT YOU.
THEY'VE--THEY'VE PASSED US!
THANK GOD!
NO TIME FOR THAT. CRANK UP THAT WAVE.
WHAT?
THEY'RE HEADING FOR BOSS MOON...

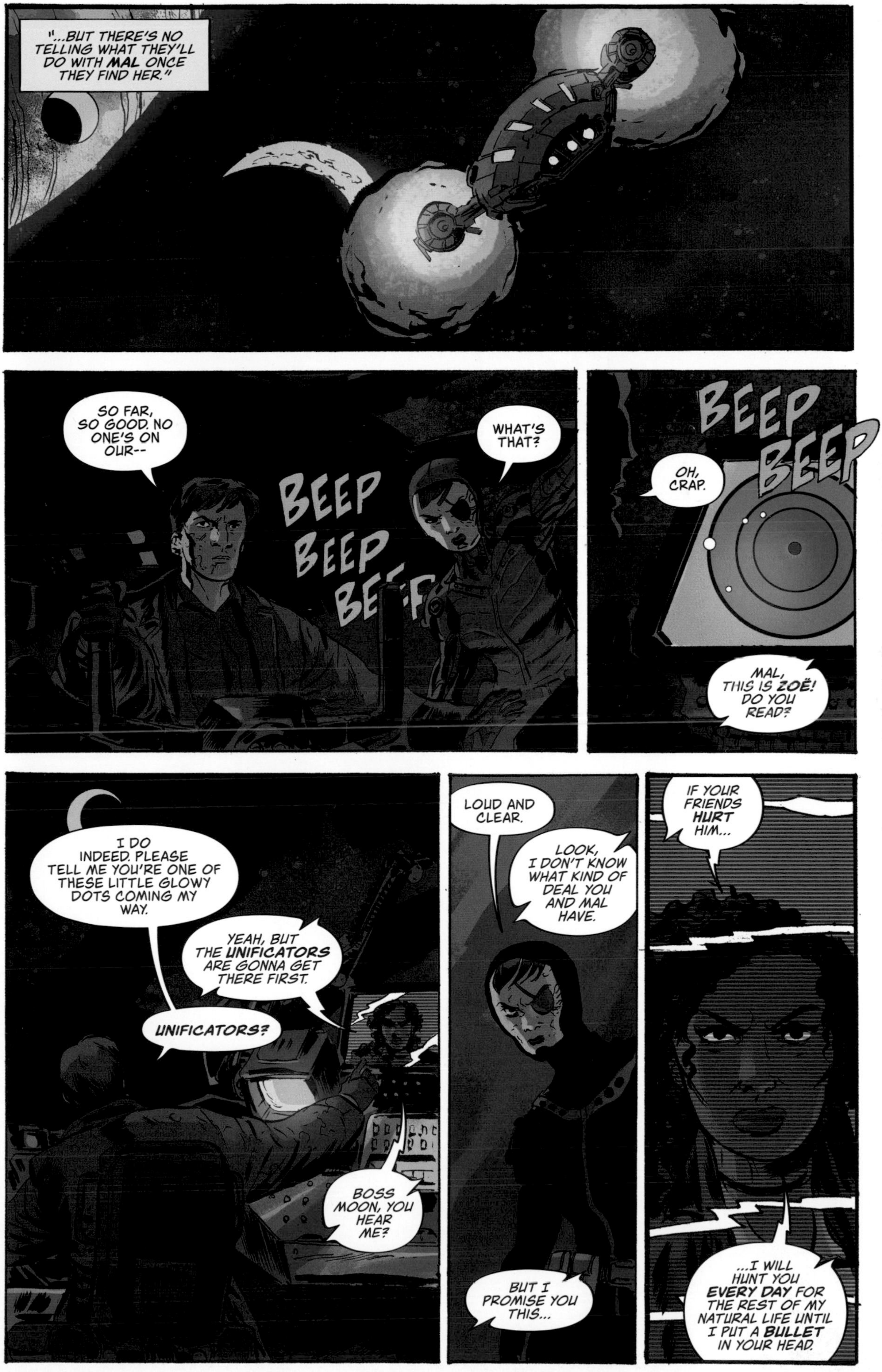
"...BUT THERE'S NO TELLING WHAT THEY'LL DO WITH MAL ONCE THEY FIND HER."
SO FAR, SO GOOD. NO ONE'S ON OUR--
BEEP BEEP BEEP
WHAT'S THAT?
BEEP BEEP
OH, CRAP.
MAL, THIS IS ZOË! DO YOU READ?
I DO INDEED. PLEASE TELL ME YOU'RE ONE OF THESE LITTLE GLOWY DOTS COMING MY WAY.
YEAH, BUT THE UNIFICATORS ARE GONNA GET THERE FIRST.
UNIFICATORS?
BOSS MOON, YOU HEAR ME?
LOUD AND CLEAR.
LOOK, I DON'T KNOW WHAT KIND OF DEAL YOU AND MAL HAVE.
BUT I PROMISE YOU THIS...
IF YOUR FRIENDS HURT HIM...
...I WILL HUNT YOU EVERY DAY FOR THE REST OF MY NATURAL LIFE UNTIL I PUT A BULLET IN YOUR HEAD.

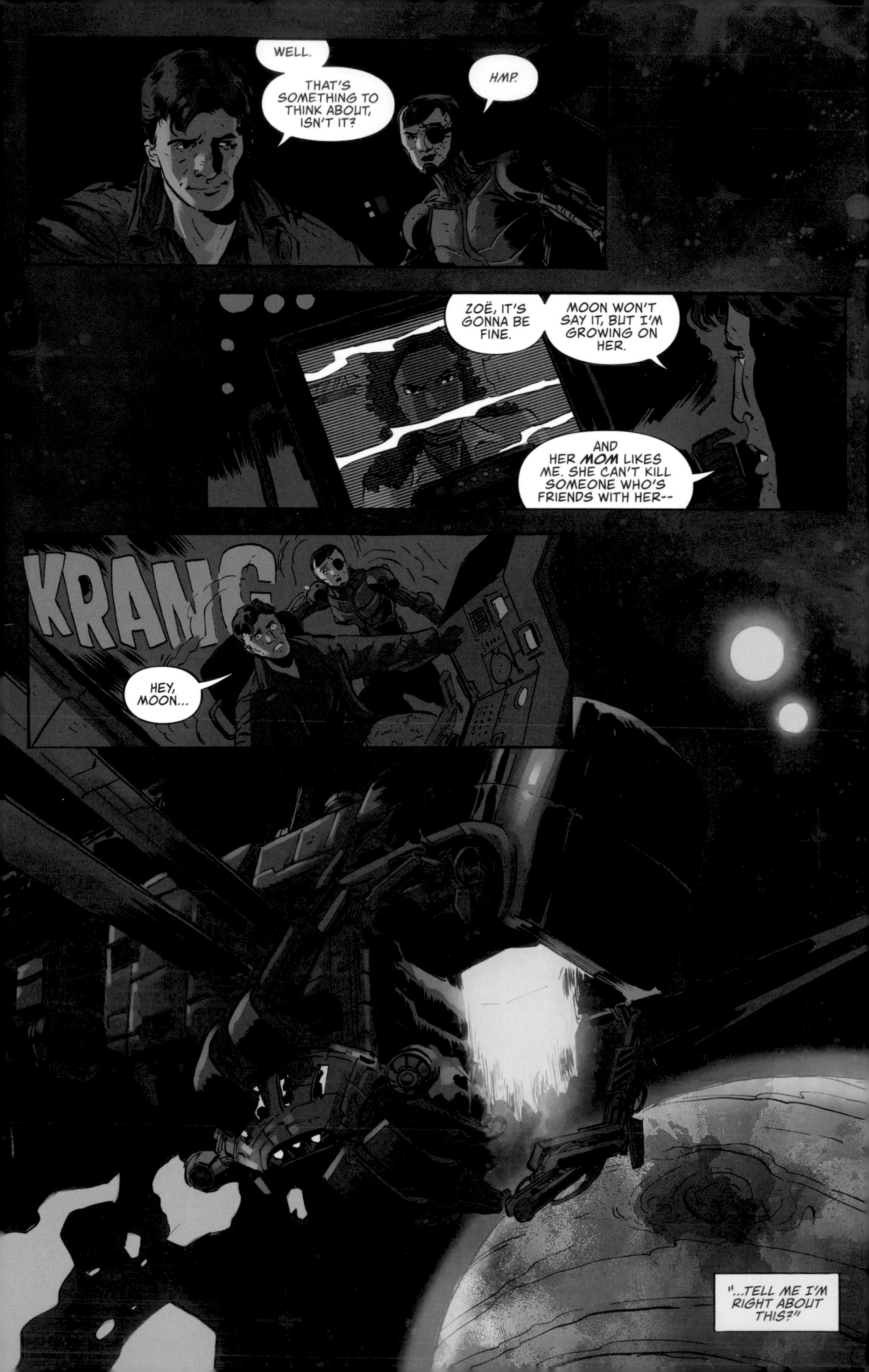
WELL.
THAT'S SOMETHING TO THINK ABOUT, ISN'T IT?
HMP.
ZOË, IT'S GONNA BE FINE.
MOON WON'T SAY IT, BUT I'M GROWING ON HER.
AND HER *MOM* LIKES ME. SHE CAN'T KILL SOMEONE WHO'S FRIENDS WITH HER--
KRANG
HEY, MOON...
"...TELL ME I'M RIGHT ABOUT THIS?"

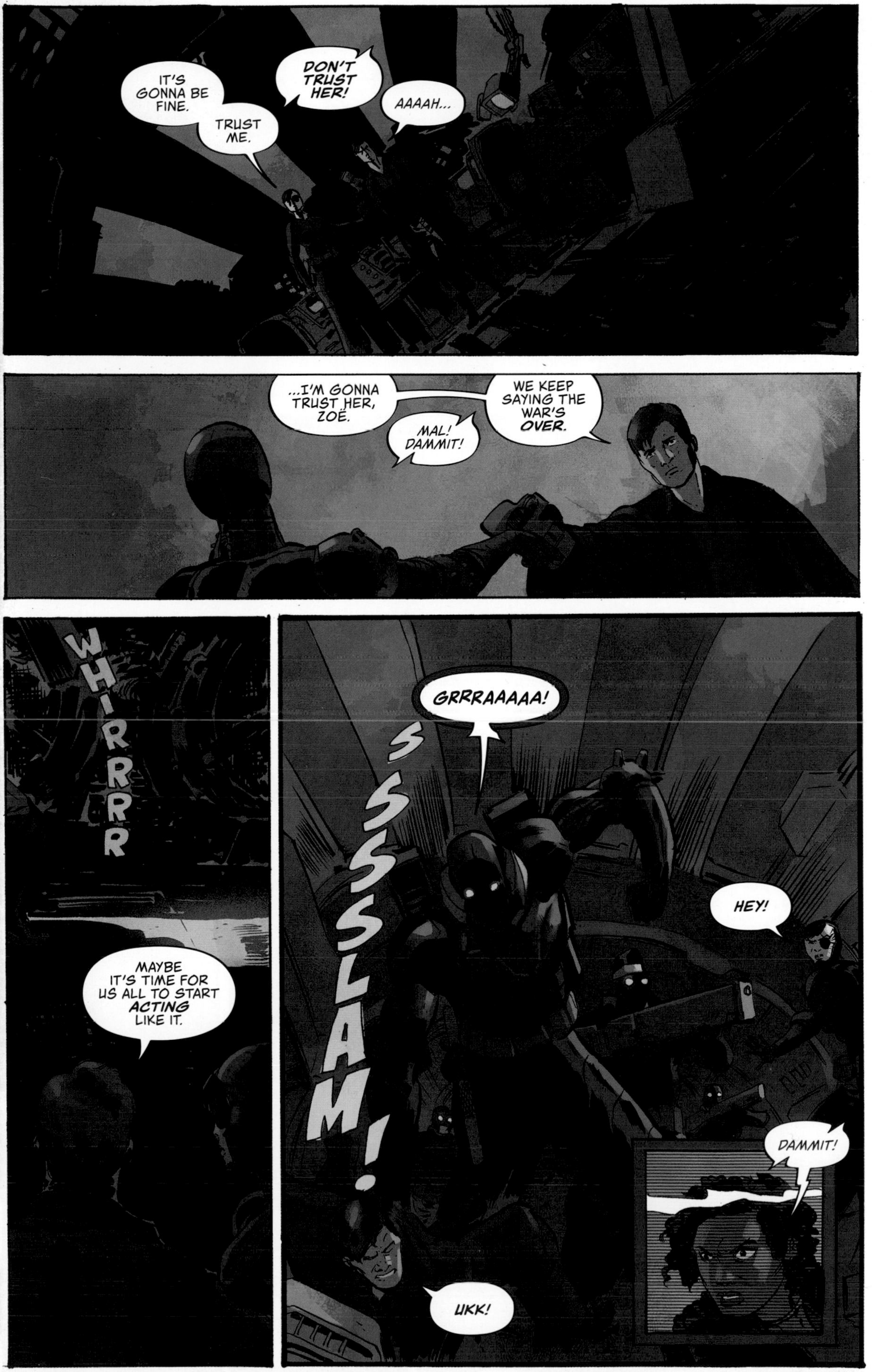
IT'S GONNA BE FINE.
TRUST ME.
DON'T TRUST HER!
AAAAH...
...I'M GONNA TRUST HER, ZOË.
MAL! DAMMIT!
WE KEEP SAYING THE WAR'S OVER.
WHIRRR
MAYBE IT'S TIME FOR US ALL TO START ACTING LIKE IT.
GRRRAAAAA!
SSSLAM!
HEY!
DAMMIT!
UKK!

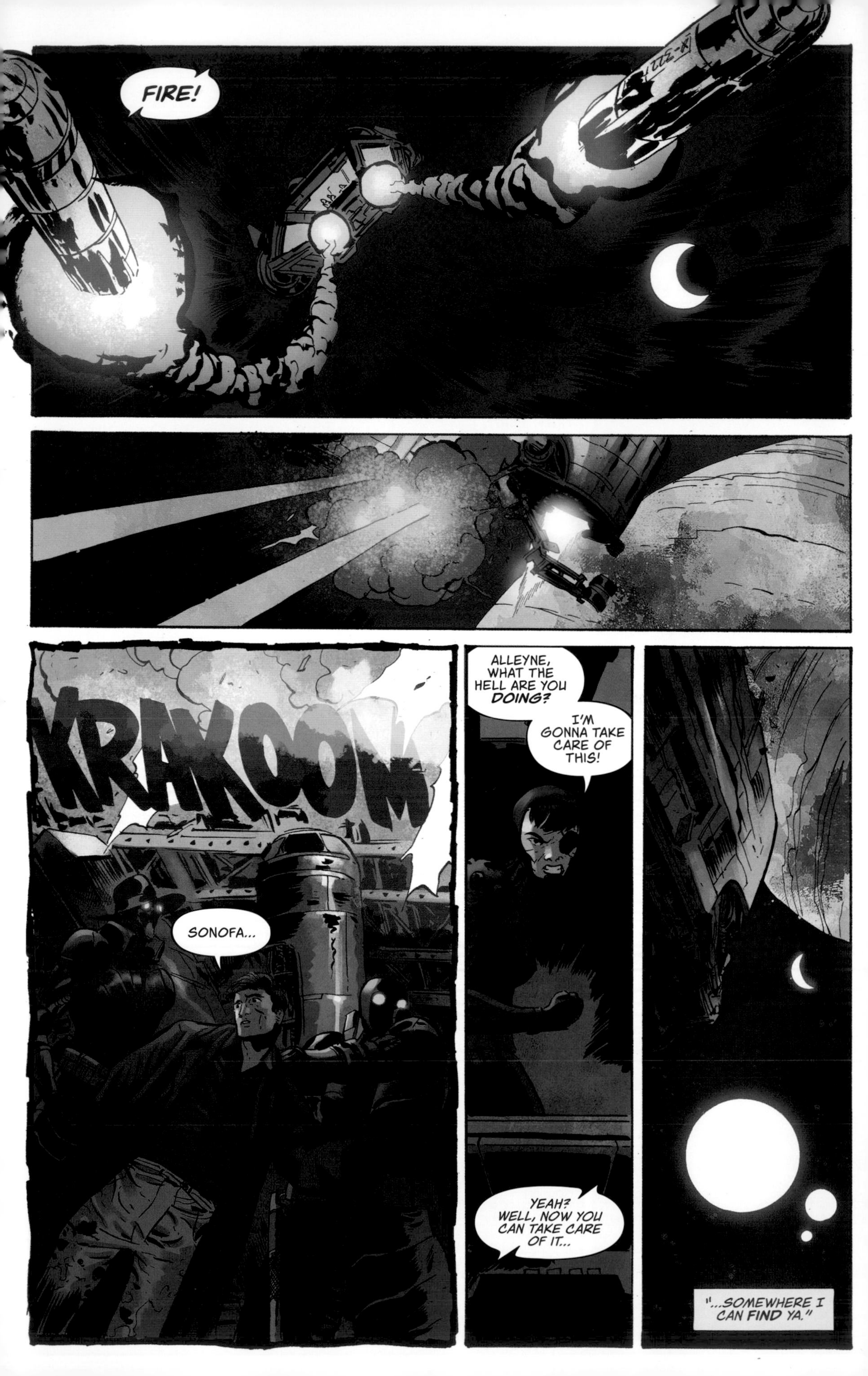
FIRE!
KRAKOOM
SONOFA...
ALLEYNE, WHAT THE HELL ARE YOU DOING?
I'M GONNA TAKE CARE OF THIS!
YEAH? WELL, NOW YOU CAN TAKE CARE OF IT...
"...SOMEWHERE I CAN FIND YA."

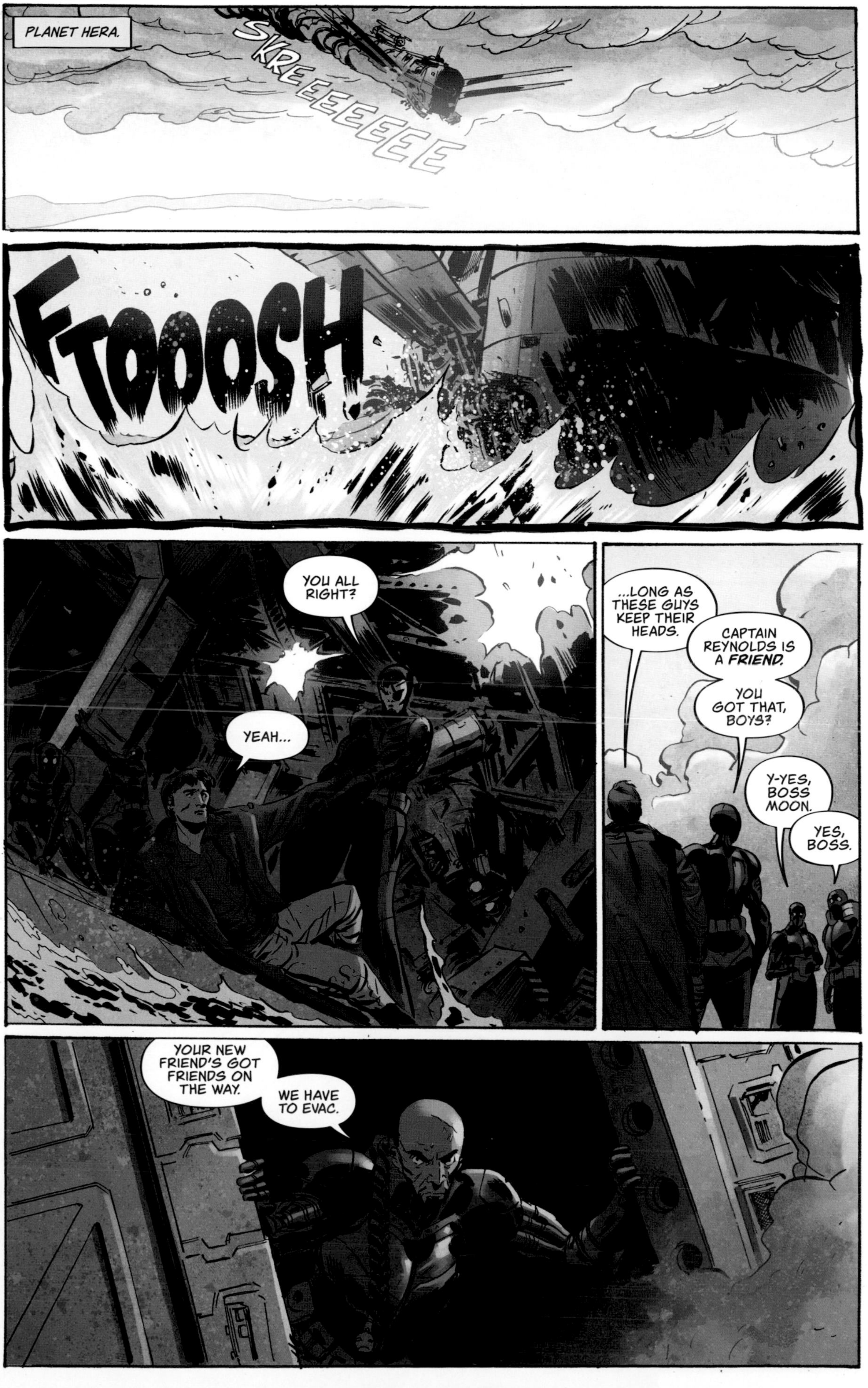
PLANET HERA.
SKREEEEEEEE
FTOOOSH!
YOU ALL RIGHT?
YEAH...
...LONG AS THESE GUYS KEEP THEIR HEADS.
CAPTAIN REYNOLDS IS A **FRIEND.**
YOU GOT THAT, BOYS?
Y-YES, BOSS MOON.
YES, BOSS.
YOUR NEW FRIEND'S GOT FRIENDS ON THE WAY.
WE HAVE TO EVAC.

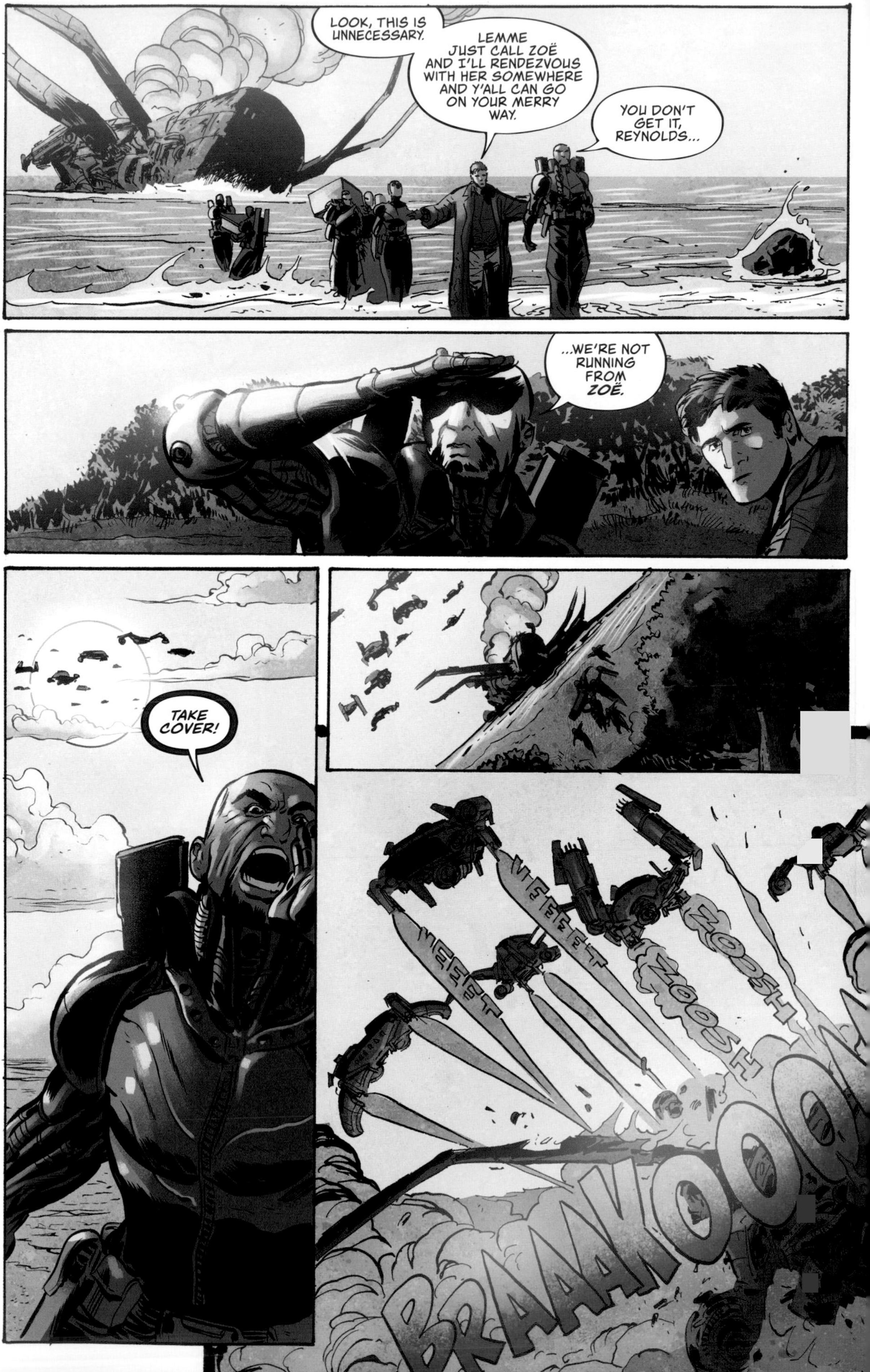
LOOK, THIS IS UNNECESSARY.
LEMME JUST CALL ZOË AND I'LL RENDEZVOUS WITH HER SOMEWHERE AND Y'ALL CAN GO ON YOUR MERRY WAY.
YOU DON'T GET IT, REYNOLDS...
...WE'RE NOT RUNNING FROM ZOË.
TAKE COVER!
ZOOSH
BRAAAKOOOO

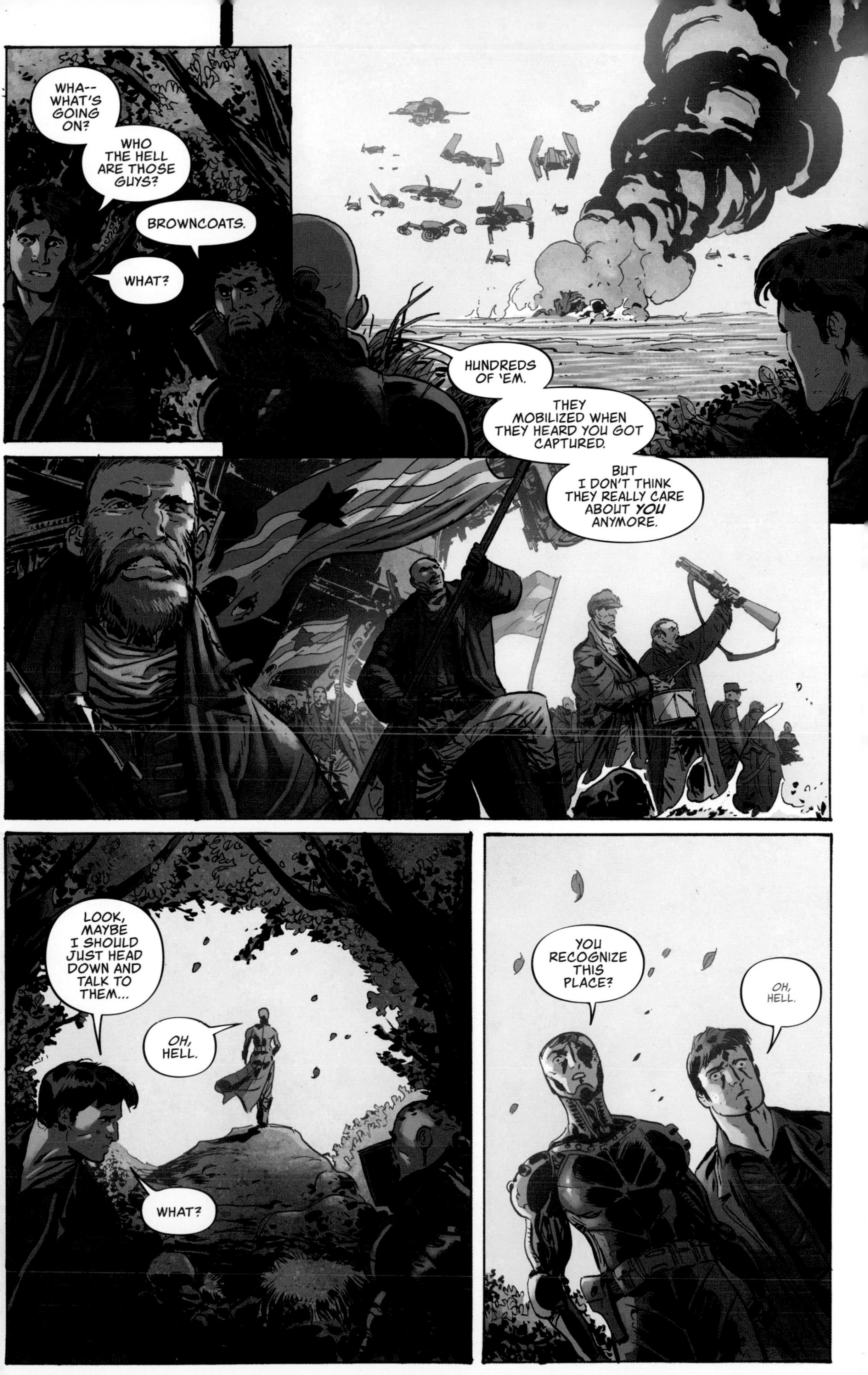
WHA-- WHAT'S GOING ON?
WHO THE HELL ARE THOSE GUYS?
BROWNCOATS.
WHAT?
HUNDREDS OF 'EM.
THEY MOBILIZED WHEN THEY HEARD YOU GOT CAPTURED.
BUT I DON'T THINK THEY REALLY CARE ABOUT YOU ANYMORE.
LOOK, MAYBE I SHOULD JUST HEAD DOWN AND TALK TO THEM...
OH, HELL.
WHAT?
YOU RECOGNIZE THIS PLACE?
OH, HELL.

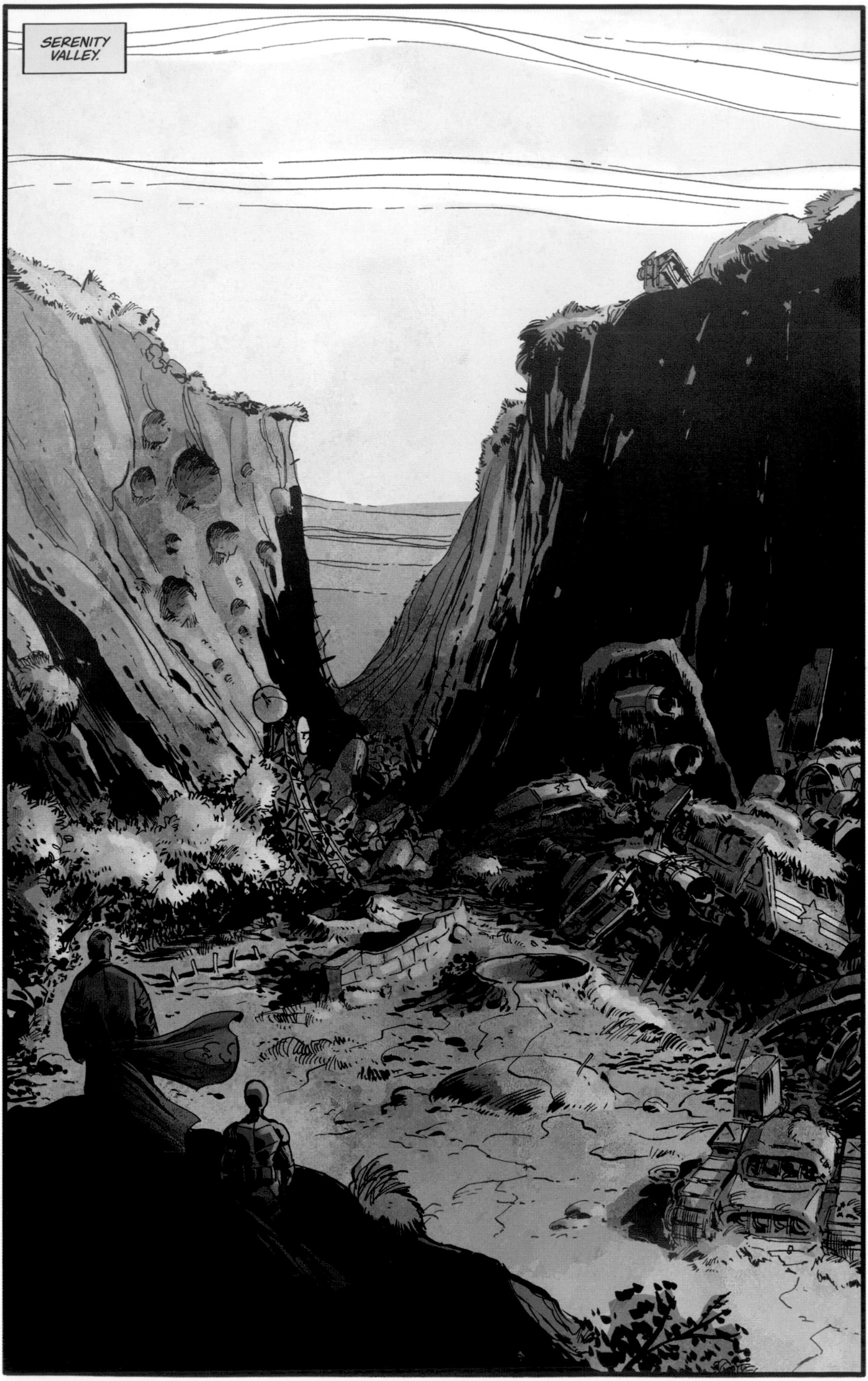
SERENITY VALLEY.

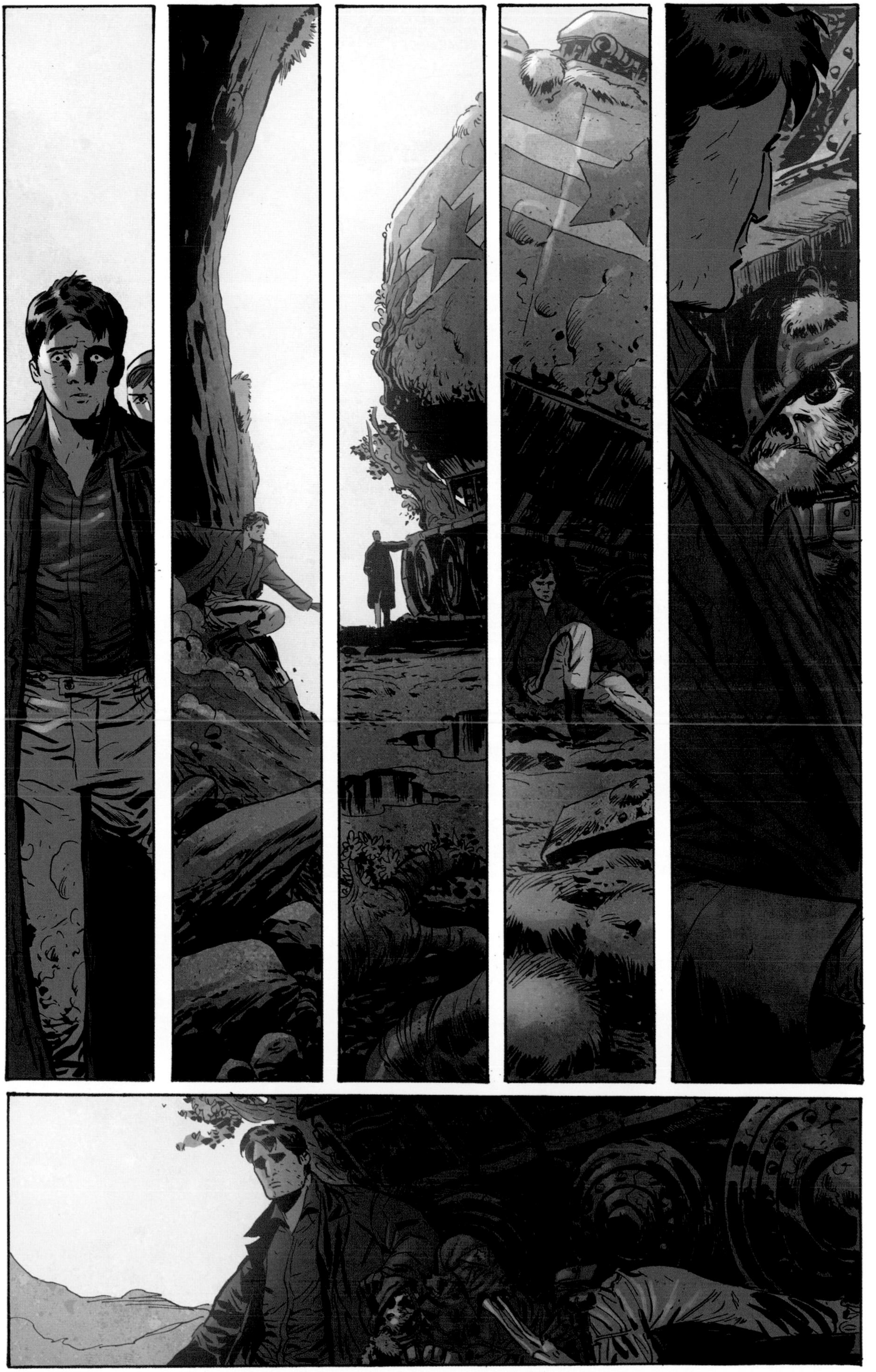

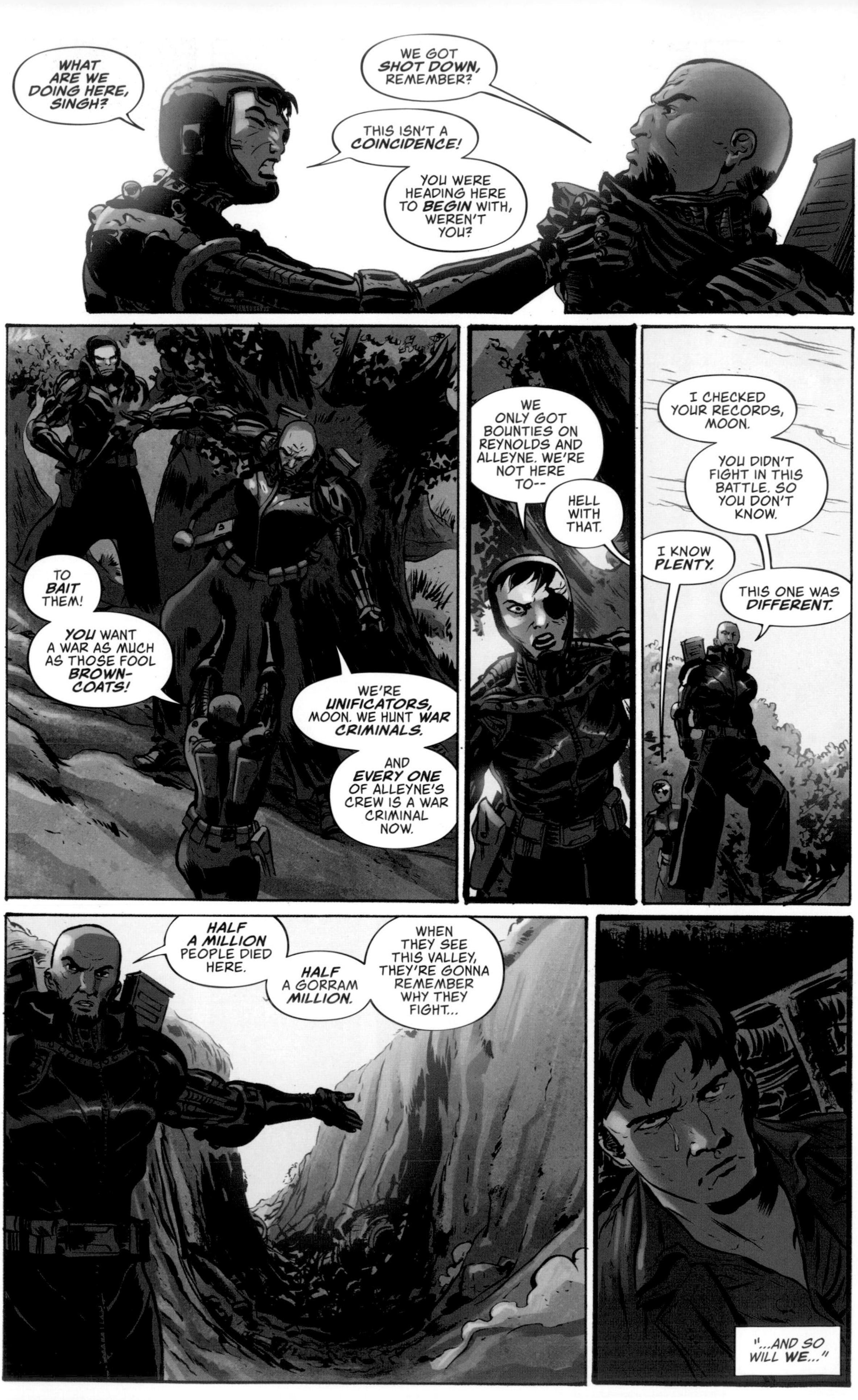
WHAT ARE WE DOING HERE, SINGH?
WE GOT SHOT DOWN, REMEMBER?
THIS ISN'T A COINCIDENCE!
YOU WERE HEADING HERE TO BEGIN WITH, WEREN'T YOU?
TO BAIT THEM!
YOU WANT A WAR AS MUCH AS THOSE FOOL BROWN-COATS!
WE'RE UNIFICATORS, MOON. WE HUNT WAR CRIMINALS.
AND EVERY ONE OF ALLEYNE'S CREW IS A WAR CRIMINAL NOW.
WE ONLY GOT BOUNTIES ON REYNOLDS AND ALLEYNE. WE'RE NOT HERE TO--
HELL WITH THAT.
I CHECKED YOUR RECORDS, MOON.
YOU DIDN'T FIGHT IN THIS BATTLE. SO YOU DON'T KNOW.
I KNOW PLENTY.
THIS ONE WAS DIFFERENT.
HALF A MILLION PEOPLE DIED HERE.
HALF A GORRAM MILLION.
WHEN THEY SEE THIS VALLEY, THEY'RE GONNA REMEMBER WHY THEY FIGHT...
"...AND SO WILL WE..."

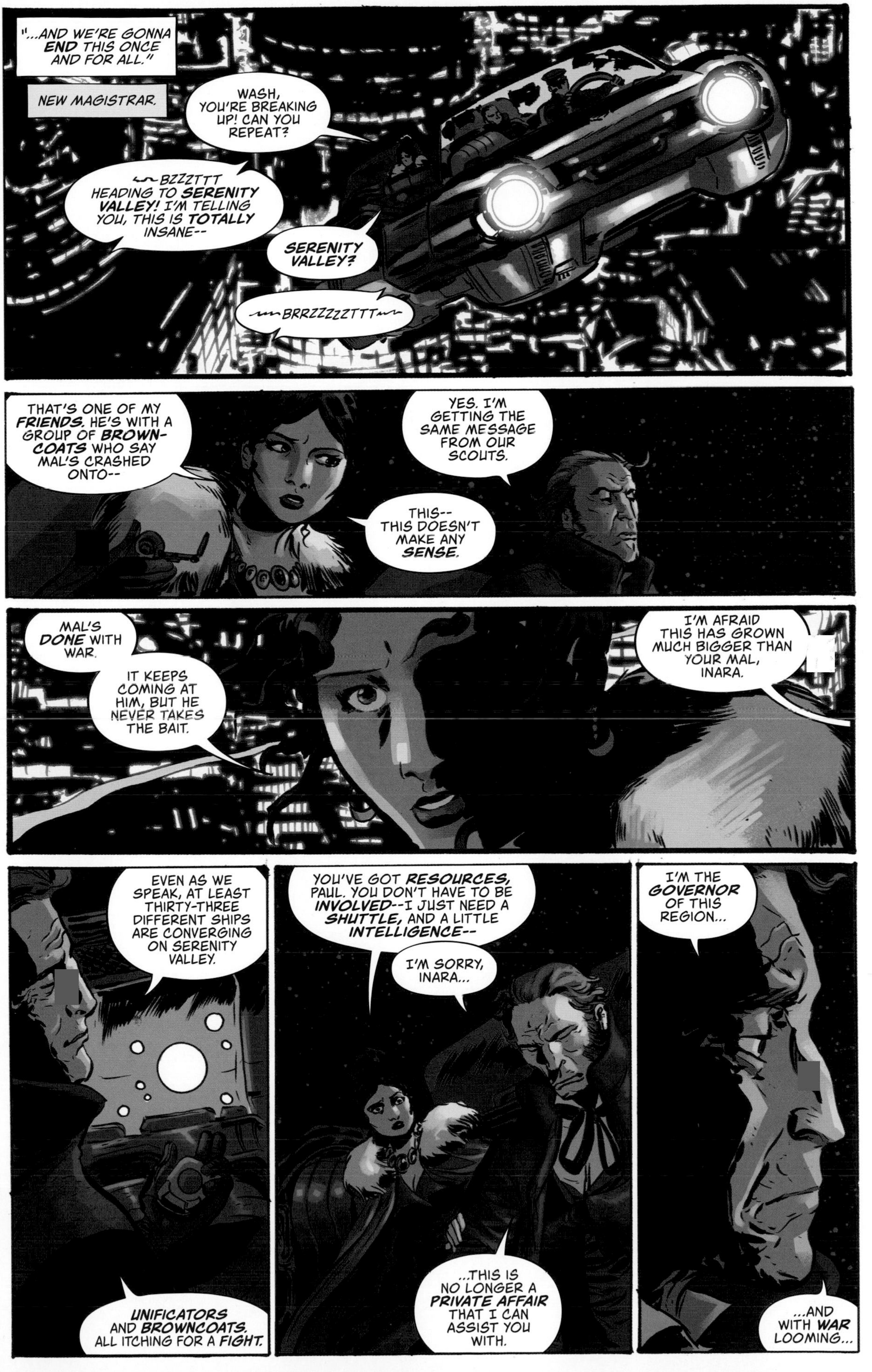
"...AND WE'RE GONNA END THIS ONCE AND FOR ALL."
NEW MAGISTRAR.
WASH, YOU'RE BREAKING UP! CAN YOU REPEAT?
BZZZTTT HEADING TO SERENITY VALLEY! I'M TELLING YOU, THIS IS TOTALLY INSANE--
SERENITY VALLEY?
BRRZZZZZZTTT
THAT'S ONE OF MY FRIENDS. HE'S WITH A GROUP OF BROWN-COATS WHO SAY MAL'S CRASHED ONTO--
YES. I'M GETTING THE SAME MESSAGE FROM OUR SCOUTS.
THIS-- THIS DOESN'T MAKE ANY SENSE.
MAL'S DONE WITH WAR.
IT KEEPS COMING AT HIM, BUT HE NEVER TAKES THE BAIT.
I'M AFRAID THIS HAS GROWN MUCH BIGGER THAN YOUR MAL, INARA.
EVEN AS WE SPEAK, AT LEAST THIRTY-THREE DIFFERENT SHIPS ARE CONVERGING ON SERENITY VALLEY.
UNIFICATORS AND BROWNCOATS. ALL ITCHING FOR A FIGHT.
YOU'VE GOT RESOURCES, PAUL. YOU DON'T HAVE TO BE INVOLVED--I JUST NEED A SHUTTLE, AND A LITTLE INTELLIGENCE--
I'M SORRY, INARA...
...THIS IS NO LONGER A PRIVATE AFFAIR THAT I CAN ASSIST YOU WITH.
I'M THE GOVERNOR OF THIS REGION...
...AND WITH WAR LOOMING...

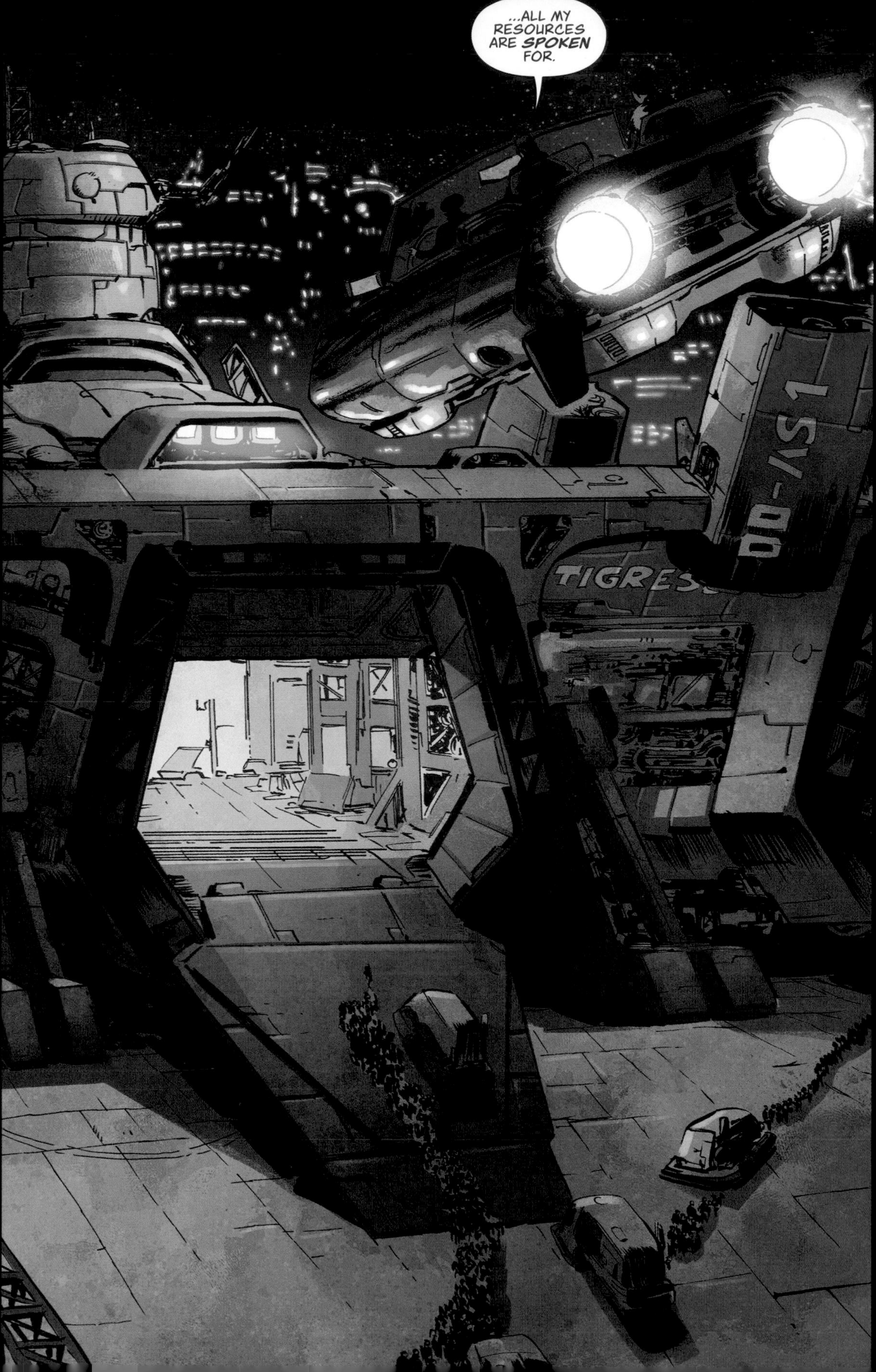
...ALL MY RESOURCES ARE SPOKEN FOR.
TIGRES

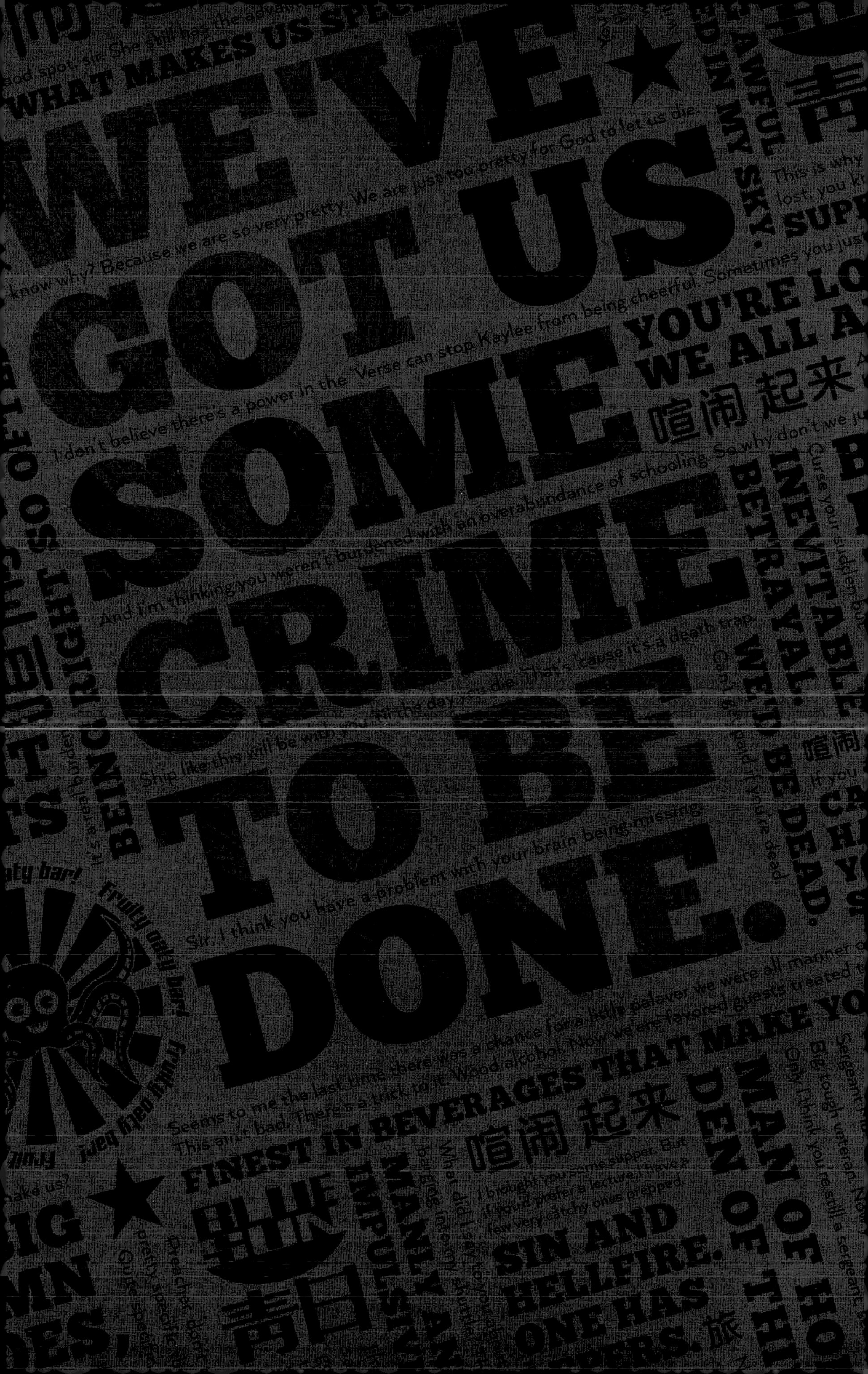
WE'VE GOT US SOME CRIME TO BE DONE.
WHAT MAKES US SPECIAL
good spot, sir. She still has the advantage
know why? Because we are so very pretty. We are just too pretty for God to let us die.
I don't believe there's a power in the 'Verse can stop Kaylee from being cheerful. Sometimes you just
And I'm thinking you weren't burdened with an overabundance of schooling. So why don't we just
Ship like this will be with you till the day you die. That's 'cause it's a death trap.
Sir, I think you have a problem with your brain being missing.
It's a real burden
BEING RIGHT
YOU'RE LO
WE ALL A
喧闹起来
INEVITABLE BETRAYAL.
WE'D BE DEAD.
AWFUL
IN MY SKY.
This is why
lost, you know
Curse your sudden but
Can't get paid if you're dead.
Seems to me the last time there was a chance for a little palaver we were all manner of
This ain't bad. There's a trick to it. Wood alcohol. Now we're favored guests treated
FINEST IN REVERAGES THAT MAKE YO
喧闹起来
I brought you some supper. But if you'd prefer a lecture, I have a few very catchy ones prepped
SIN AND HELLFIRE. ONE HAS
MAN OF THE HO
DEN
EMPULSIA
MANLY
What did I say
Big tough veteran.
Sergeant
Only I think you're still a sergeant.
Fruity Oaty Bar!
青日
旅

CHAPTER TEN

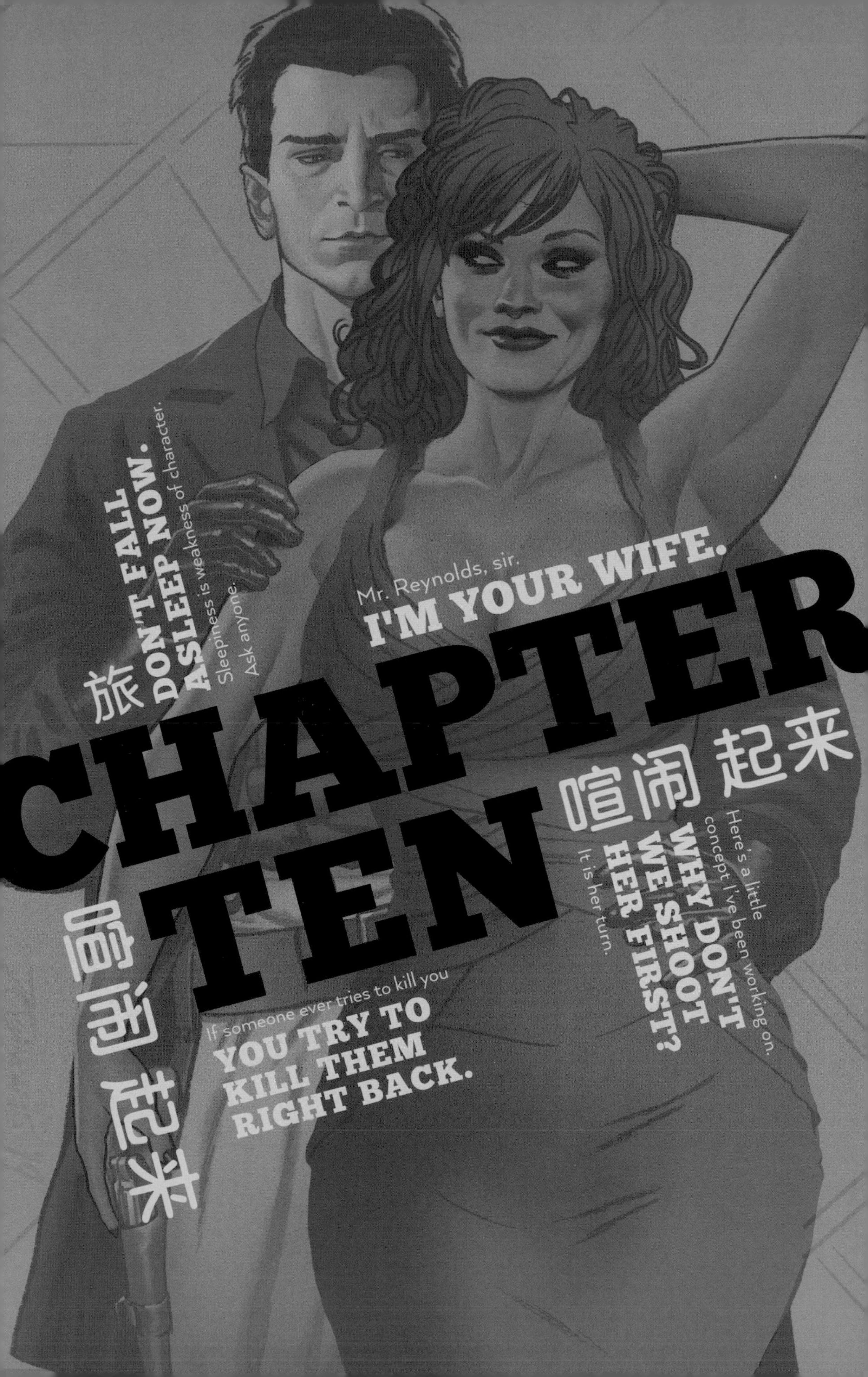

旅
DON'T FALL ASLEEP NOW.
Sleepiness is weakness of character. Ask anyone.
Mr. Reynolds, sir.
I'M YOUR WIFE.
喧闹起来
Here's a little concept I've been working on.
WHY DON'T WE SHOOT HER FIRST?
It is her turn.
喧闹起来
If someone ever tries to kill you
YOU TRY TO KILL THEM RIGHT BACK.

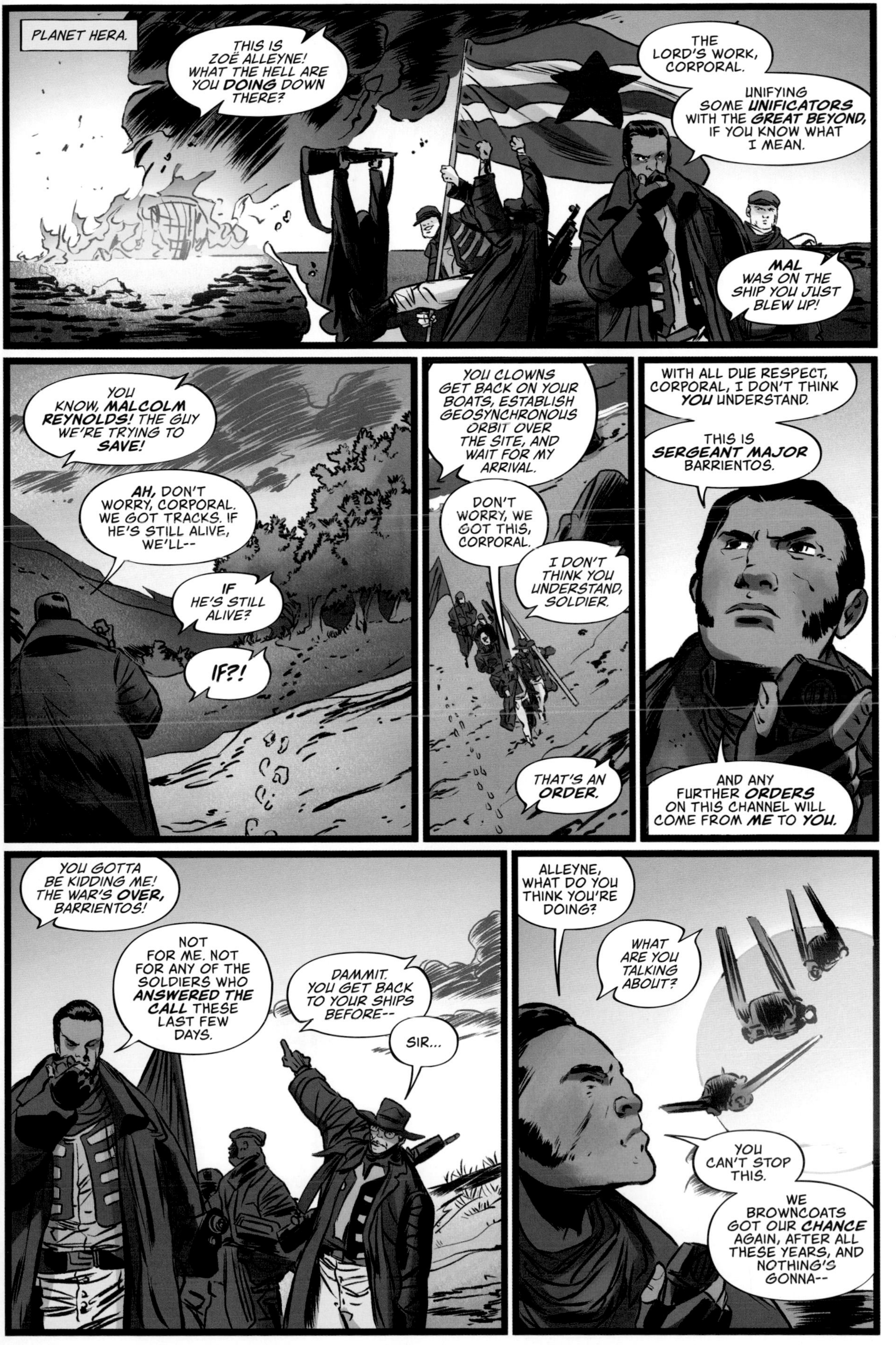
PLANET HERA.
THIS IS ZOË ALLEYNE! WHAT THE HELL ARE YOU DOING DOWN THERE?
THE LORD'S WORK, CORPORAL.
UNIFYING SOME UNIFICATORS WITH THE GREAT BEYOND, IF YOU KNOW WHAT I MEAN.
MAL WAS ON THE SHIP YOU JUST BLEW UP!
YOU KNOW, MALCOLM REYNOLDS! THE GUY WE'RE TRYING TO SAVE!
AH, DON'T WORRY, CORPORAL. WE GOT TRACKS. IF HE'S STILL ALIVE, WE'LL--
IF HE'S STILL ALIVE?
IF?!
YOU CLOWNS GET BACK ON YOUR BOATS, ESTABLISH GEOSYNCHRONOUS ORBIT OVER THE SITE, AND WAIT FOR MY ARRIVAL.
DON'T WORRY, WE GOT THIS, CORPORAL.
I DON'T THINK YOU UNDERSTAND, SOLDIER.
THAT'S AN ORDER.
WITH ALL DUE RESPECT, CORPORAL, I DON'T THINK YOU UNDERSTAND.
THIS IS SERGEANT MAJOR BARRIENTOS.
AND ANY FURTHER ORDERS ON THIS CHANNEL WILL COME FROM ME TO YOU.
YOU GOTTA BE KIDDING ME! THE WAR'S OVER, BARRIENTOS!
NOT FOR ME. NOT FOR ANY OF THE SOLDIERS WHO ANSWERED THE CALL THESE LAST FEW DAYS.
DAMMIT. YOU GET BACK TO YOUR SHIPS BEFORE--
SIR...
ALLEYNE, WHAT DO YOU THINK YOU'RE DOING?
WHAT ARE YOU TALKING ABOUT?
YOU CAN'T STOP THIS.
WE BROWNCOATS GOT OUR CHANCE AGAIN, AFTER ALL THESE YEARS, AND NOTHING'S GONNA--

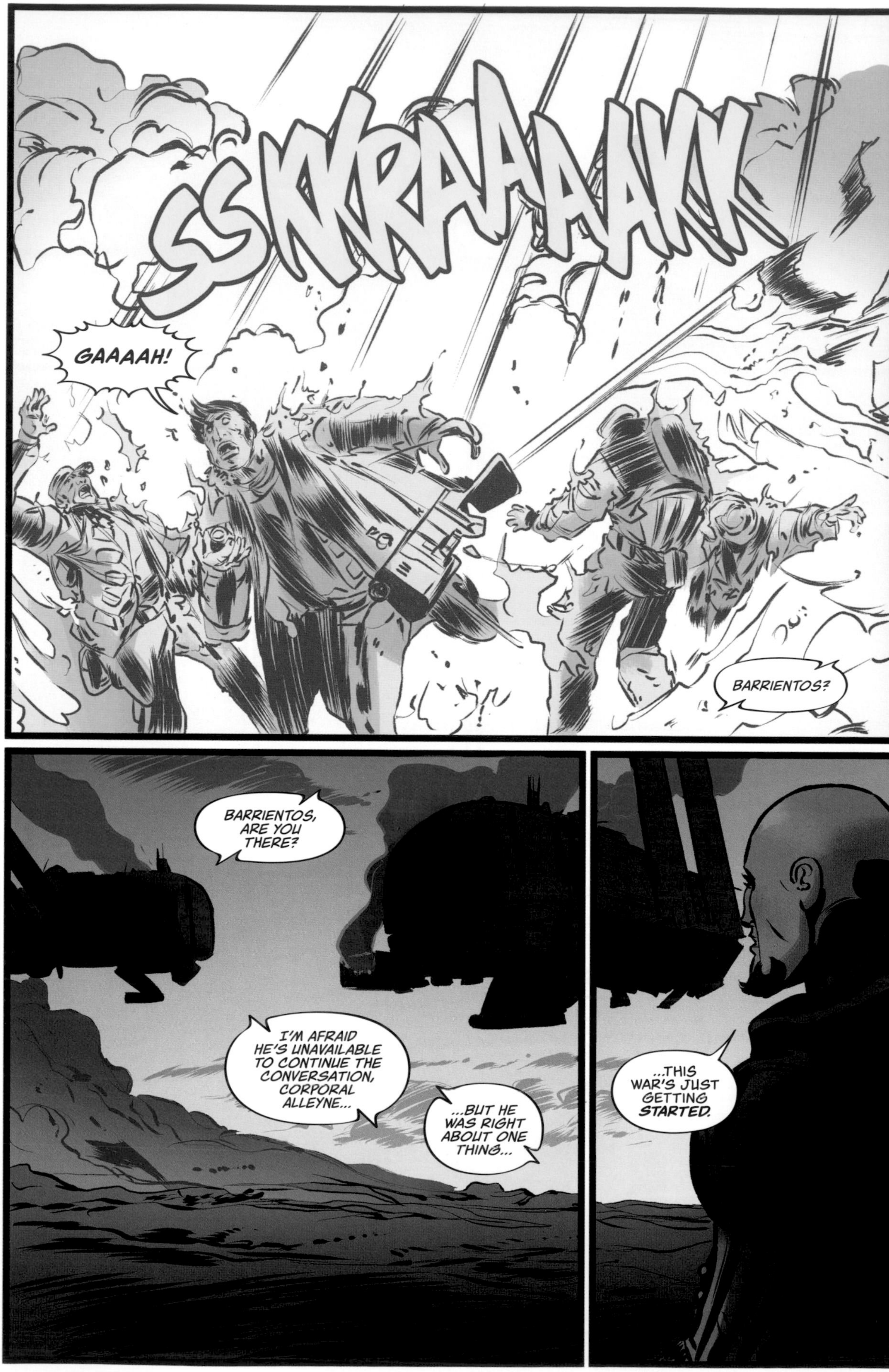
SSKKRAAAAKK
GAAAAH!
BARRIENTOS?
BARRIENTOS, ARE YOU THERE?
I'M AFRAID HE'S UNAVAILABLE TO CONTINUE THE CONVERSATION, CORPORAL ALLEYNE...
...BUT HE WAS RIGHT ABOUT ONE THING...
...THIS WAR'S JUST GETTING STARTED.

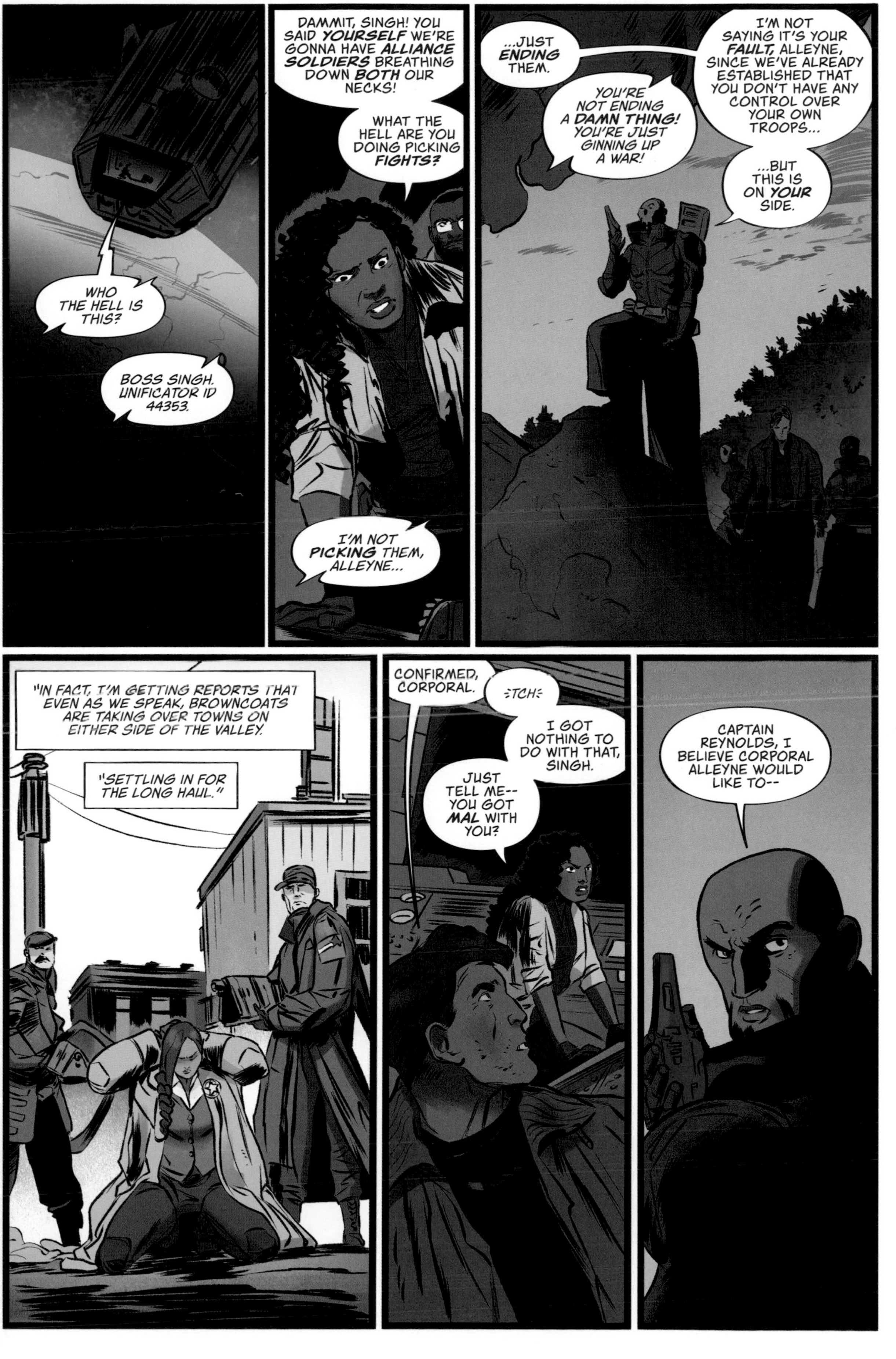
WHO THE HELL IS THIS?
BOSS SINGH. UNIFICATOR ID 44353.
DAMMIT, SINGH! YOU SAID YOURSELF WE'RE GONNA HAVE ALLIANCE SOLDIERS BREATHING DOWN BOTH OUR NECKS!
WHAT THE HELL ARE YOU DOING PICKING FIGHTS?
I'M NOT PICKING THEM, ALLEYNE...
...JUST ENDING THEM.
YOU'RE NOT ENDING A DAMN THING! YOU'RE JUST GINNING UP A WAR!
I'M NOT SAYING IT'S YOUR FAULT, ALLEYNE, SINCE WE'VE ALREADY ESTABLISHED THAT YOU DON'T HAVE ANY CONTROL OVER YOUR OWN TROOPS...
...BUT THIS IS ON YOUR SIDE.
"IN FACT, I'M GETTING REPORTS THAT EVEN AS WE SPEAK, BROWNCOATS ARE TAKING OVER TOWNS ON EITHER SIDE OF THE VALLEY.
"SETTLING IN FOR THE LONG HAUL."
CONFIRMED, CORPORAL.
=TCH=
I GOT NOTHING TO DO WITH THAT, SINGH.
JUST TELL ME--YOU GOT MAL WITH YOU?
CAPTAIN REYNOLDS, I BELIEVE CORPORAL ALLEYNE WOULD LIKE TO--

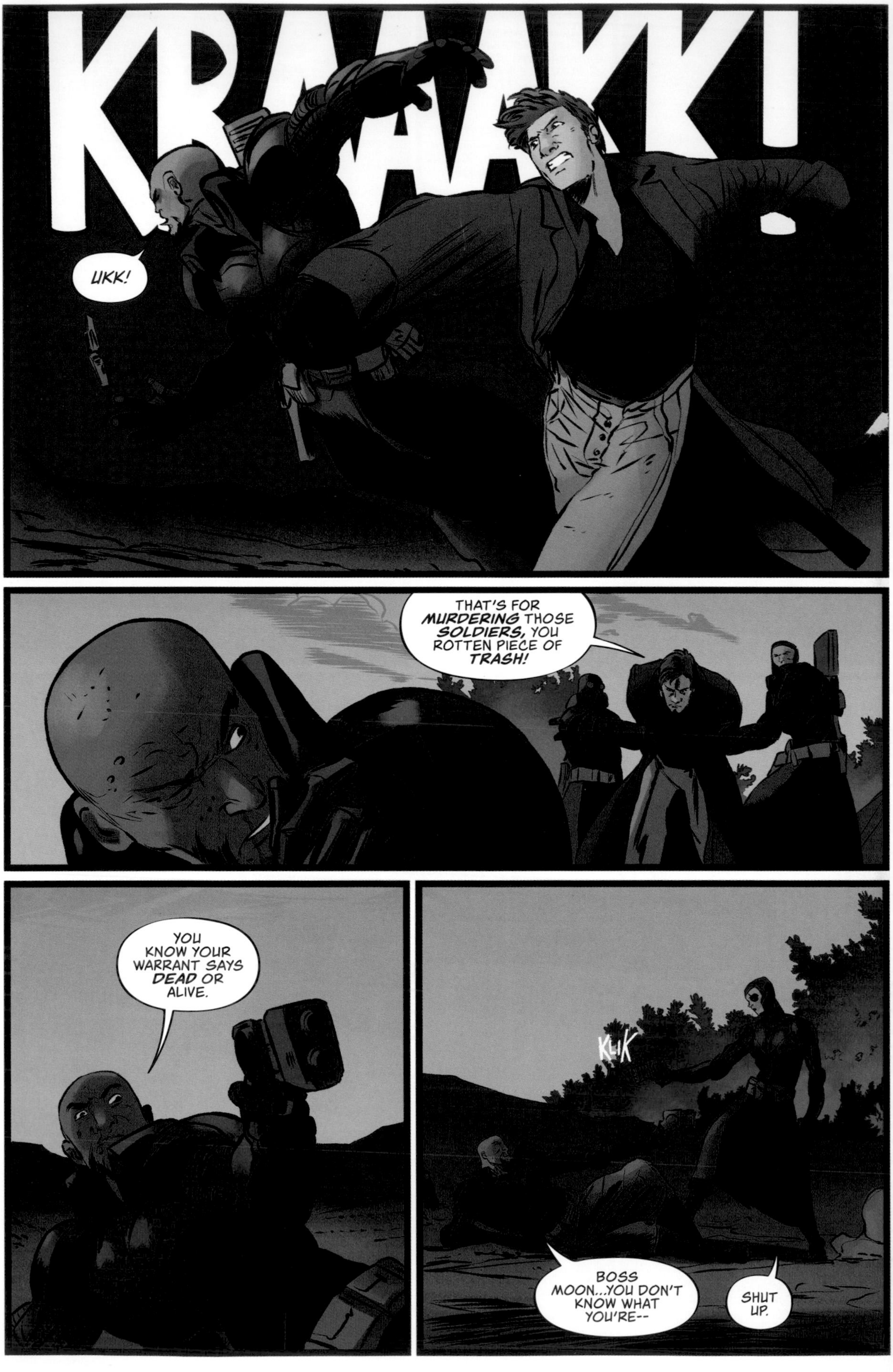
KRAAKK!
UKK!
THAT'S FOR MURDERING THOSE SOLDIERS, YOU ROTTEN PIECE OF TRASH!
YOU KNOW YOUR WARRANT SAYS DEAD OR ALIVE.
KLIK
BOSS MOON...YOU DON'T KNOW WHAT YOU'RE--
SHUT UP.

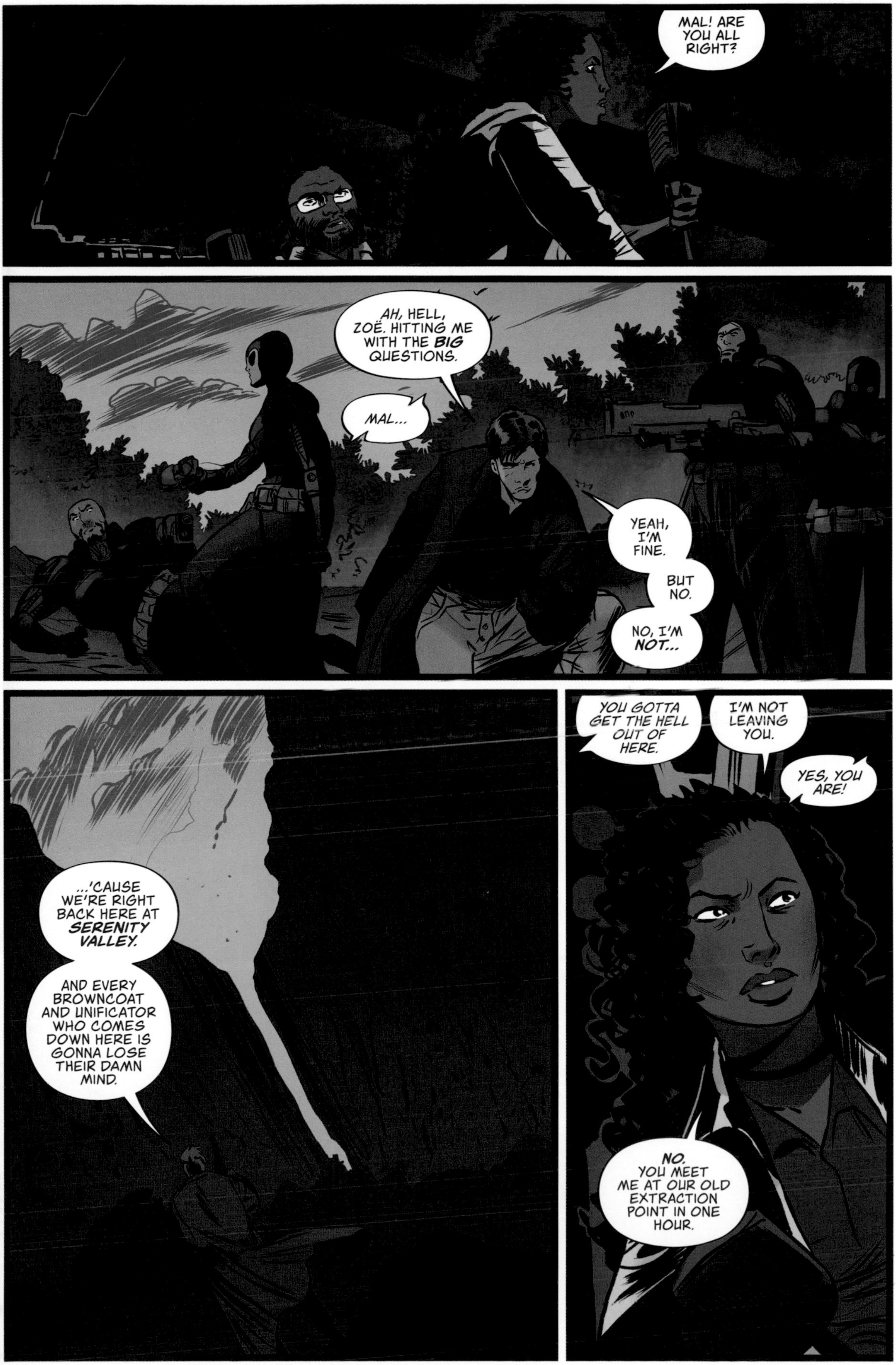
MAL! ARE YOU ALL RIGHT?
AH, HELL, ZOË. HITTING ME WITH THE BIG QUESTIONS.
MAL...
YEAH, I'M FINE.
BUT NO.
NO, I'M NOT...
...'CAUSE WE'RE RIGHT BACK HERE AT SERENITY VALLEY.
AND EVERY BROWNCOAT AND UNIFICATOR WHO COMES DOWN HERE IS GONNA LOSE THEIR DAMN MIND.
YOU GOTTA GET THE HELL OUT OF HERE.
I'M NOT LEAVING YOU.
YES, YOU ARE!
NO. YOU MEET ME AT OUR OLD EXTRACTION POINT IN ONE HOUR.

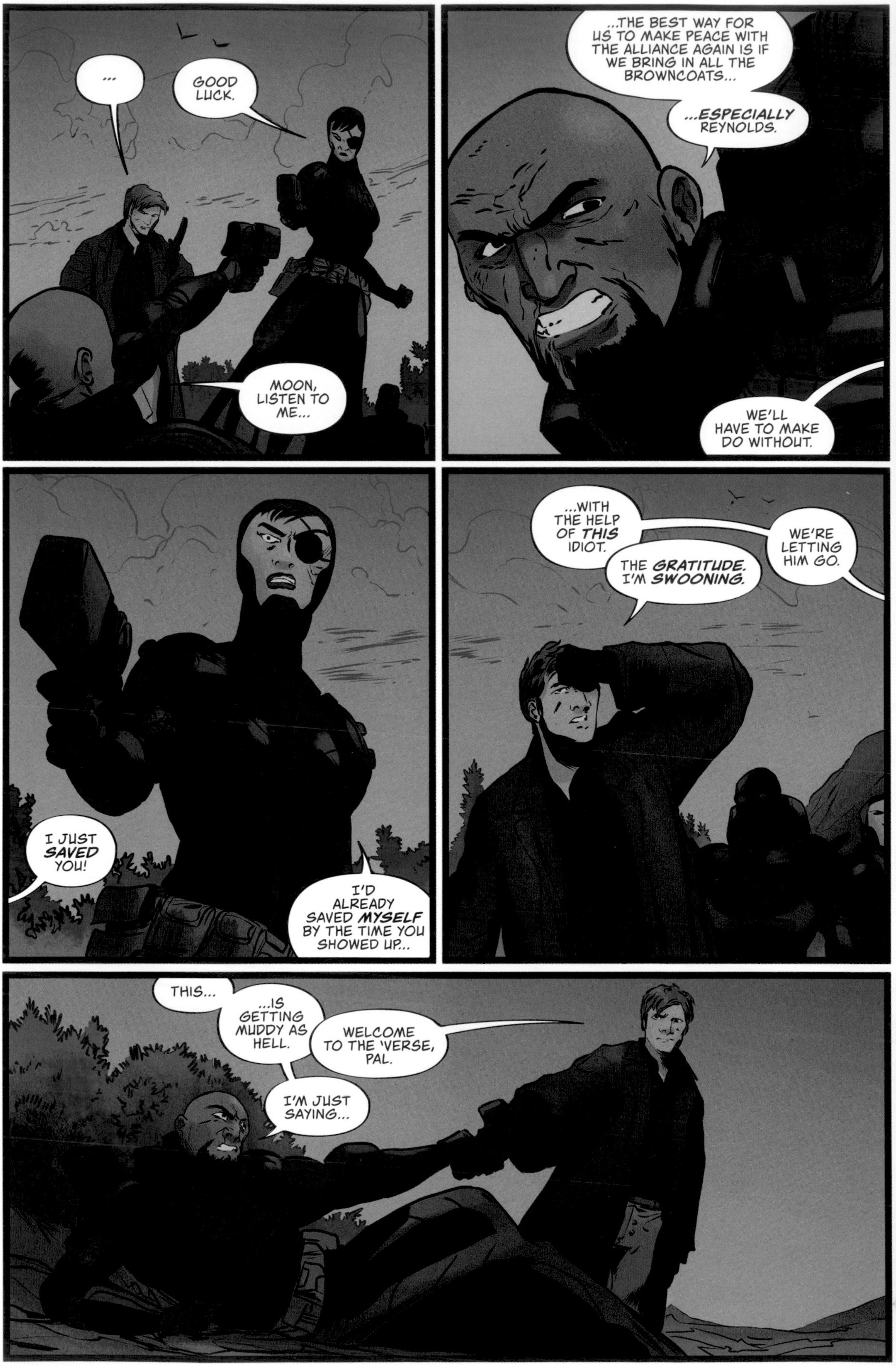
...
GOOD LUCK.
MOON, LISTEN TO ME...
...THE BEST WAY FOR US TO MAKE PEACE WITH THE ALLIANCE AGAIN IS IF WE BRING IN ALL THE BROWNCOATS...
...ESPECIALLY REYNOLDS.
WE'LL HAVE TO MAKE DO WITHOUT.
I JUST SAVED YOU!
I'D ALREADY SAVED MYSELF BY THE TIME YOU SHOWED UP...
...WITH THE HELP OF THIS IDIOT.
THE GRATITUDE. I'M SWOONING.
WE'RE LETTING HIM GO.
THIS...
...IS GETTING MUDDY AS HELL.
WELCOME TO THE 'VERSE, PAL.
I'M JUST SAYING...

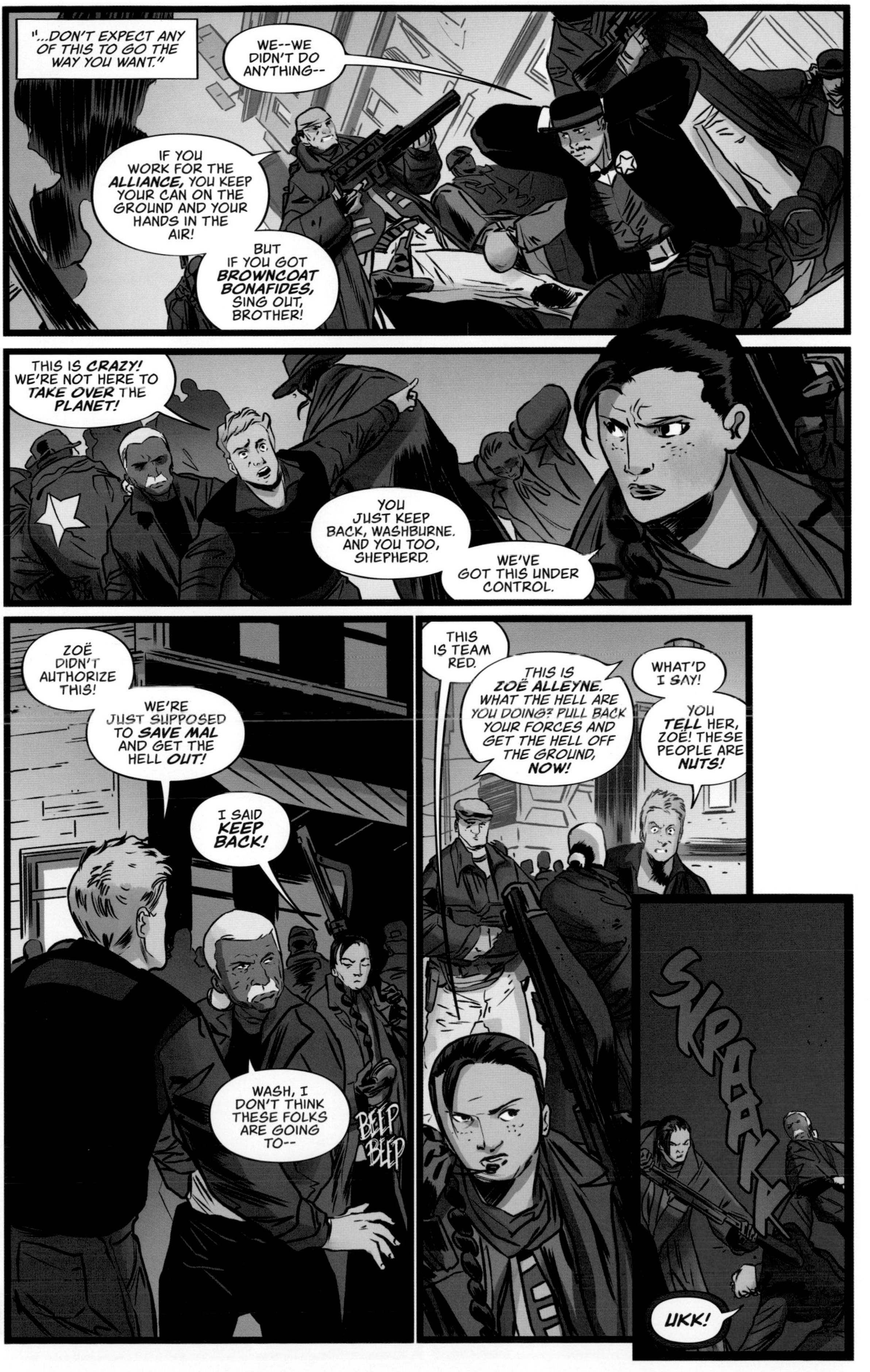
"...DON'T EXPECT ANY OF THIS TO GO THE WAY YOU WANT."
WE--WE DIDN'T DO ANYTHING--
IF YOU WORK FOR THE ALLIANCE, YOU KEEP YOUR CAN ON THE GROUND AND YOUR HANDS IN THE AIR!
BUT IF YOU GOT BROWNCOAT BONAFIDES, SING OUT, BROTHER!
THIS IS CRAZY! WE'RE NOT HERE TO TAKE OVER THE PLANET!
YOU JUST KEEP BACK, WASHBURNE. AND YOU TOO, SHEPHERD.
WE'VE GOT THIS UNDER CONTROL.
ZOË DIDN'T AUTHORIZE THIS!
WE'RE JUST SUPPOSED TO SAVE MAL AND GET THE HELL OUT!
I SAID KEEP BACK!
WASH, I DON'T THINK THESE FOLKS ARE GOING TO--
BEEP BEEP
THIS IS TEAM RED.
THIS IS ZOË ALLEYNE. WHAT THE HELL ARE YOU DOING? PULL BACK YOUR FORCES AND GET THE HELL OFF THE GROUND, NOW!
WHAT'D I SAY!
YOU TELL HER, ZOË! THESE PEOPLE ARE NUTS!
SKRAAK
UKK!

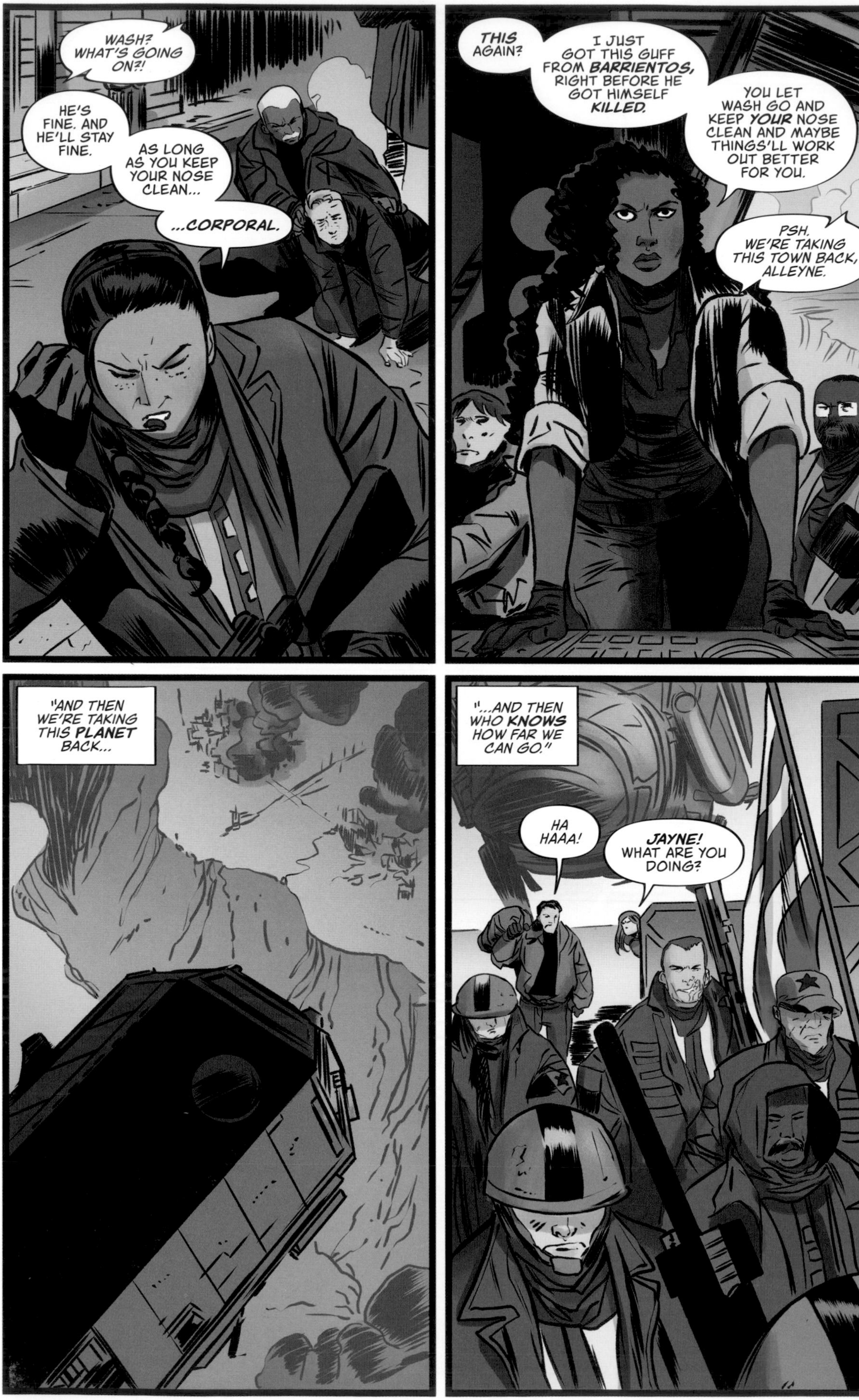
WASH? WHAT'S GOING ON?!
HE'S FINE. AND HE'LL STAY FINE.
AS LONG AS YOU KEEP YOUR NOSE CLEAN...
...CORPORAL.
THIS AGAIN?
I JUST GOT THIS GUFF FROM BARRIENTOS, RIGHT BEFORE HE GOT HIMSELF KILLED.
YOU LET WASH GO AND KEEP YOUR NOSE CLEAN AND MAYBE THINGS'LL WORK OUT BETTER FOR YOU.
PSH. WE'RE TAKING THIS TOWN BACK, ALLEYNE.
"AND THEN WE'RE TAKING THIS PLANET BACK...
"...AND THEN WHO KNOWS HOW FAR WE CAN GO."
HA HAAA!
JAYNE! WHAT ARE YOU DOING?

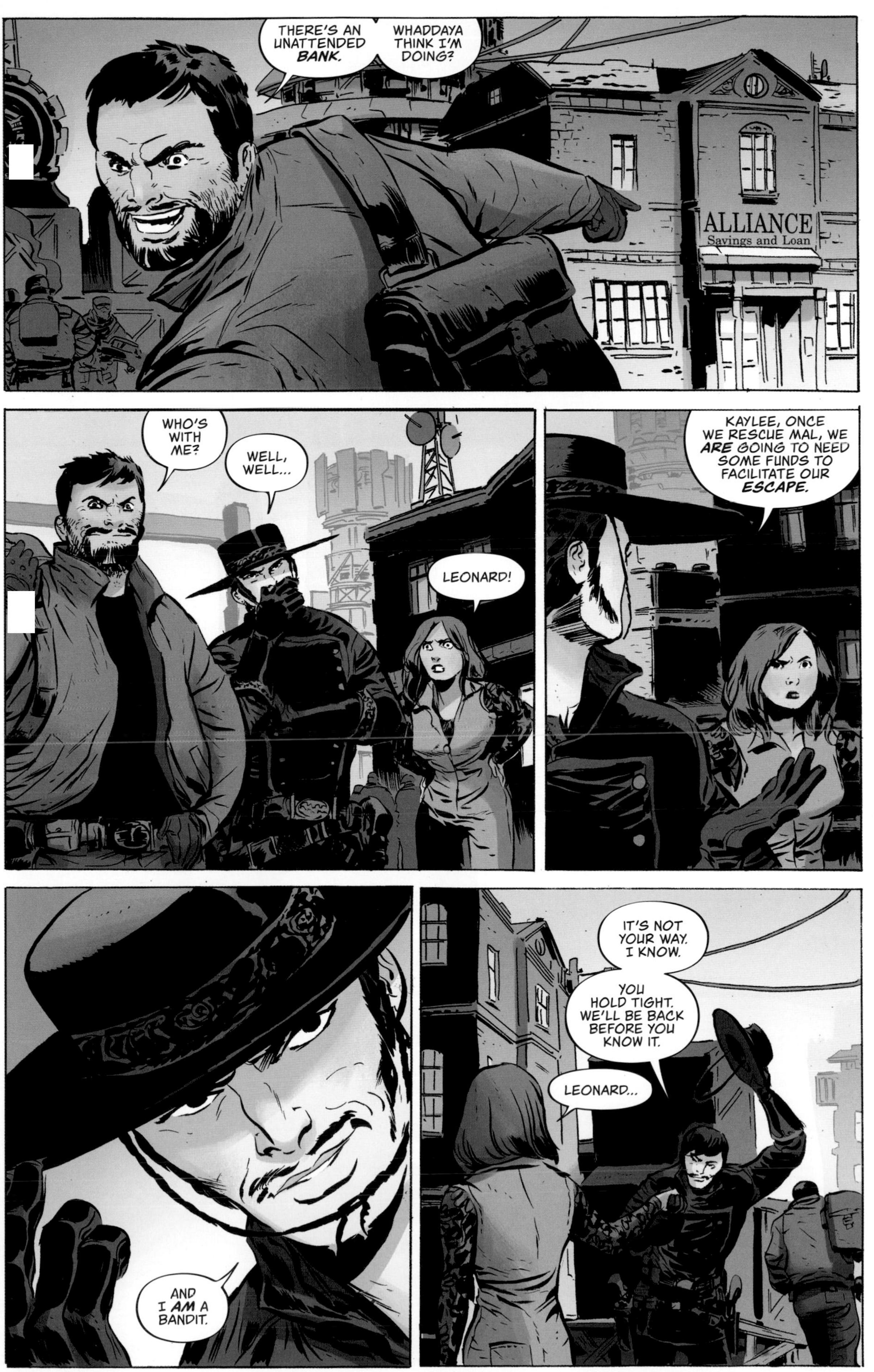

THERE'S AN UNATTENDED BANK.
WHADDAYA THINK I'M DOING?
ALLIANCE
Savings and Loan
WHO'S WITH ME?
WELL, WELL...
LEONARD!
KAYLEE, ONCE WE RESCUE MAL, WE ARE GOING TO NEED SOME FUNDS TO FACILITATE OUR ESCAPE.
AND I AM A BANDIT.
IT'S NOT YOUR WAY. I KNOW.
YOU HOLD TIGHT. WE'LL BE BACK BEFORE YOU KNOW IT.
LEONARD...

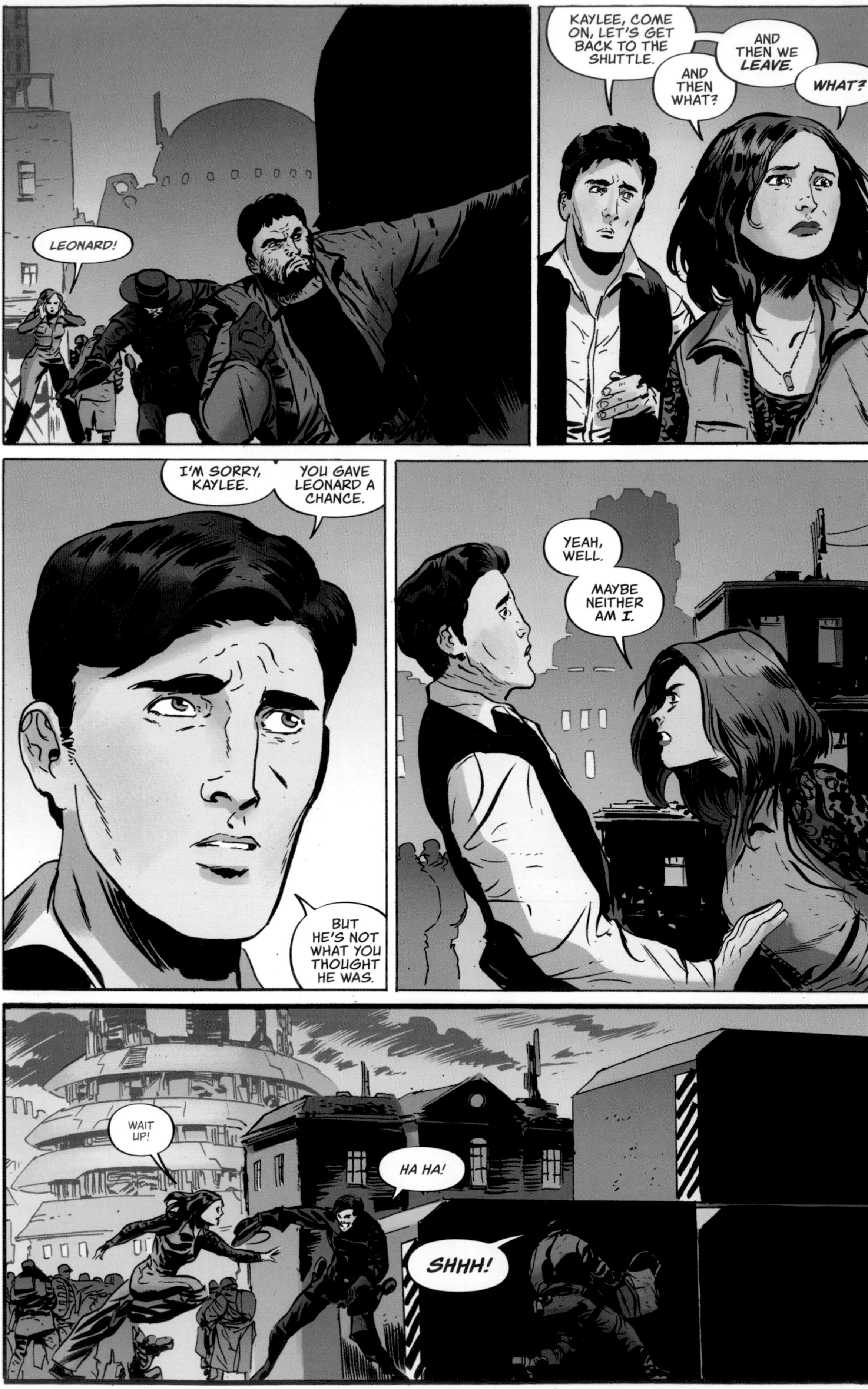
LEONARD!
KAYLEE, COME ON, LET'S GET BACK TO THE SHUTTLE.
AND THEN WHAT?
AND THEN WE LEAVE.
WHAT?
I'M SORRY, KAYLEE.
YOU GAVE LEONARD A CHANCE.
BUT HE'S NOT WHAT YOU THOUGHT HE WAS.
YEAH, WELL.
MAYBE NEITHER AM I.
WAIT UP!
HA HA!
SHHH!

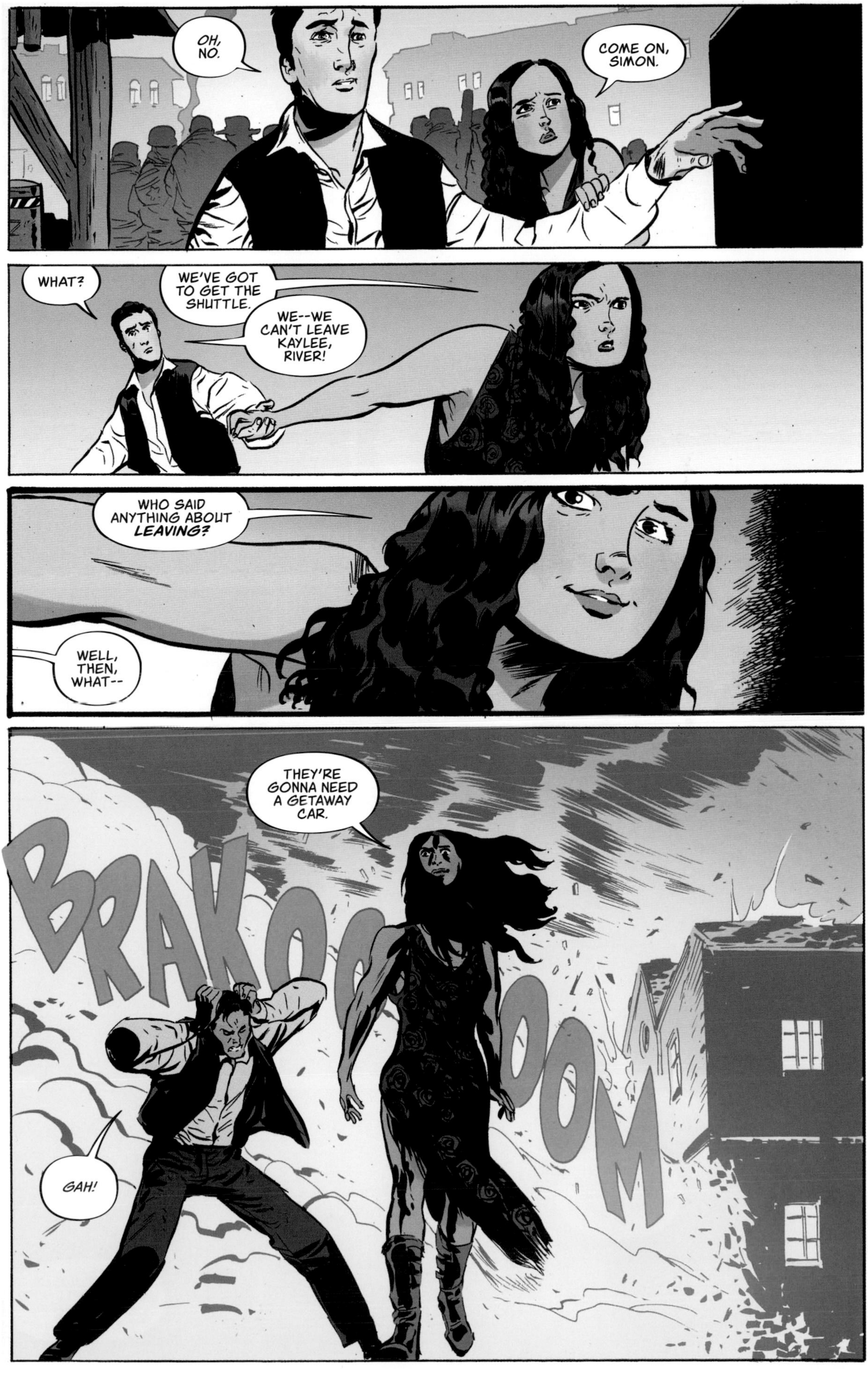

OH, NO.
COME ON, SIMON.
WHAT?
WE'VE GOT TO GET THE SHUTTLE.
WE--WE CAN'T LEAVE KAYLEE, RIVER!
WHO SAID ANYTHING ABOUT *LEAVING?*
WELL, THEN, WHAT--
THEY'RE GONNA NEED A GETAWAY CAR.
BRAKOOOOM
GAH!

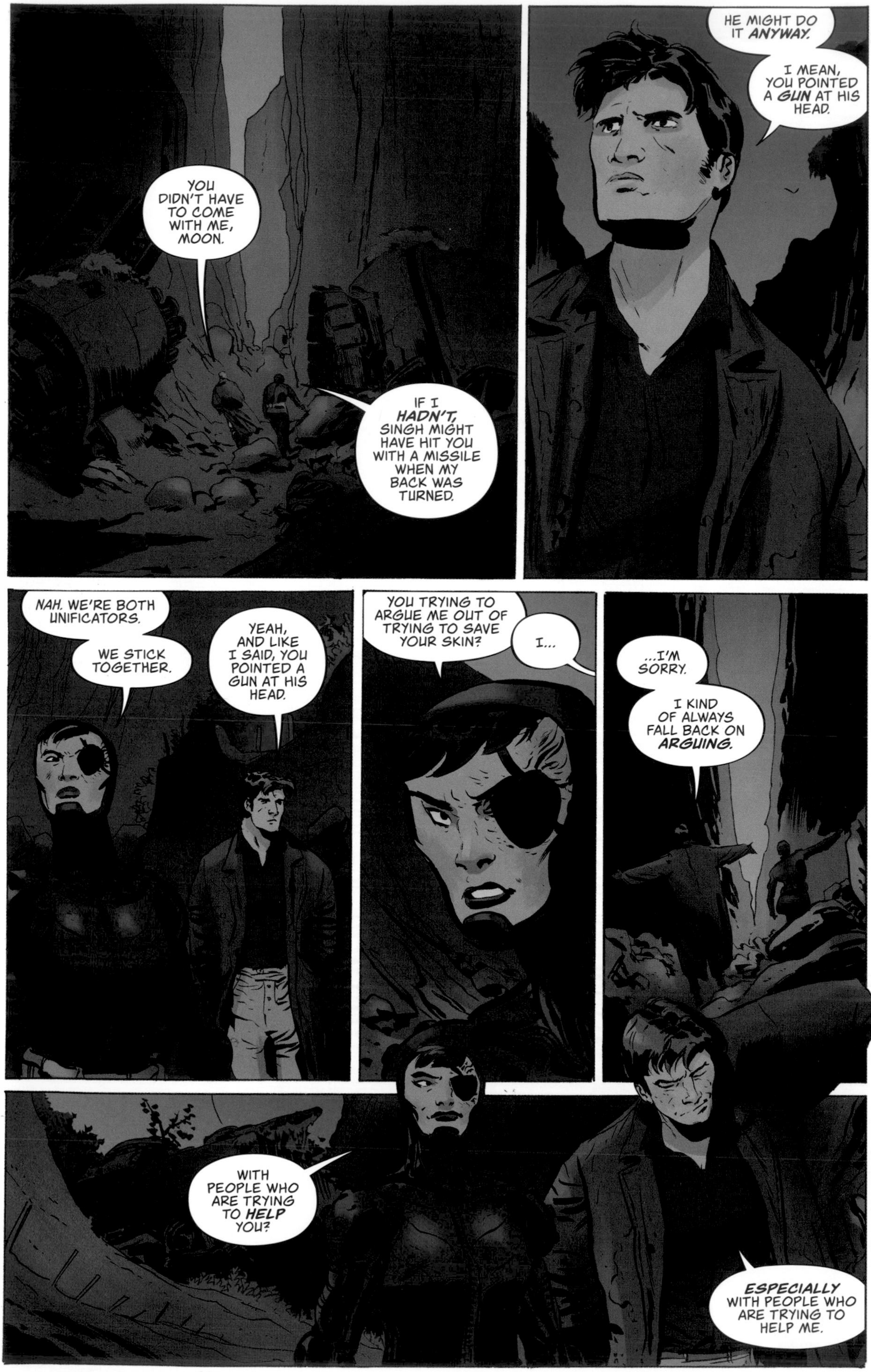
YOU DIDN'T HAVE TO COME WITH ME, MOON.
IF I HADN'T, SINGH MIGHT HAVE HIT YOU WITH A MISSILE WHEN MY BACK WAS TURNED.
HE MIGHT DO IT ANYWAY.
I MEAN, YOU POINTED A GUN AT HIS HEAD.
NAH. WE'RE BOTH UNIFICATORS.
WE STICK TOGETHER.
YEAH, AND LIKE I SAID, YOU POINTED A GUN AT HIS HEAD.
YOU TRYING TO ARGUE ME OUT OF TRYING TO SAVE YOUR SKIN?
I...
...I'M SORRY.
I KIND OF ALWAYS FALL BACK ON ARGUING.
WITH PEOPLE WHO ARE TRYING TO HELP YOU?
ESPECIALLY WITH PEOPLE WHO ARE TRYING TO HELP ME.

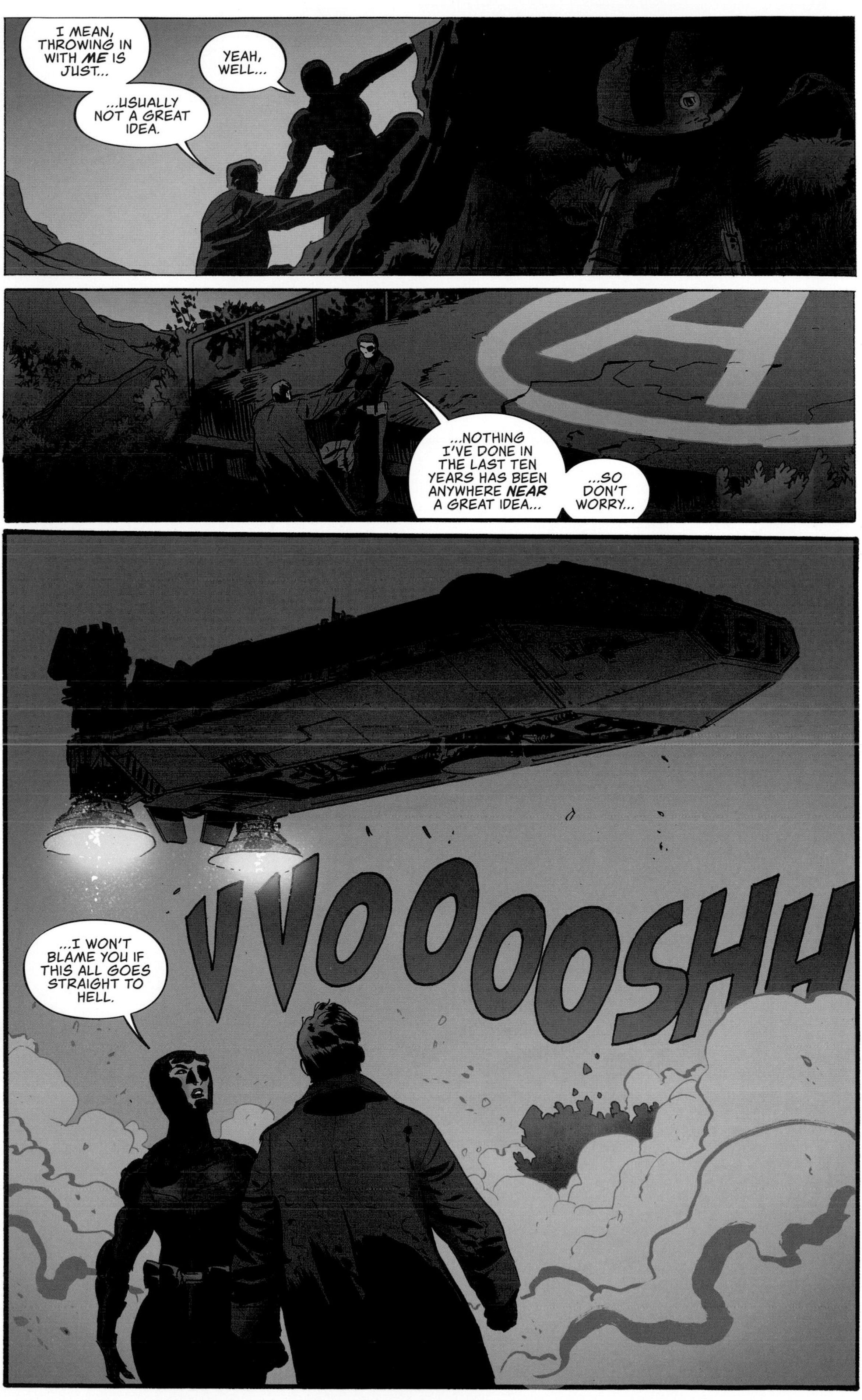
I MEAN, THROWING IN WITH *ME* IS JUST...
...USUALLY NOT A GREAT IDEA.
YEAH, WELL...
...NOTHING I'VE DONE IN THE LAST TEN YEARS HAS BEEN ANYWHERE *NEAR* A GREAT IDEA...
...SO DON'T WORRY...
...I WON'T BLAME YOU IF THIS ALL GOES STRAIGHT TO HELL.
VVOOOOSHH

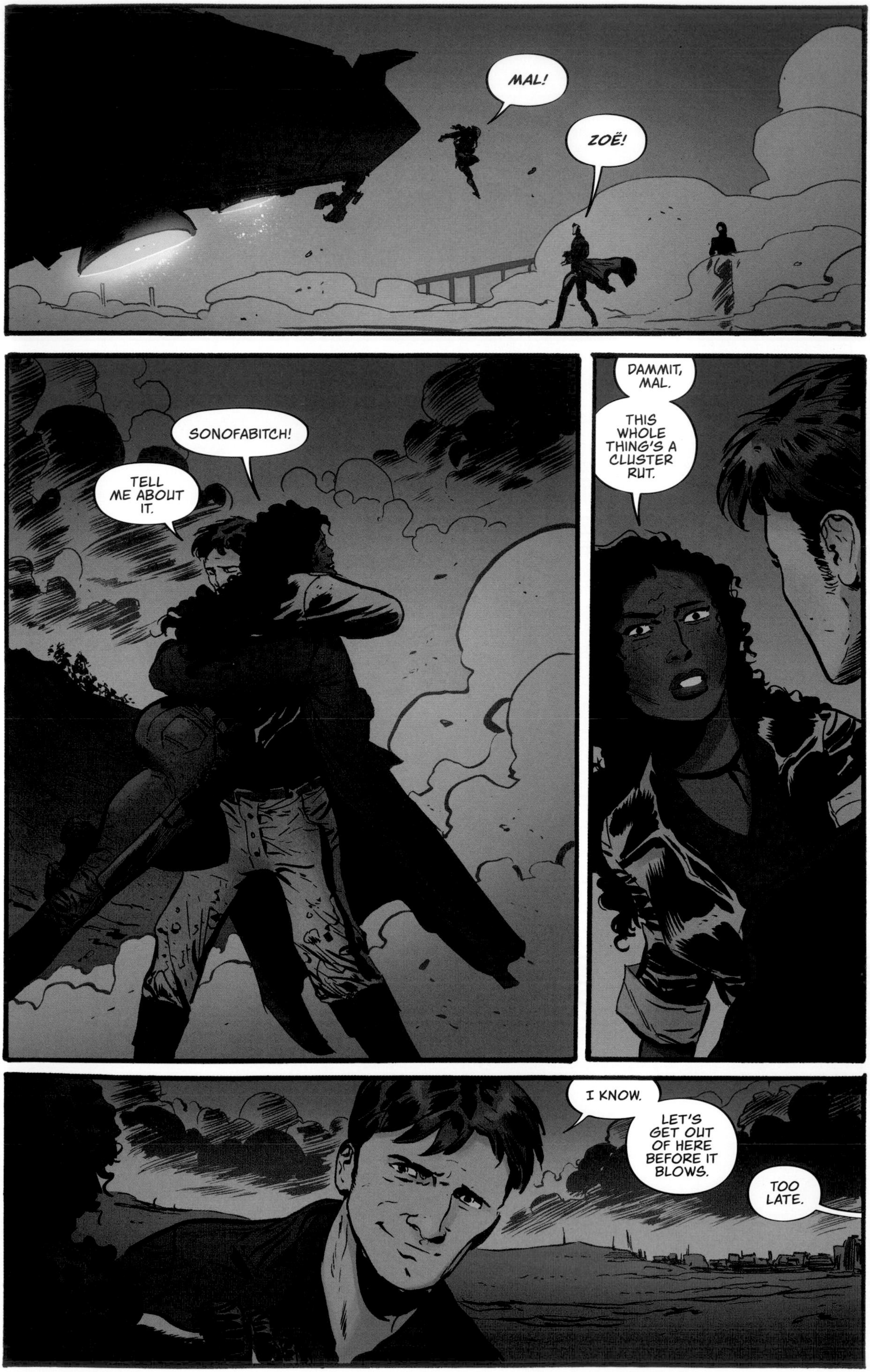
MAL!
ZOË!
SONOFABITCH!
TELL ME ABOUT IT.
DAMMIT, MAL.
THIS WHOLE THING'S A CLUSTER RUT.
I KNOW.
LET'S GET OUT OF HERE BEFORE IT BLOWS.
TOO LATE.

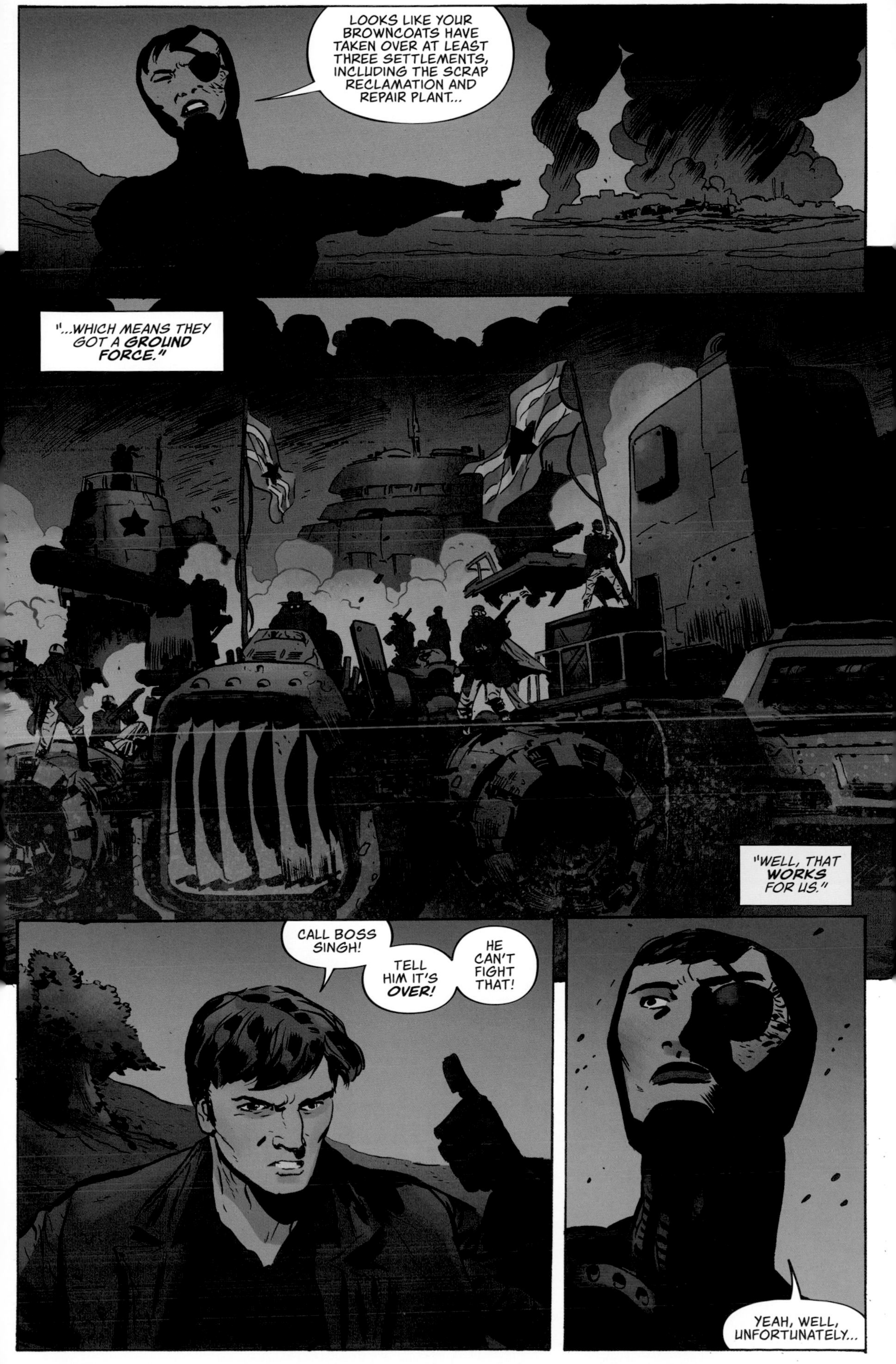
LOOKS LIKE YOUR BROWNCOATS HAVE TAKEN OVER AT LEAST THREE SETTLEMENTS, INCLUDING THE SCRAP RECLAMATION AND REPAIR PLANT...
"...WHICH MEANS THEY GOT A GROUND FORCE."
"WELL, THAT WORKS FOR US."
CALL BOSS SINGH!
TELL HIM IT'S OVER!
HE CAN'T FIGHT THAT!
YEAH, WELL, UNFORTUNATELY...

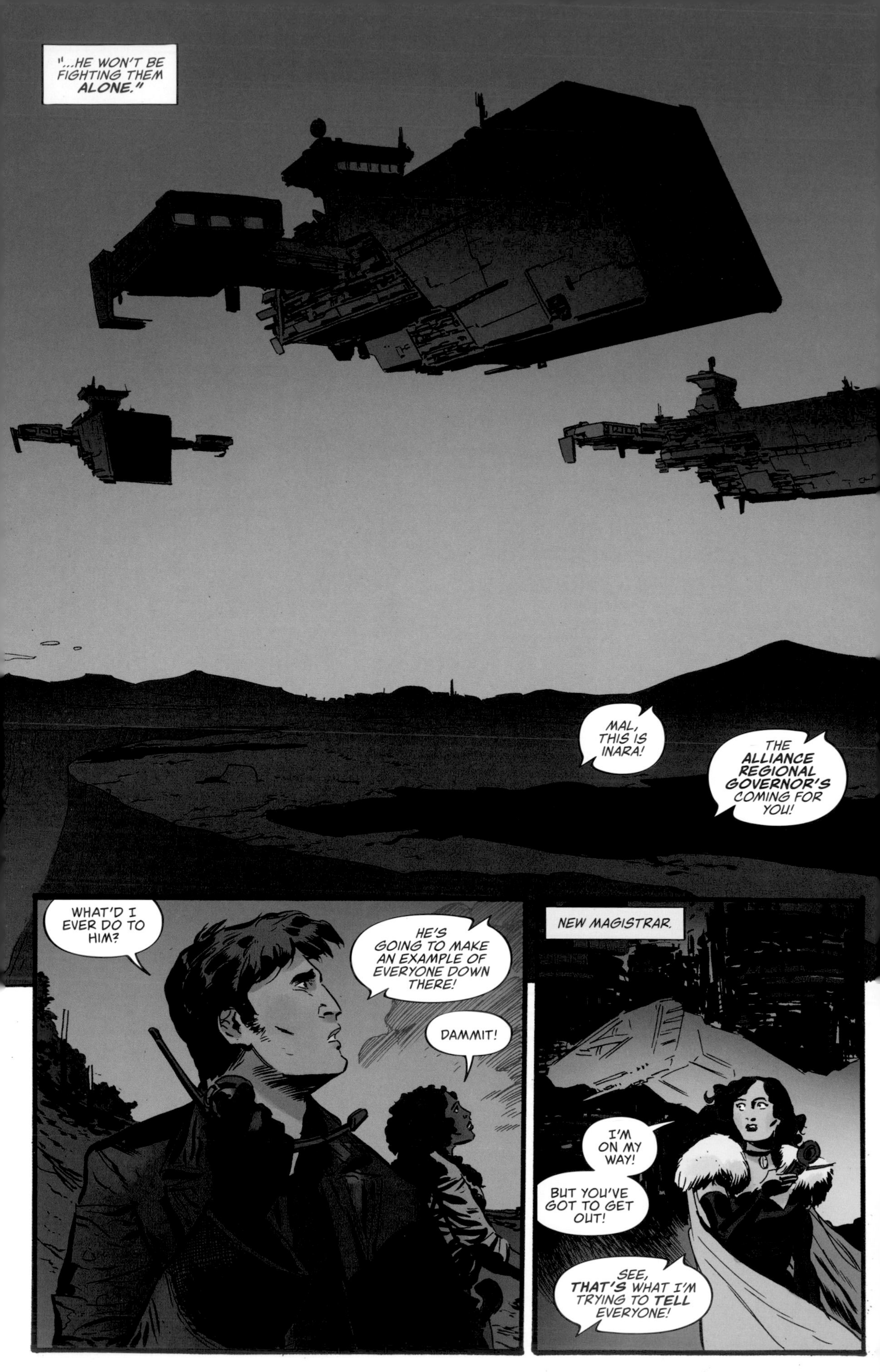
"...HE WON'T BE FIGHTING THEM **ALONE.**"
MAL, THIS IS INARA!
THE **ALLIANCE REGIONAL GOVERNOR'S** COMING FOR YOU!
WHAT'D I EVER DO TO HIM?
HE'S GOING TO MAKE AN EXAMPLE OF EVERYONE DOWN THERE!
DAMMIT!
NEW MAGISTRAR.
I'M ON MY WAY!
BUT YOU'VE GOT TO GET OUT!
SEE, **THAT'S** WHAT I'M TRYING TO **TELL** EVERYONE!

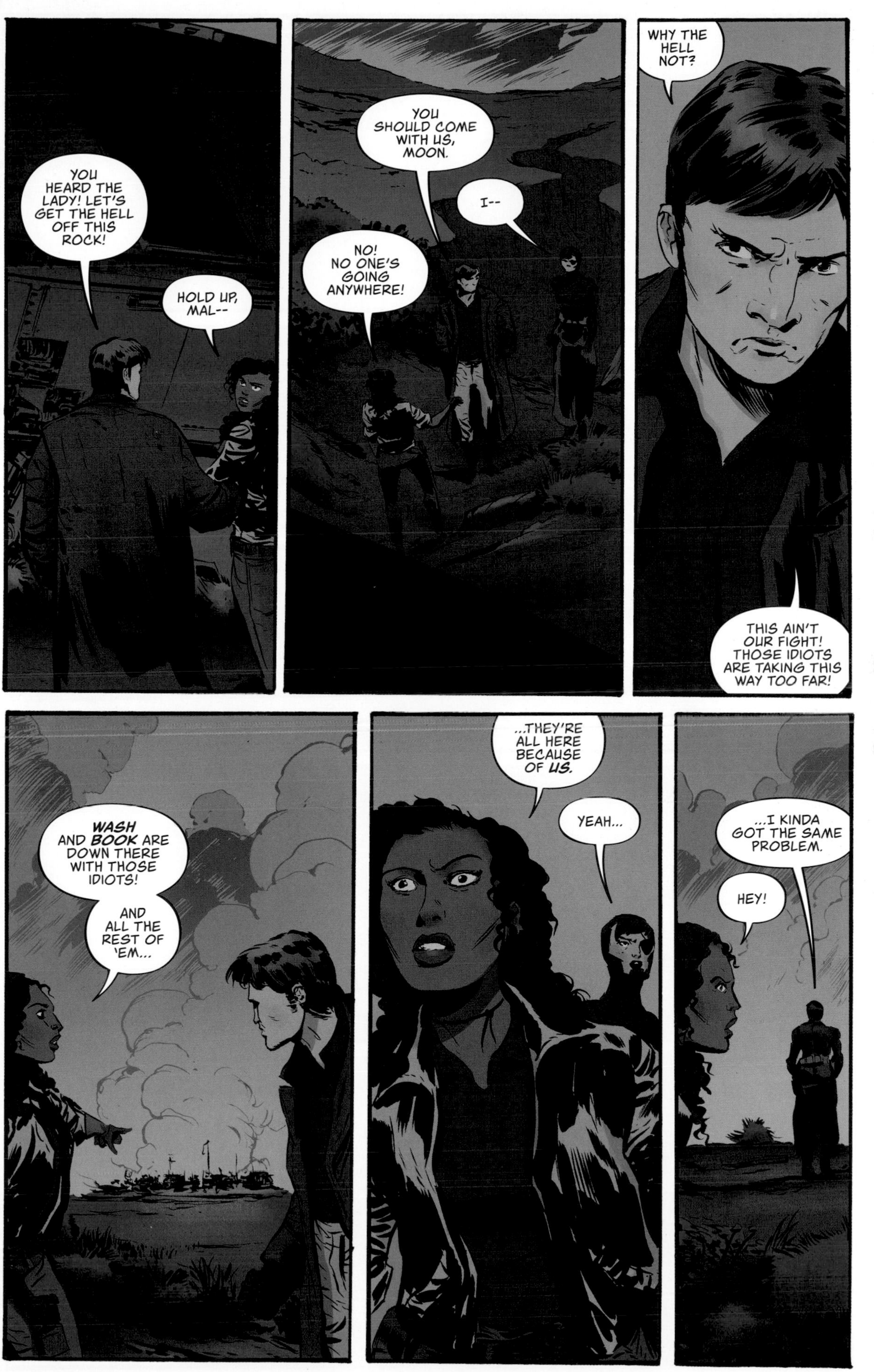
YOU HEARD THE LADY! LET'S GET THE HELL OFF THIS ROCK!
HOLD UP, MAL--
YOU SHOULD COME WITH US, MOON.
I--
NO! NO ONE'S GOING ANYWHERE!
WHY THE HELL NOT?
THIS AIN'T OUR FIGHT! THOSE IDIOTS ARE TAKING THIS WAY TOO FAR!
WASH AND BOOK ARE DOWN THERE WITH THOSE IDIOTS!
AND ALL THE REST OF 'EM...
...THEY'RE ALL HERE BECAUSE OF US.
YEAH...
...I KINDA GOT THE SAME PROBLEM.
HEY!

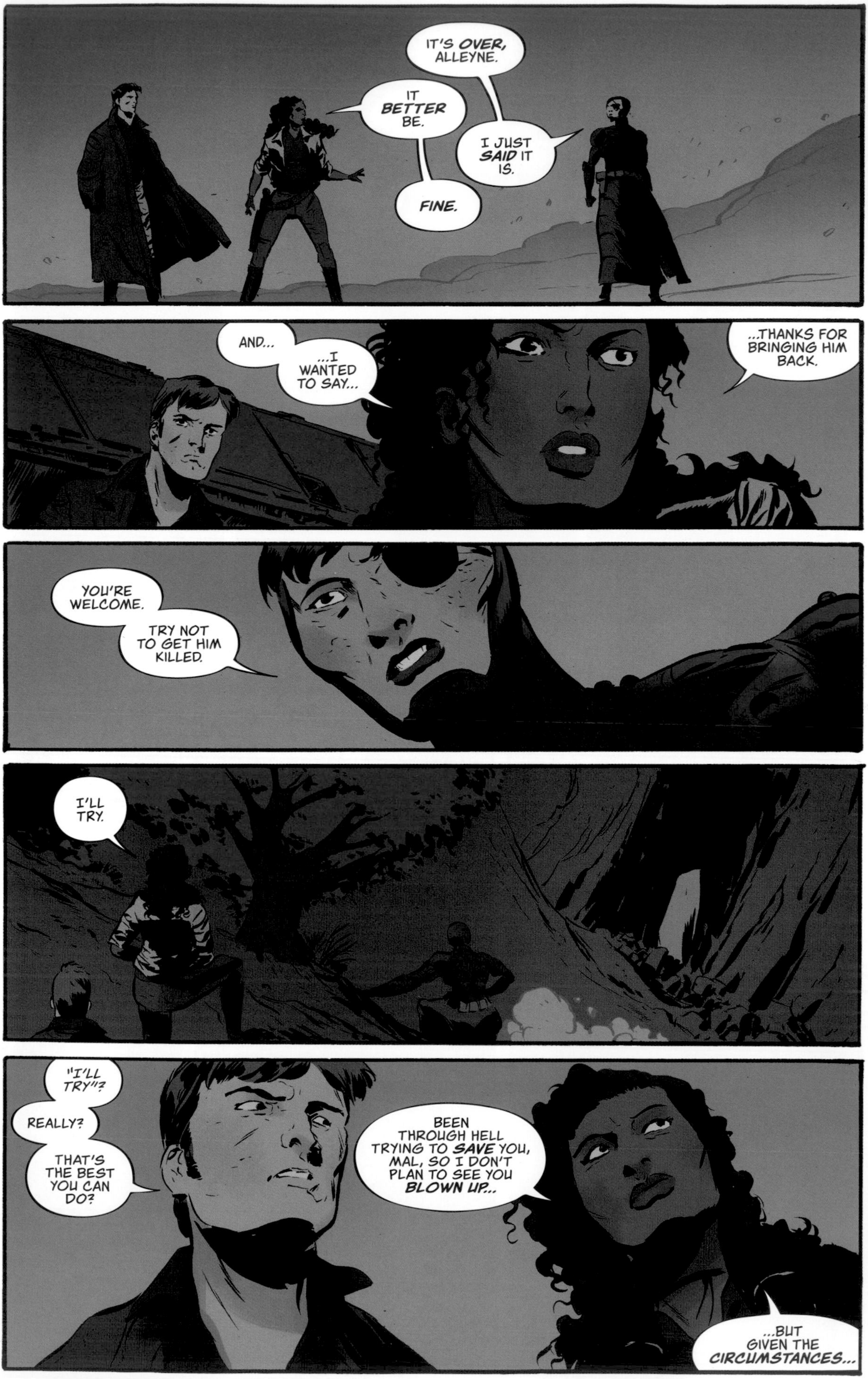
IT'S *OVER,* ALLEYNE.
IT *BETTER* BE.
I JUST *SAID* IT IS.
FINE.
AND...
...I WANTED TO SAY...
...THANKS FOR BRINGING HIM BACK.
YOU'RE WELCOME.
TRY NOT TO GET HIM KILLED.
I'LL TRY.
"I'LL TRY"?
REALLY?
THAT'S THE BEST YOU CAN DO?
BEEN THROUGH HELL TRYING TO *SAVE* YOU, MAL, SO I DON'T PLAN TO SEE YOU *BLOWN UP...*
...BUT GIVEN THE *CIRCUMSTANCES...*

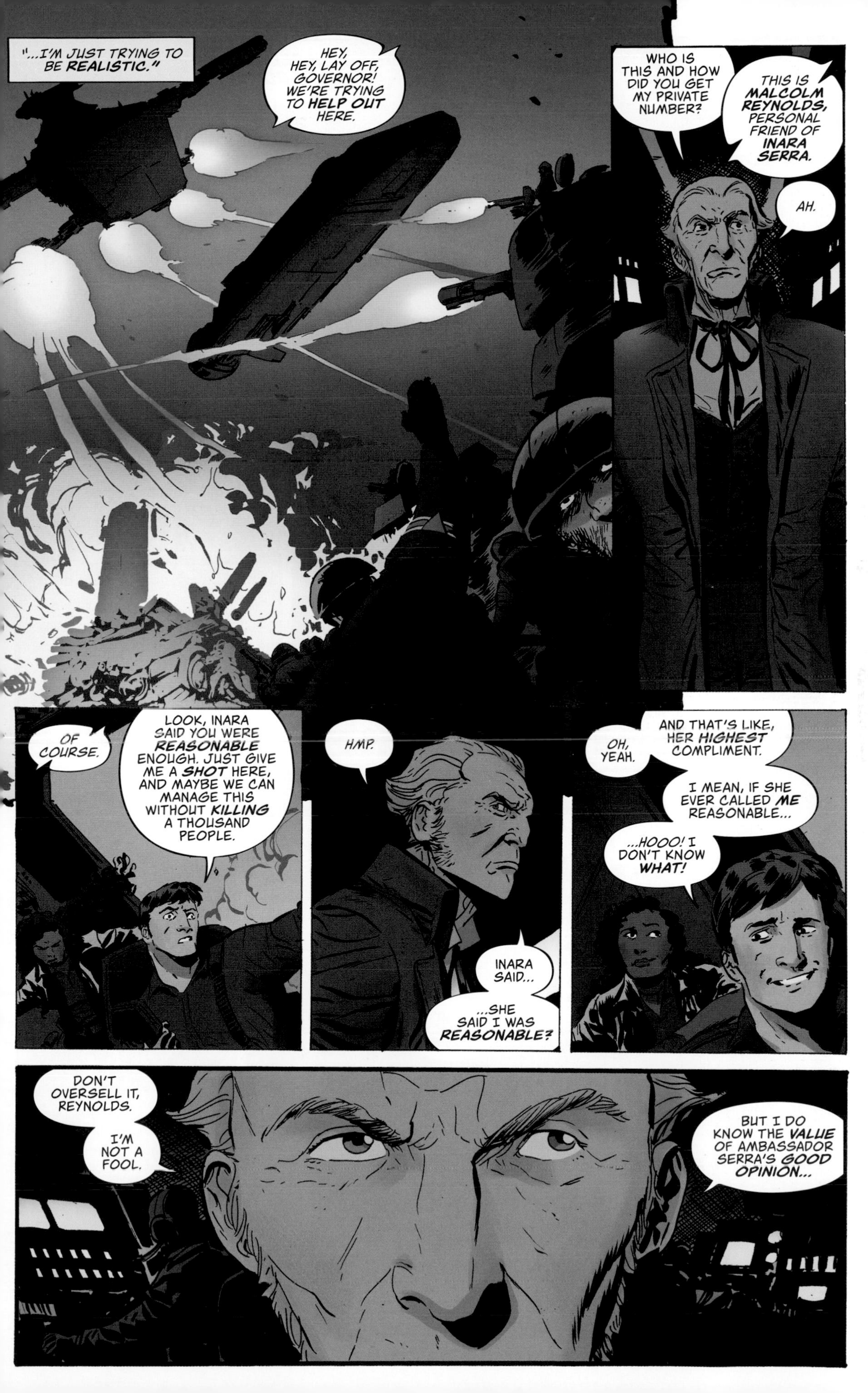
"...I'M JUST TRYING TO BE REALISTIC."
HEY, HEY, LAY OFF, GOVERNOR! WE'RE TRYING TO HELP OUT HERE.
WHO IS THIS AND HOW DID YOU GET MY PRIVATE NUMBER?
THIS IS MALCOLM REYNOLDS, PERSONAL FRIEND OF INARA SERRA.
AH.
OF COURSE.
LOOK, INARA SAID YOU WERE REASONABLE ENOUGH. JUST GIVE ME A SHOT HERE, AND MAYBE WE CAN MANAGE THIS WITHOUT KILLING A THOUSAND PEOPLE.
HMP.
INARA SAID...
...SHE SAID I WAS REASONABLE?
OH, YEAH.
AND THAT'S LIKE, HER HIGHEST COMPLIMENT.
I MEAN, IF SHE EVER CALLED ME REASONABLE...
...HOOO! I DON'T KNOW WHAT!
DON'T OVERSELL IT, REYNOLDS.
I'M NOT A FOOL.
BUT I DO KNOW THE VALUE OF AMBASSADOR SERRA'S GOOD OPINION...

"...SO I'LL GIVE YOU TEN MINUTES."

HOLD UP, YA GRUNTS!

WHO THE HELL'S THAT?

THAT, MY FRIENDS, IS CAPTAIN MALCOLM REYNOLDS...

...THE MAN YOU ALL SUPPOSEDLY CAME HERE TO RESCUE.

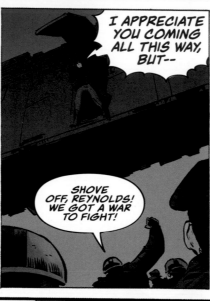

I APPRECIATE YOU COMING ALL THIS WAY, BUT--

SHOVE OFF, REYNOLDS! WE GOT A WAR TO FIGHT!

I HEAR YOU GOT A COUPLE OF SERGEANTS AMONGST YA.

BUT I'M PRETTY DAMN SURE I'M THE ONLY CAPTAIN ON THE FIELD.

SO LISTEN UP.

I'M FINE. AND RIGHT NOW, SO ARE ALL OF YOU.

AND THAT'S HOW I WANNA KEEP YOU.

SCREW THIS! KEEP ON MOVING!

SHUT UP BACK THERE!

BUT ISN'T HE TECHNICALLY ONLY A SERGEANT? I MEAN, HE JUST BOUGHT THE "CAPTAIN" TITLE WITH HIS SHIP--

SHUT UP, GOVERNOR. THIS IS WORKING, ALL RIGHT? JUST GIVE US ANOTHER FEW MINUTES AND--

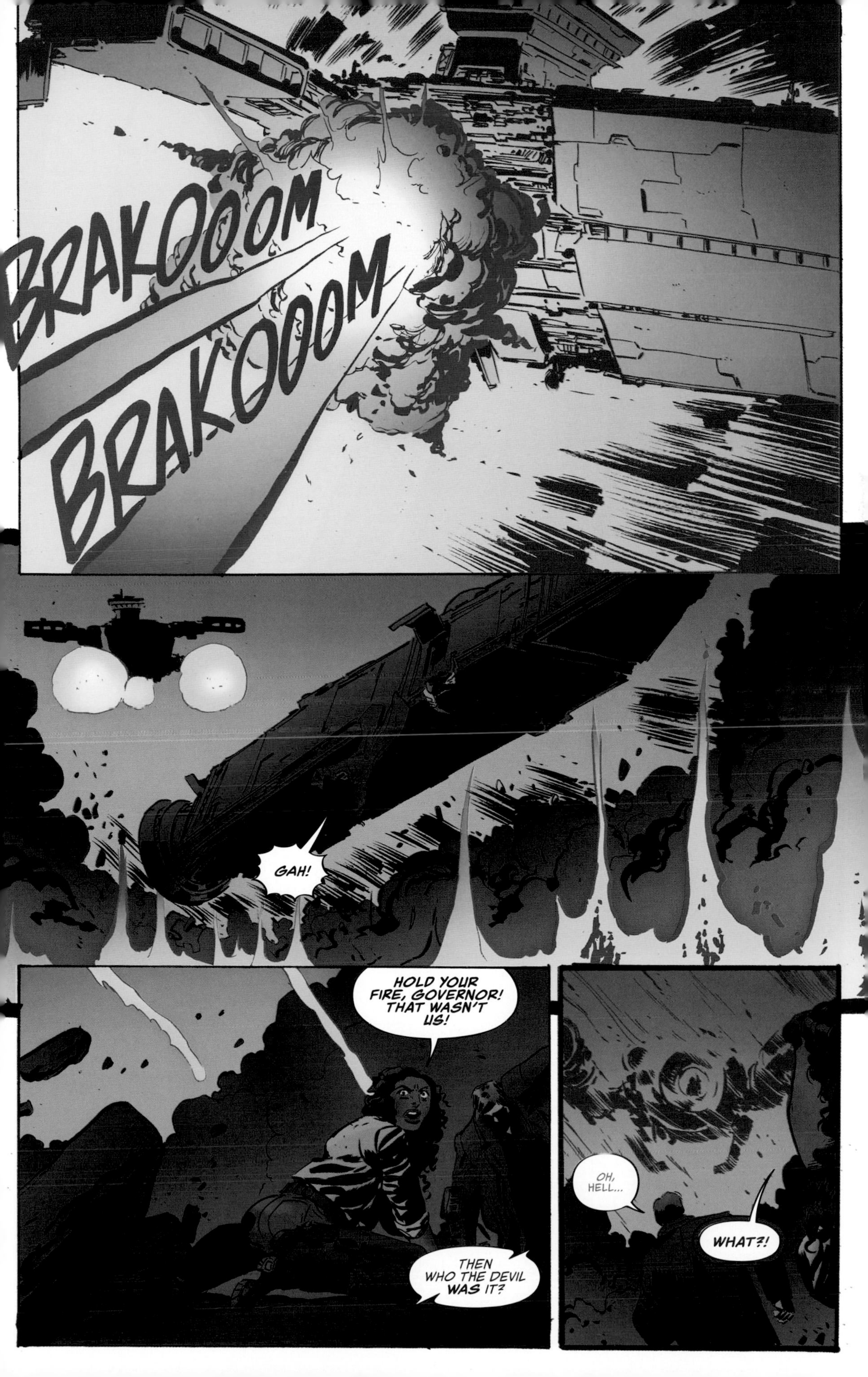
BRAKOOOM
BRAKOOOM
GAH!
HOLD YOUR FIRE, GOVERNOR! THAT WASN'T US!
THEN WHO THE DEVIL WAS IT?
OH, HELL...
WHAT?!

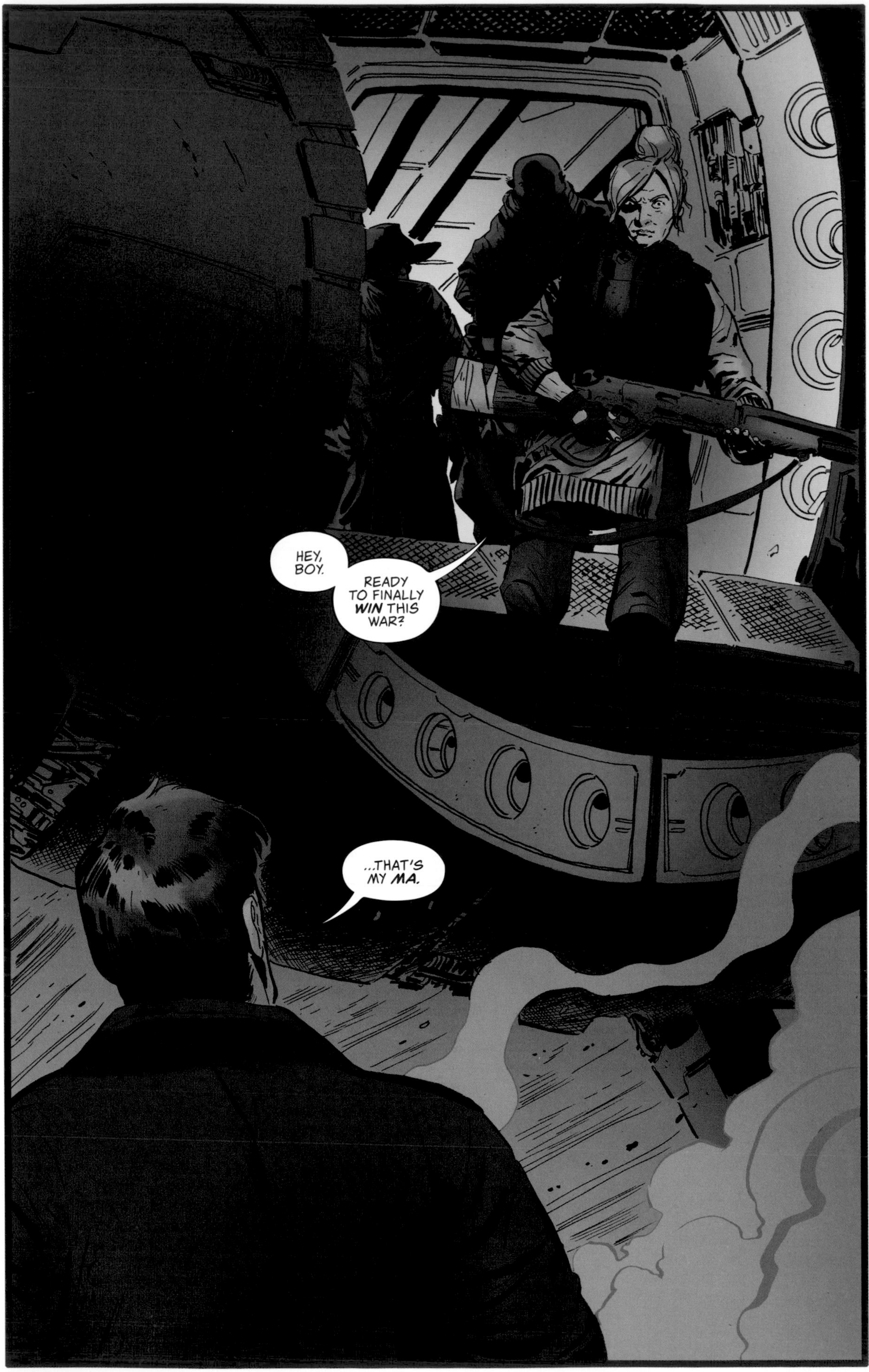
HEY, BOY.
READY TO FINALLY WIN THIS WAR?
...THAT'S MY MA.

WHAT MAKES US SPECI

WE'VE GOT US SOME CRIME TO BE DONE.

Wood spot, sir. She still has the adva

know why? Because we are so very pretty. We are just too pretty for God to let us die.

I don't believe there's a power in the 'Verse can stop Kaylee from being cheerful. Sometimes you jus

And I'm thinking you weren't burdened with an overabundance of schooling. So why don't we ju

Ship like this will be with you 'til the day you die. That's 'cause it's a death trap.

It's a real burden

BEING RIGHT SO OF

Sir, I think you have a problem with your brain being missing

Fruity oaty bar!

Seems to me the last time there was a chance for a little palaver we were all manner

This ain't bad. There's a trick to it. Wood alcohol. Now we are favored guests treated

FINEST IN BEVERAGES THAT MAKE YO

YOU'RE LO

WE ALL A

喧闹 起来

INEVITABLE BETRAYAL.

WE'D BE DEAD.

Curse your sudden

Can't get paid if you're dead

IN MY SKY. SU

This is why

lost, you ju

喧闹

BIG DMN OES,

BLUE

MANLY AN IMPULSIV

喧闹 起来

MAN OF HO

DEN OF THI

SIN AND HELLFIRE. ONE HAS PERS. 旅

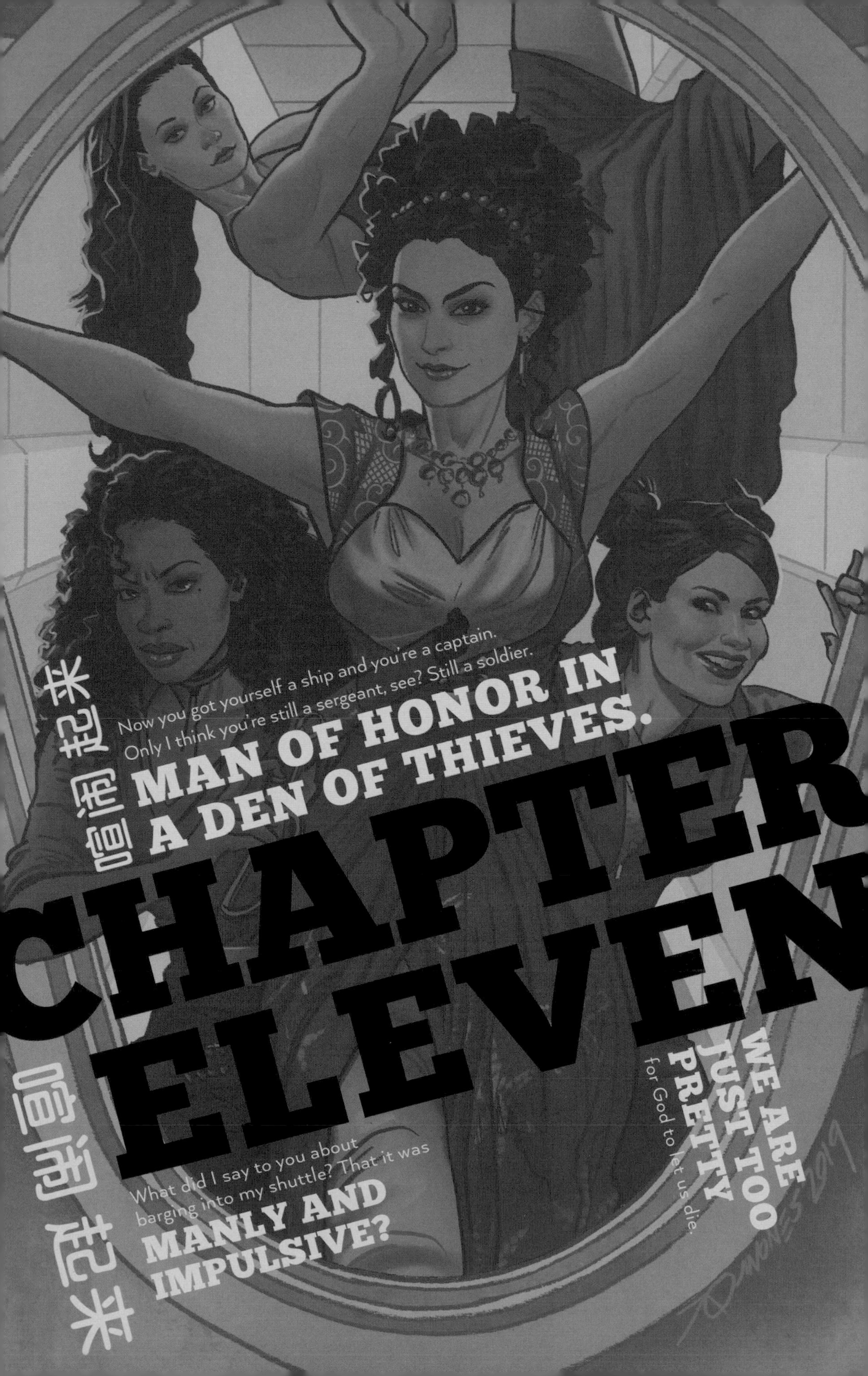

Now you got yourself a ship and you're a captain.
Only I think you're still a sergeant, see? Still a soldier.
MAN OF HONOR IN A DEN OF THIEVES.
喧闹起来
CHAPTER ELEVEN
WE ARE JUST TOO PRETTY
for God to let us die.
What did I say to you about barging into my shuttle? That it was
MANLY AND IMPULSIVE?
喧闹起来

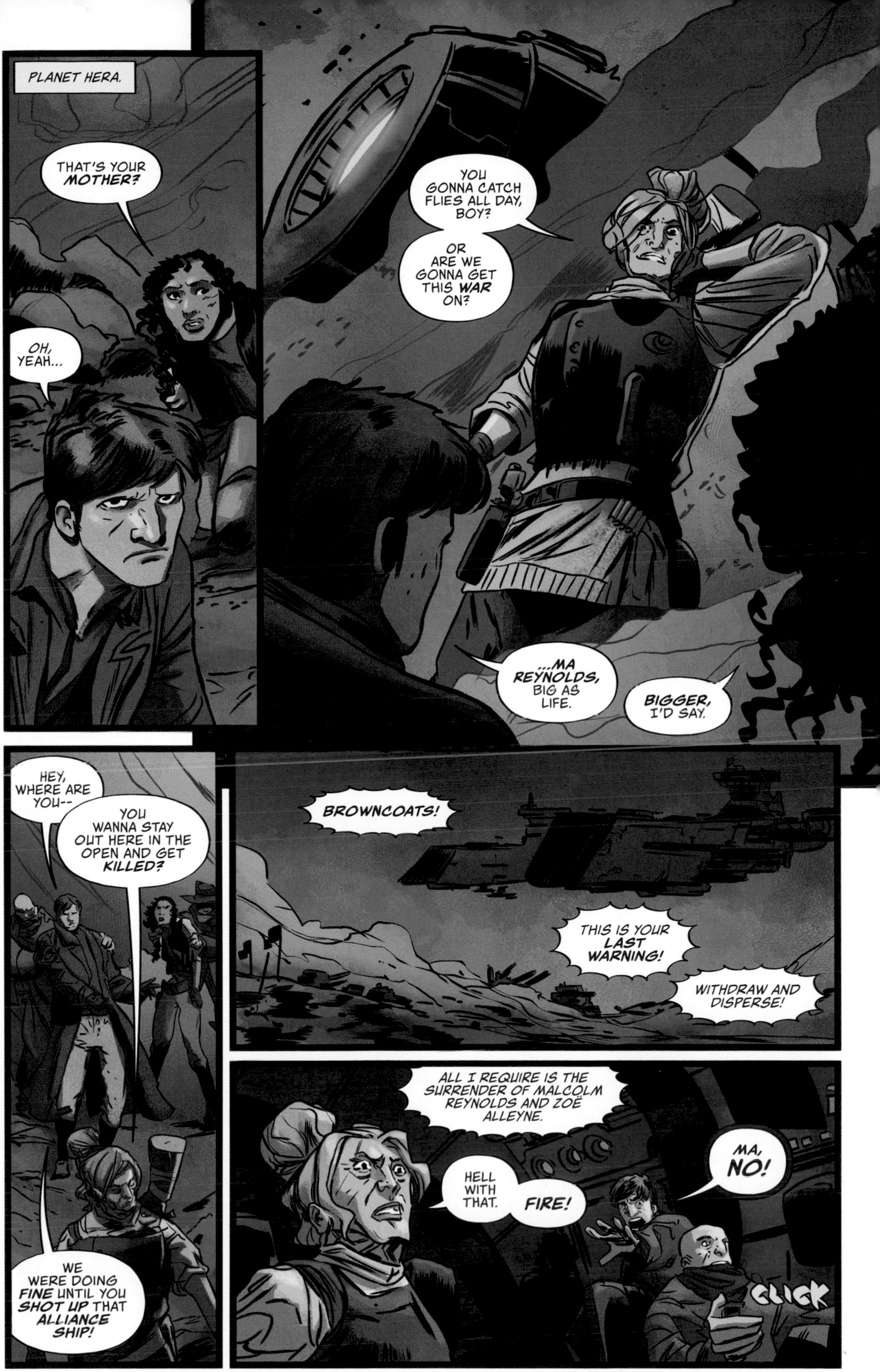
PLANET HERA.
THAT'S YOUR MOTHER?
OH, YEAH...
YOU GONNA CATCH FLIES ALL DAY, BOY?
OR ARE WE GONNA GET THIS WAR ON?
...MA REYNOLDS, BIG AS LIFE.
BIGGER, I'D SAY.
HEY, WHERE ARE YOU--
YOU WANNA STAY OUT HERE IN THE OPEN AND GET KILLED?
WE WERE DOING FINE UNTIL YOU SHOT UP THAT ALLIANCE SHIP!
BROWNCOATS!
THIS IS YOUR LAST WARNING!
WITHDRAW AND DISPERSE!
ALL I REQUIRE IS THE SURRENDER OF MALCOLM REYNOLDS AND ZOË ALLEYNE.
HELL WITH THAT.
FIRE!
MA, NO!
CLICK

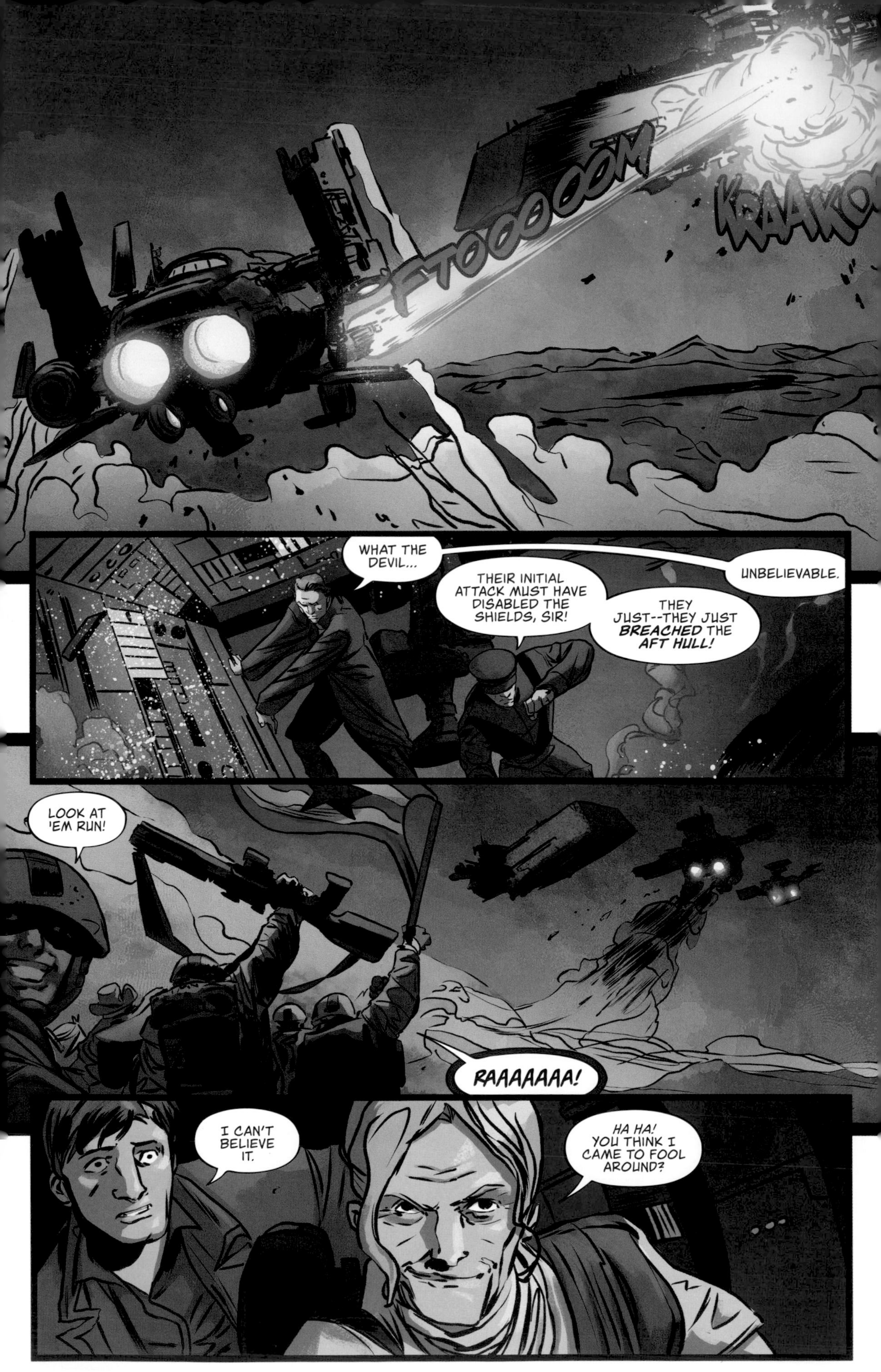

FTOOOOOOM
KRAAKO
WHAT THE DEVIL...
UNBELIEVABLE.
THEIR INITIAL ATTACK MUST HAVE DISABLED THE SHIELDS, SIR!
THEY JUST--THEY JUST **BREACHED** THE **AFT HULL!**
LOOK AT 'EM RUN!
RAAAAAAA!
I CAN'T BELIEVE IT.
HA HA! YOU THINK I CAME TO FOOL AROUND?

BUT *YOU*.

YOU LAID THE GROUNDWORK.

PROUD OF YOU, MALCOLM.

SOCK

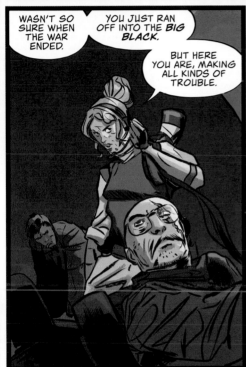

WASN'T SO SURE WHEN THE WAR ENDED.

YOU JUST RAN OFF INTO THE *BIG BLACK*.

BUT HERE YOU ARE, MAKING ALL KINDS OF TROUBLE.

BROWNCOATS, THIS IS *MAUDE REYNOLDS* FROM *PLANET SHADOW*.

YOU MIGHT HAVE NOTICED I GOT A *2508 BLUE SUN SKYCRACKER* ON THIS BOAT.

THOSE ALLIANCE BASTARDS'RE GONNA TAKE A FEW MINUTES TO THINK ABOUT THIS ONE.

I'M TOUCHING DOWN.

YOU WANNA *GET ORGANIZED* AND ACTUALLY *WIN* THIS THING, COME *PARLEY*.

THIS IS NUTS.

THIS ISN'T HAPPENING.

GET AHOLD OF YOURSELF, BOY.

I WAS TRYING TO *STOP* THIS STUPID WAR!

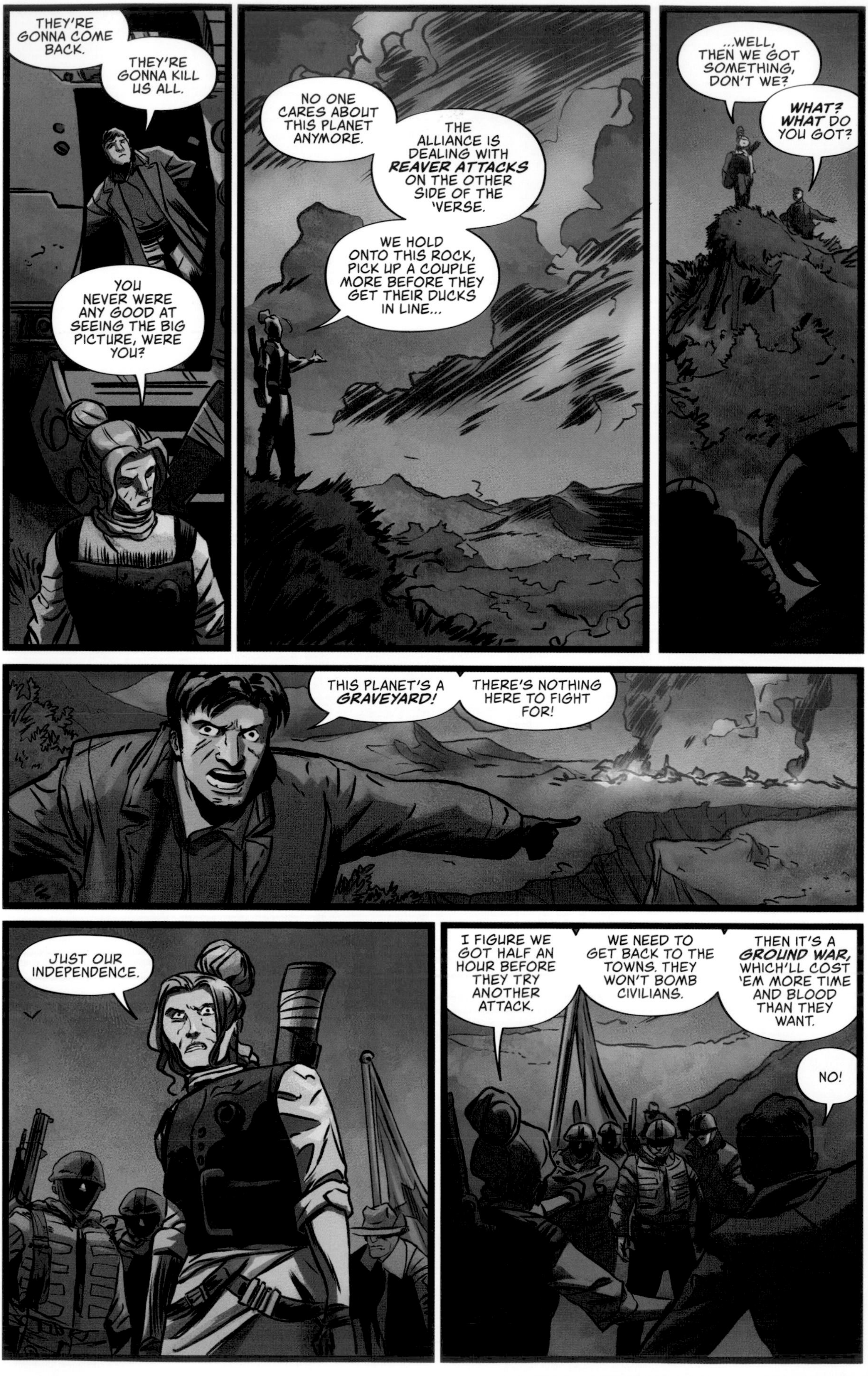
THEY'RE GONNA COME BACK.
THEY'RE GONNA KILL US ALL.
YOU NEVER WERE ANY GOOD AT SEEING THE BIG PICTURE, WERE YOU?
NO ONE CARES ABOUT THIS PLANET ANYMORE.
THE ALLIANCE IS DEALING WITH REAVER ATTACKS ON THE OTHER SIDE OF THE 'VERSE.
WE HOLD ONTO THIS ROCK, PICK UP A COUPLE MORE BEFORE THEY GET THEIR DUCKS IN LINE...
...WELL, THEN WE GOT SOMETHING, DON'T WE?
WHAT? WHAT DO YOU GOT?
THIS PLANET'S A GRAVEYARD!
THERE'S NOTHING HERE TO FIGHT FOR!
JUST OUR INDEPENDENCE.
I FIGURE WE GOT HALF AN HOUR BEFORE THEY TRY ANOTHER ATTACK.
WE NEED TO GET BACK TO THE TOWNS. THEY WON'T BOMB CIVILIANS.
THEN IT'S A GROUND WAR, WHICH'LL COST 'EM MORE TIME AND BLOOD THAN THEY WANT.
NO!

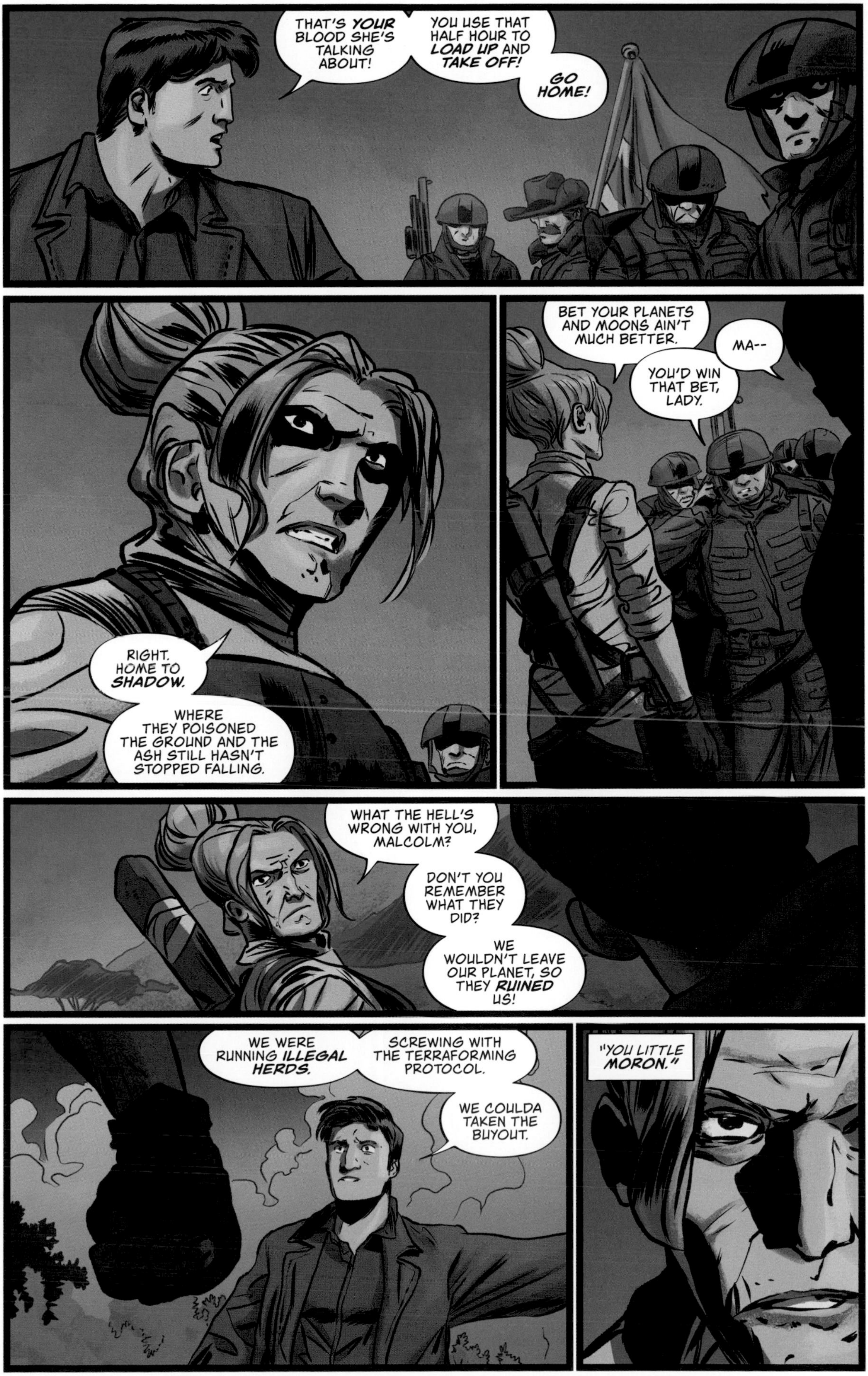
THAT'S *YOUR* BLOOD SHE'S TALKING ABOUT!
YOU USE THAT HALF HOUR TO *LOAD UP* AND *TAKE OFF!*
GO HOME!
RIGHT. HOME TO *SHADOW.*
WHERE THEY POISONED THE GROUND AND THE ASH STILL HASN'T STOPPED FALLING.
BET YOUR PLANETS AND MOONS AIN'T MUCH BETTER.
MA--
YOU'D WIN THAT BET, LADY.
WHAT THE HELL'S WRONG WITH YOU, MALCOLM?
DON'T YOU REMEMBER WHAT THEY DID?
WE WOULDN'T LEAVE OUR PLANET, SO THEY *RUINED* US!
WE WERE RUNNING *ILLEGAL HERDS.*
SCREWING WITH THE TERRAFORMING PROTOCOL.
WE COULDA TAKEN THE BUYOUT.
"YOU LITTLE MORON."

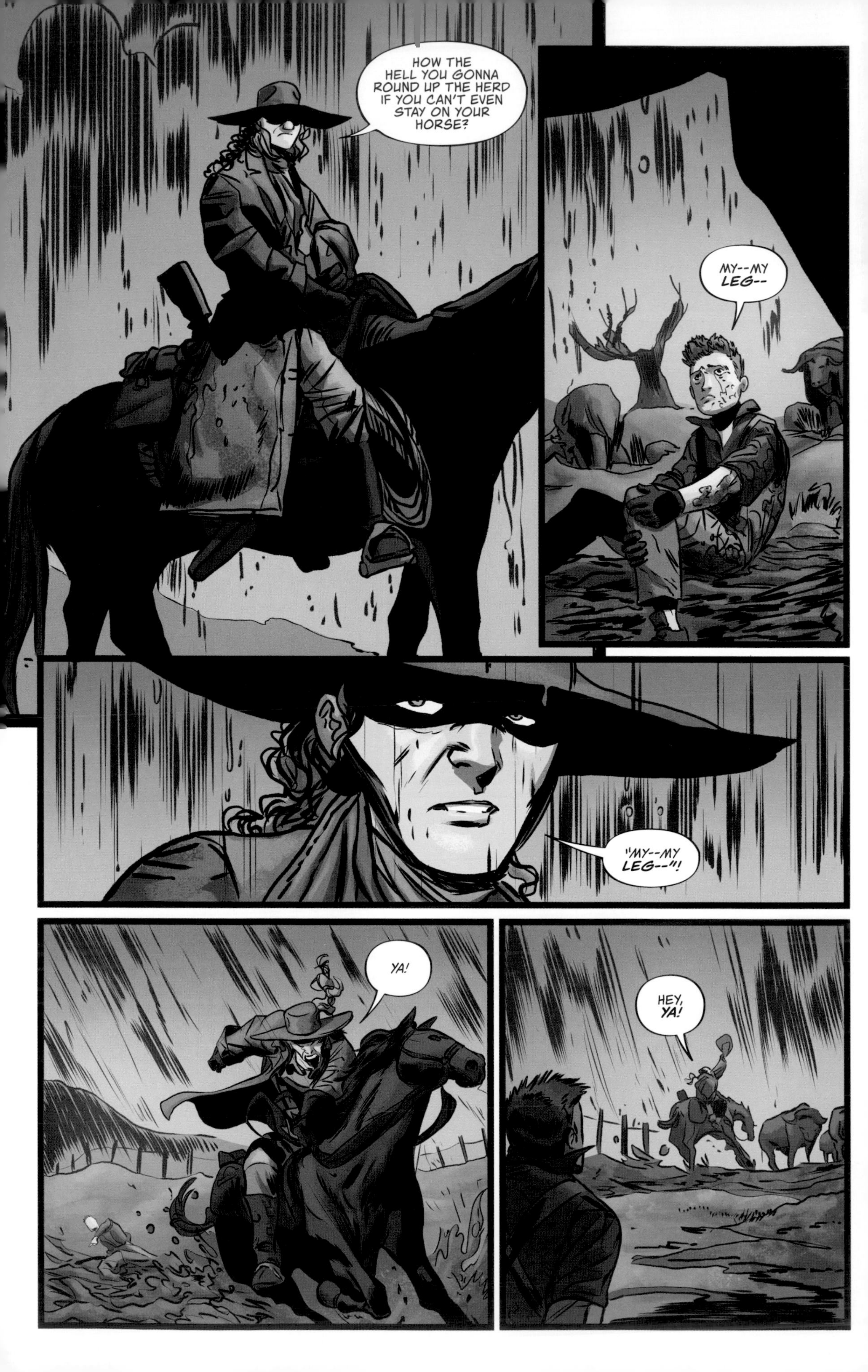
HOW THE HELL YOU GONNA ROUND UP THE HERD IF YOU CAN'T EVEN STAY ON YOUR HORSE?
MY--MY LEG--
"MY--MY LEG--"!
YA!
HEY, YA!

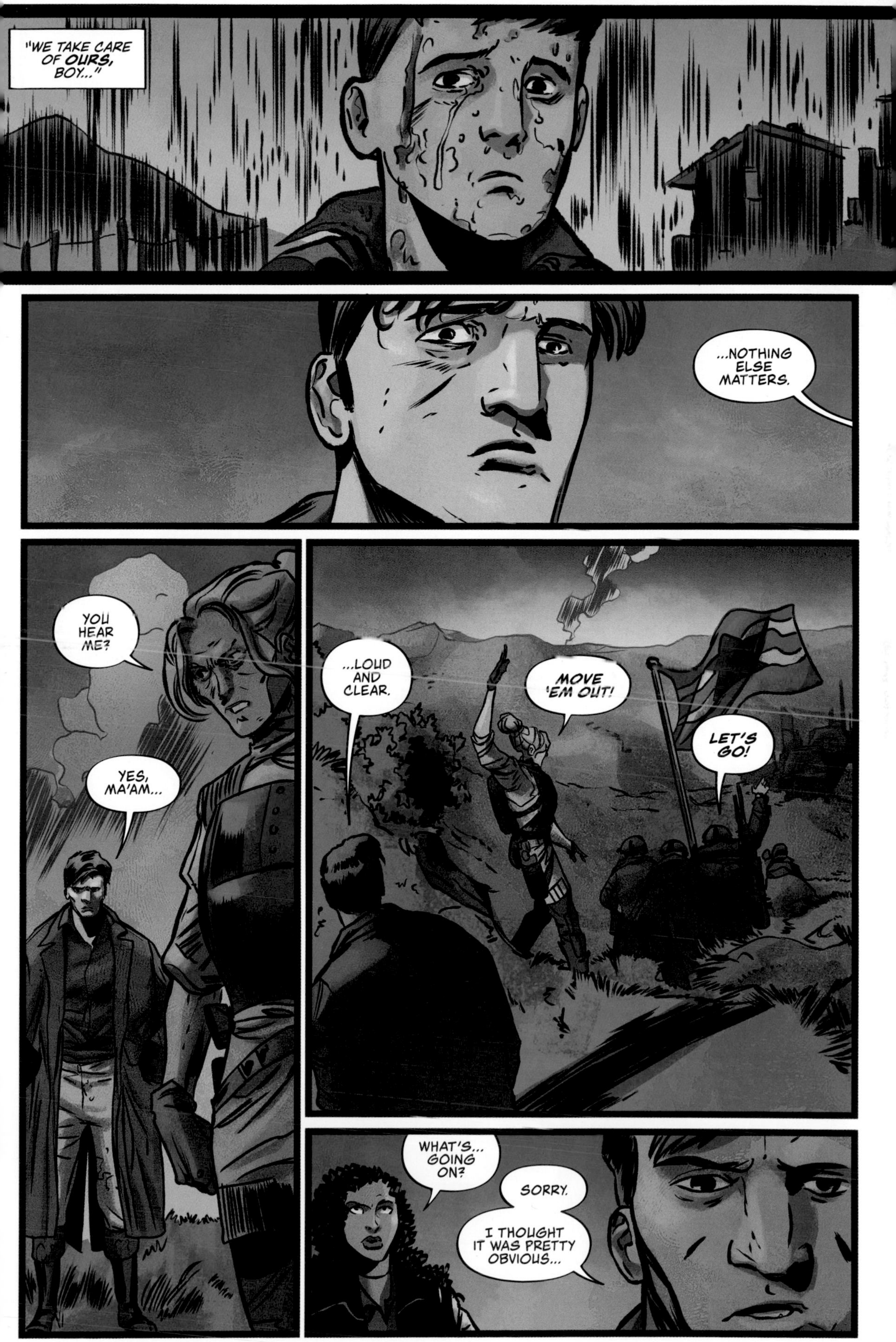
"WE TAKE CARE OF OURS, BOY..."
...NOTHING ELSE MATTERS.
YOU HEAR ME?
YES, MA'AM...
...LOUD AND CLEAR.
MOVE 'EM OUT!
LET'S GO!
WHAT'S... GOING ON?
SORRY.
I THOUGHT IT WAS PRETTY OBVIOUS...

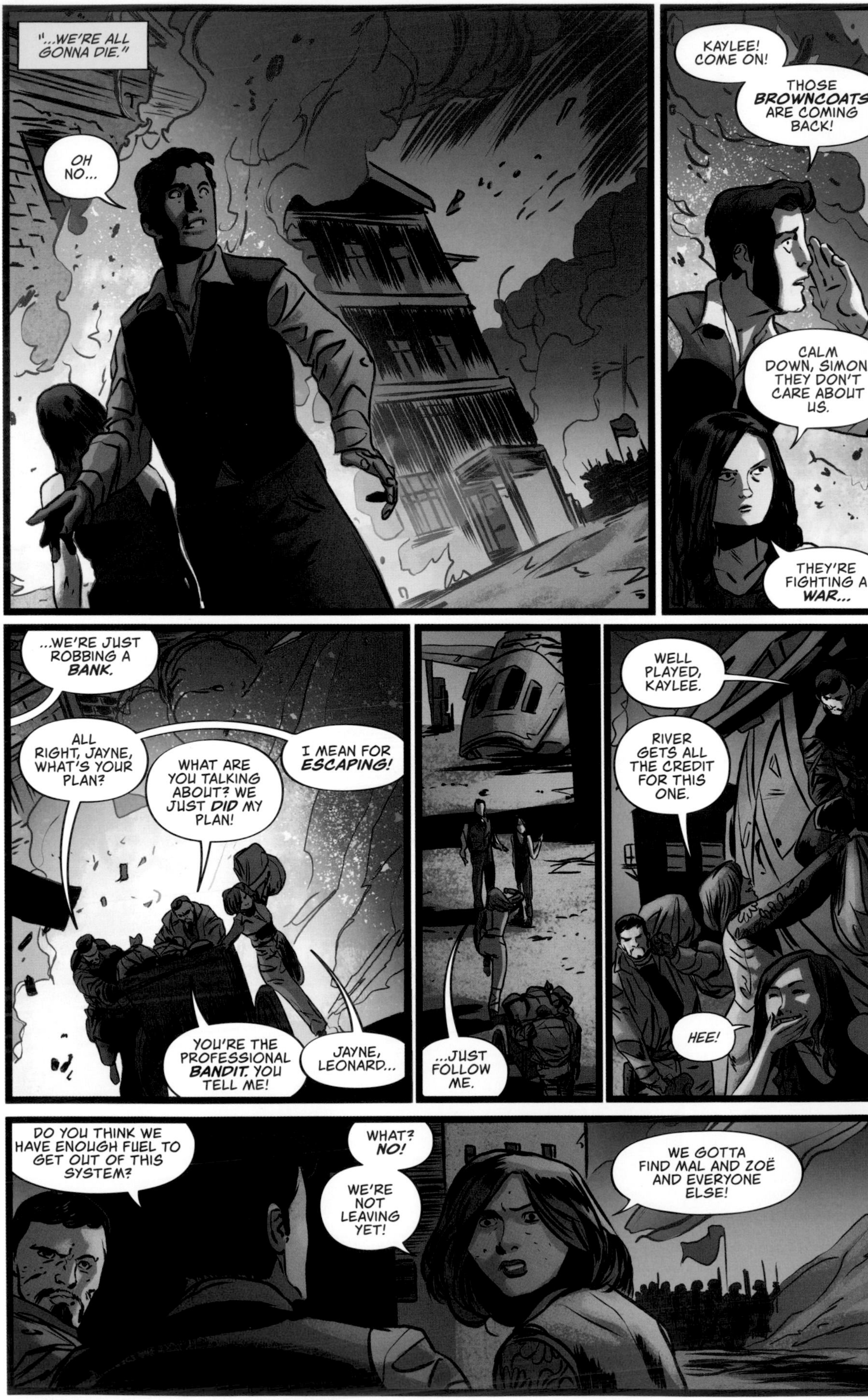
"...WE'RE ALL GONNA DIE."
OH NO...
KAYLEE! COME ON!
THOSE BROWNCOATS ARE COMING BACK!
CALM DOWN, SIMON. THEY DON'T CARE ABOUT US.
THEY'RE FIGHTING A WAR...
...WE'RE JUST ROBBING A BANK.
ALL RIGHT, JAYNE, WHAT'S YOUR PLAN?
WHAT ARE YOU TALKING ABOUT? WE JUST DID MY PLAN!
I MEAN FOR ESCAPING!
YOU'RE THE PROFESSIONAL BANDIT. YOU TELL ME!
JAYNE, LEONARD...
...JUST FOLLOW ME.
WELL PLAYED, KAYLEE.
RIVER GETS ALL THE CREDIT FOR THIS ONE.
HEE!
DO YOU THINK WE HAVE ENOUGH FUEL TO GET OUT OF THIS SYSTEM?
WHAT? NO!
WE'RE NOT LEAVING YET!
WE GOTTA FIND MAL AND ZOË AND EVERYONE ELSE!

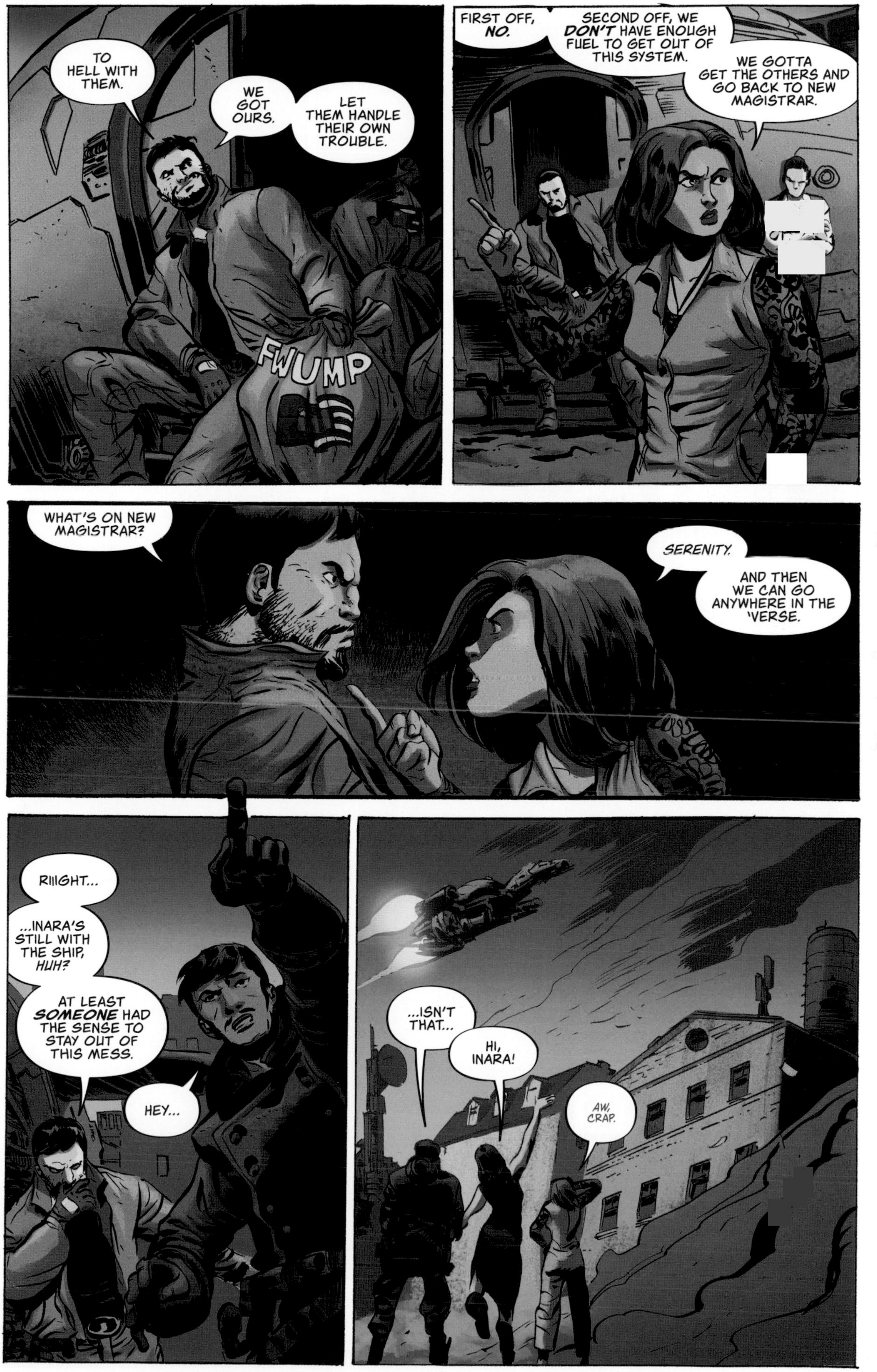
TO HELL WITH THEM.
WE GOT OURS.
LET THEM HANDLE THEIR OWN TROUBLE.
FWUMP
FIRST OFF, NO.
SECOND OFF, WE DON'T HAVE ENOUGH FUEL TO GET OUT OF THIS SYSTEM.
WE GOTTA GET THE OTHERS AND GO BACK TO NEW MAGISTRAR.
WHAT'S ON NEW MAGISTRAR?
SERENITY.
AND THEN WE CAN GO ANYWHERE IN THE 'VERSE.
RIIIGHT...
...INARA'S STILL WITH THE SHIP, HUH?
AT LEAST SOMEONE HAD THE SENSE TO STAY OUT OF THIS MESS.
HEY...
...ISN'T THAT...
HI, INARA!
AW, CRAP.

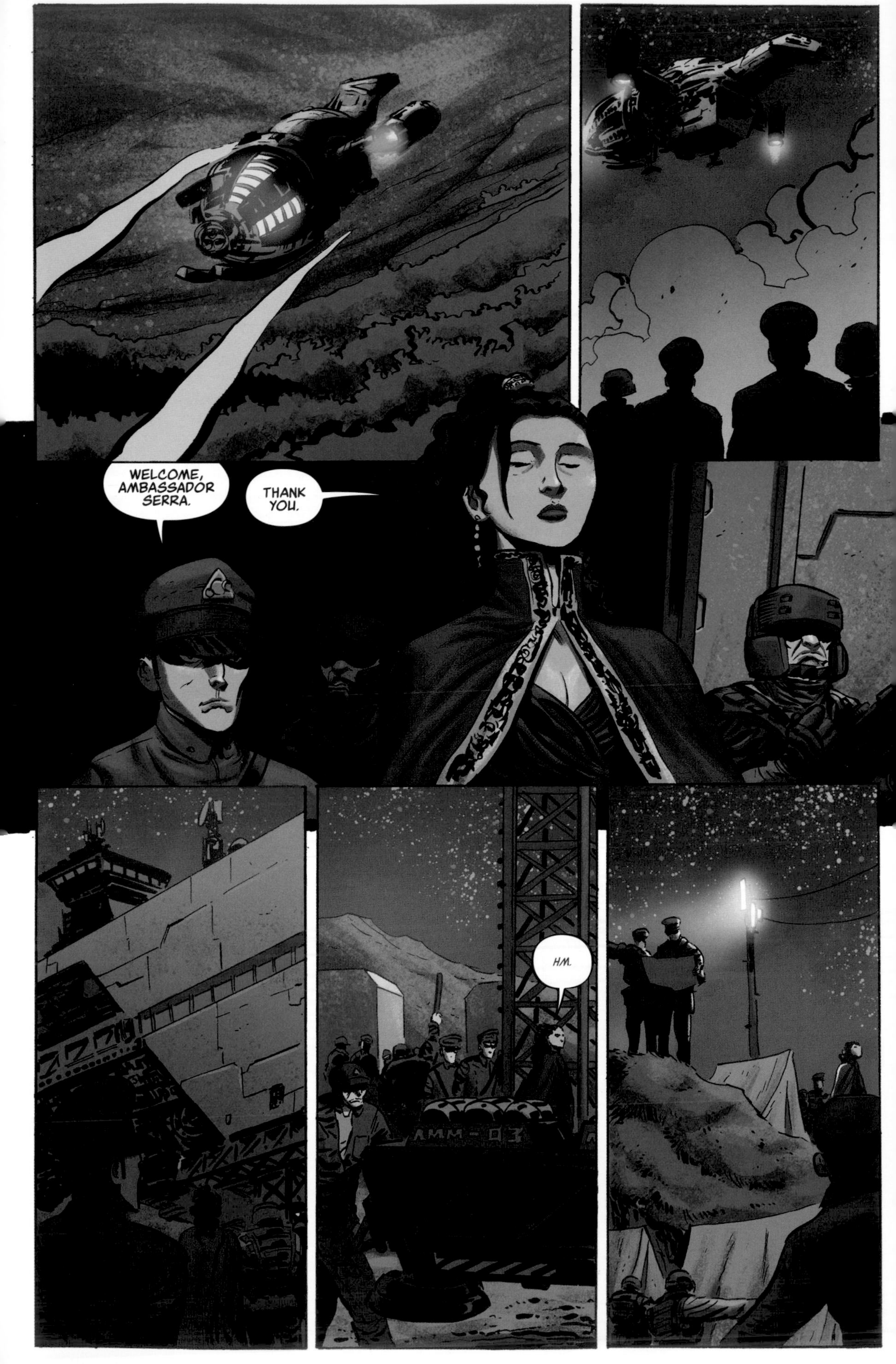
WELCOME, AMBASSADOR SERRA.
THANK YOU.
HM.

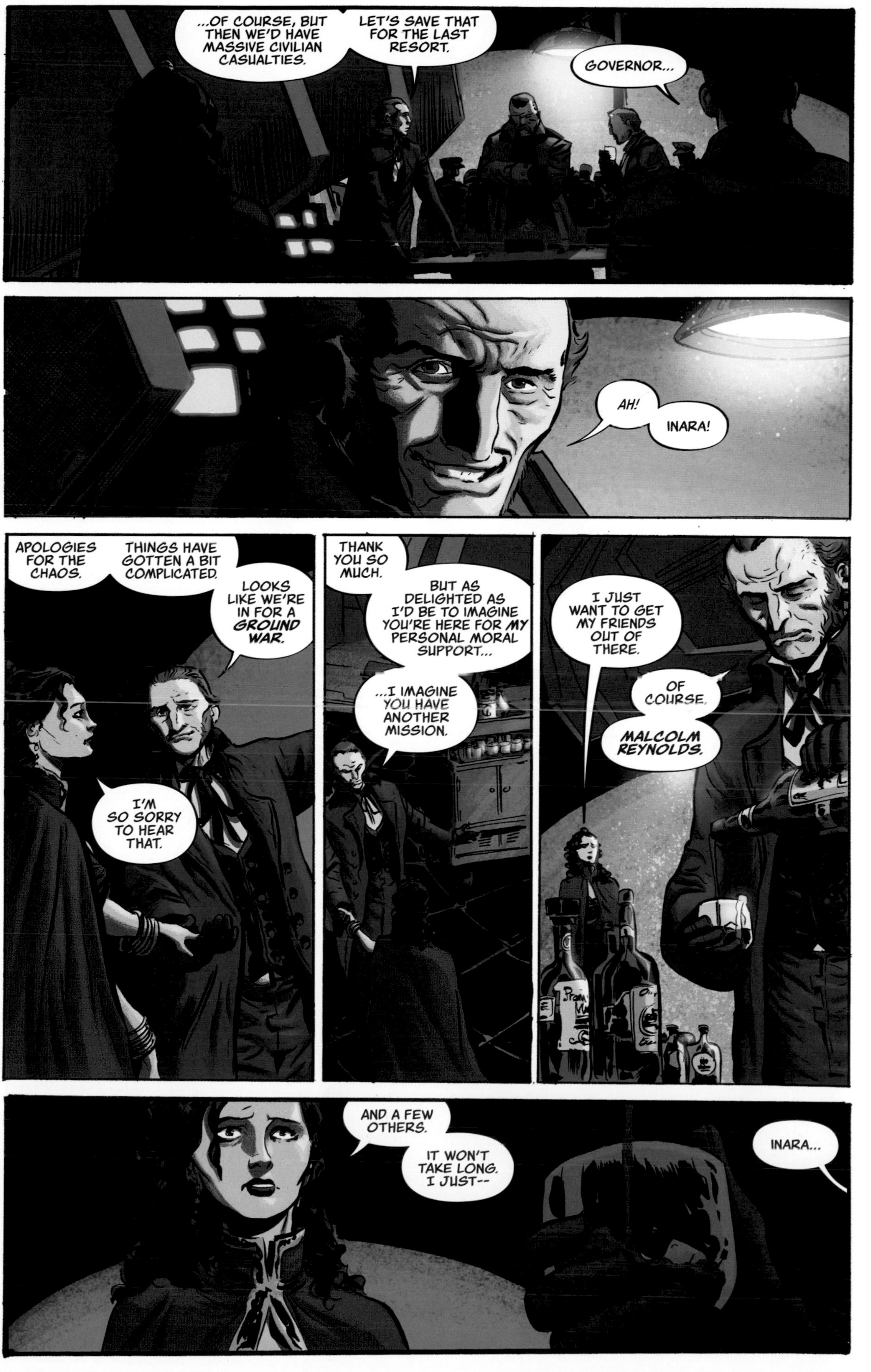
...OF COURSE, BUT THEN WE'D HAVE MASSIVE CIVILIAN CASUALTIES.
LET'S SAVE THAT FOR THE LAST RESORT.
GOVERNOR...
AH!
INARA!
APOLOGIES FOR THE CHAOS.
THINGS HAVE GOTTEN A BIT COMPLICATED.
LOOKS LIKE WE'RE IN FOR A GROUND WAR.
I'M SO SORRY TO HEAR THAT.
THANK YOU SO MUCH.
BUT AS DELIGHTED AS I'D BE TO IMAGINE YOU'RE HERE FOR MY PERSONAL MORAL SUPPORT...
...I IMAGINE YOU HAVE ANOTHER MISSION.
I JUST WANT TO GET MY FRIENDS OUT OF THERE.
OF COURSE.
MALCOLM REYNOLDS.
AND A FEW OTHERS.
IT WON'T TAKE LONG. I JUST--
INARA...

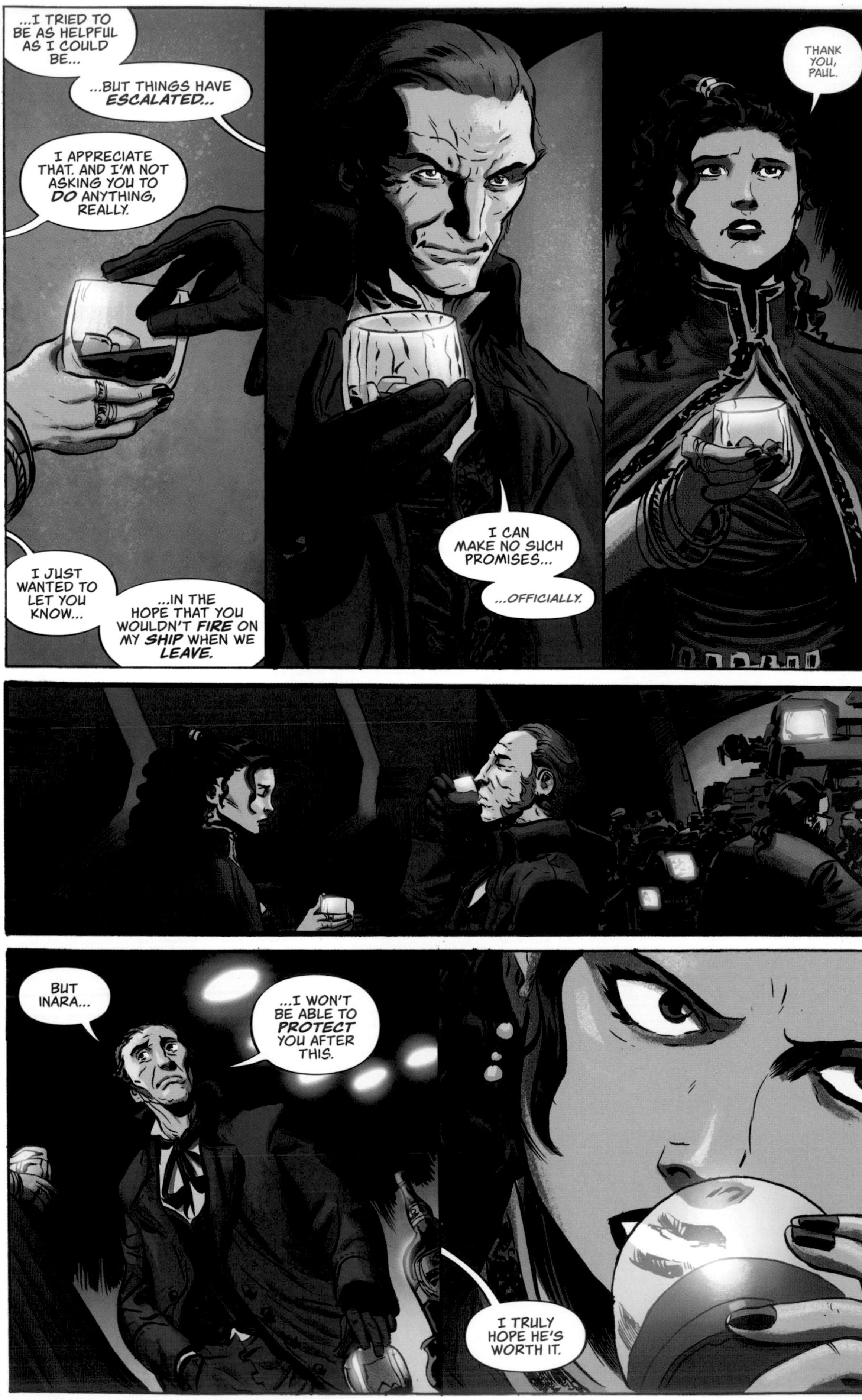
...I TRIED TO BE AS HELPFUL AS I COULD BE...
...BUT THINGS HAVE *ESCALATED...*
I APPRECIATE THAT. AND I'M NOT ASKING YOU TO *DO* ANYTHING, REALLY.
I JUST WANTED TO LET YOU KNOW...
...IN THE HOPE THAT YOU WOULDN'T *FIRE* ON MY *SHIP* WHEN WE *LEAVE.*
I CAN MAKE NO SUCH PROMISES...
...OFFICIALLY.
THANK YOU, PAUL.
BUT INARA...
...I WON'T BE ABLE TO *PROTECT* YOU AFTER THIS.
I TRULY HOPE HE'S WORTH IT.

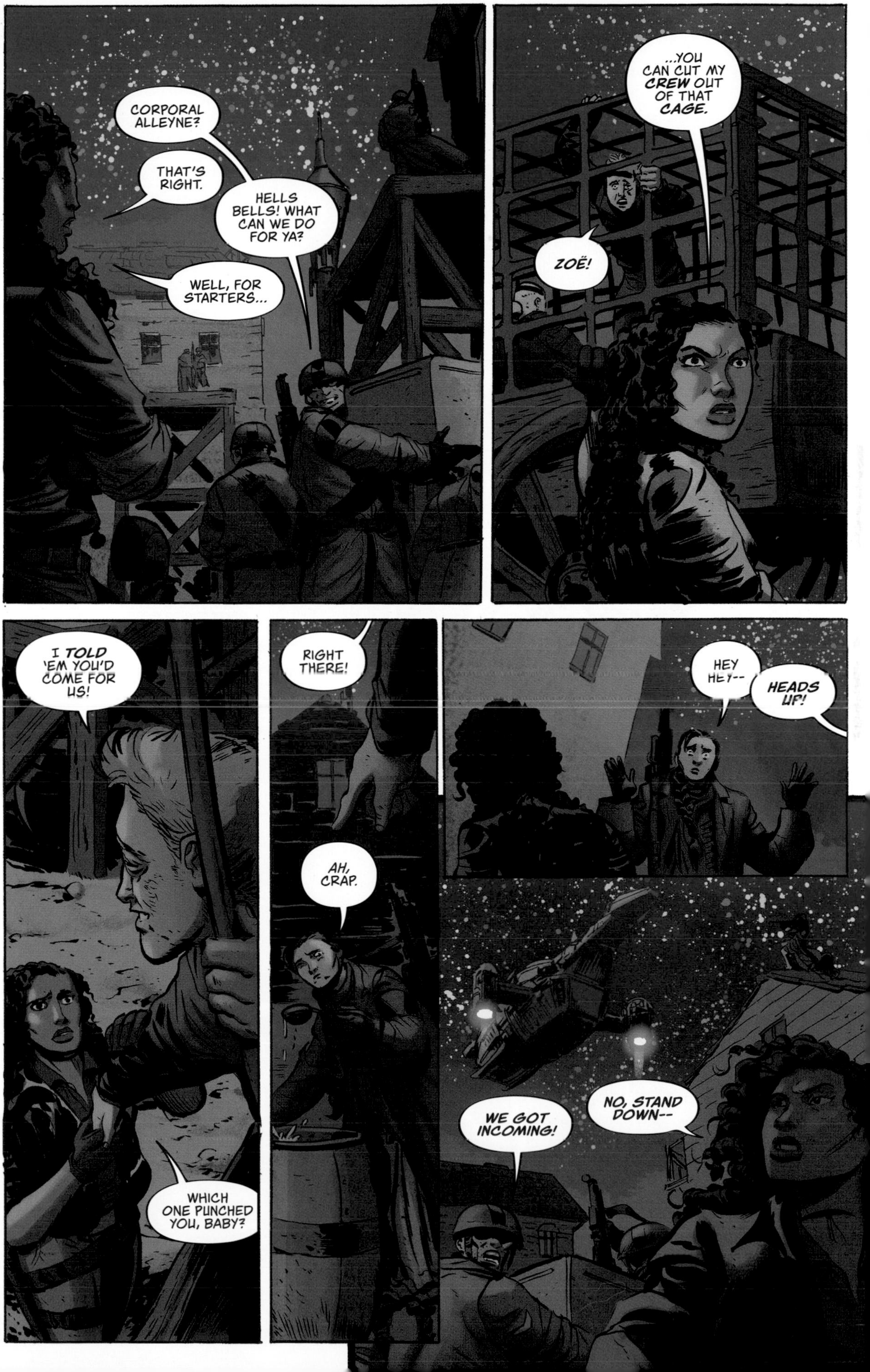
CORPORAL ALLEYNE?
THAT'S RIGHT.
HELLS BELLS! WHAT CAN WE DO FOR YA?
WELL, FOR STARTERS...
...YOU CAN CUT MY **CREW** OUT OF THAT **CAGE.**
ZOË!
I *TOLD* 'EM YOU'D COME FOR US!
WHICH ONE PUNCHED YOU, BABY?
RIGHT THERE!
AH, CRAP.
HEY HEY--
HEADS UP!
NO, STAND DOWN--
WE GOT INCOMING!

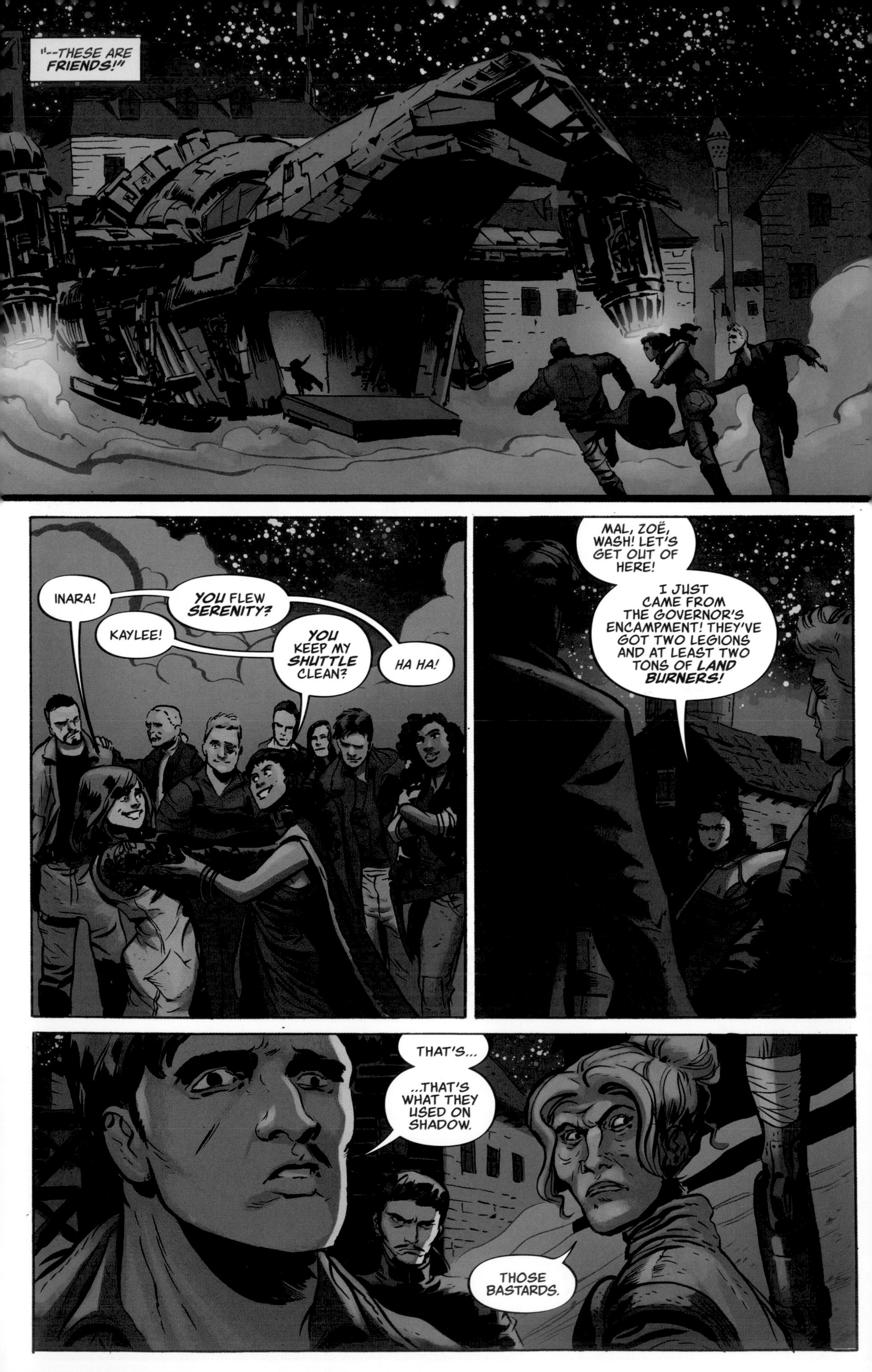
"--THESE ARE FRIENDS!"
INARA!
YOU FLEW SERENITY?
KAYLEE!
YOU KEEP MY SHUTTLE CLEAN?
HA HA!
MAL, ZOË, WASH! LET'S GET OUT OF HERE!
I JUST CAME FROM THE GOVERNOR'S ENCAMPMENT! THEY'VE GOT TWO LEGIONS AND AT LEAST TWO TONS OF LAND BURNERS!
THAT'S...
...THAT'S WHAT THEY USED ON SHADOW.
THOSE BASTARDS.

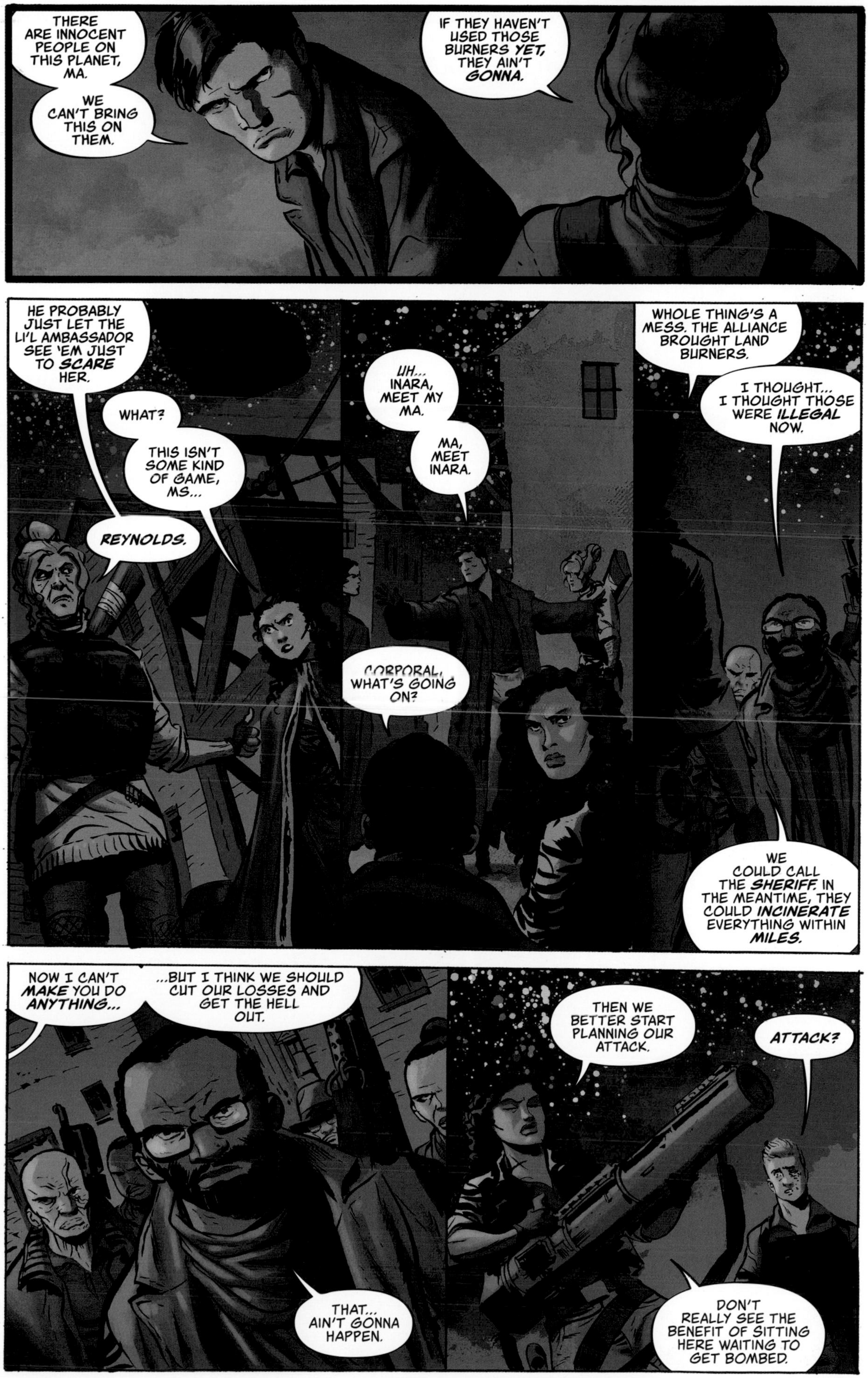
THERE ARE INNOCENT PEOPLE ON THIS PLANET, MA.
WE CAN'T BRING THIS ON THEM.
IF THEY HAVEN'T USED THOSE BURNERS YET, THEY AIN'T GONNA.
HE PROBABLY JUST LET THE LI'L AMBASSADOR SEE 'EM JUST TO SCARE HER.
WHAT?
THIS ISN'T SOME KIND OF GAME, MS...
REYNOLDS.
UH... INARA, MEET MY MA.
MA, MEET INARA.
CORPORAL, WHAT'S GOING ON?
WHOLE THING'S A MESS. THE ALLIANCE BROUGHT LAND BURNERS.
I THOUGHT... I THOUGHT THOSE WERE ILLEGAL NOW.
WE COULD CALL THE SHERIFF. IN THE MEANTIME, THEY COULD INCINERATE EVERYTHING WITHIN MILES.
NOW I CAN'T MAKE YOU DO ANYTHING...
...BUT I THINK WE SHOULD CUT OUR LOSSES AND GET THE HELL OUT.
THAT... AIN'T GONNA HAPPEN.
THEN WE BETTER START PLANNING OUR ATTACK.
ATTACK?
DON'T REALLY SEE THE BENEFIT OF SITTING HERE WAITING TO GET BOMBED.

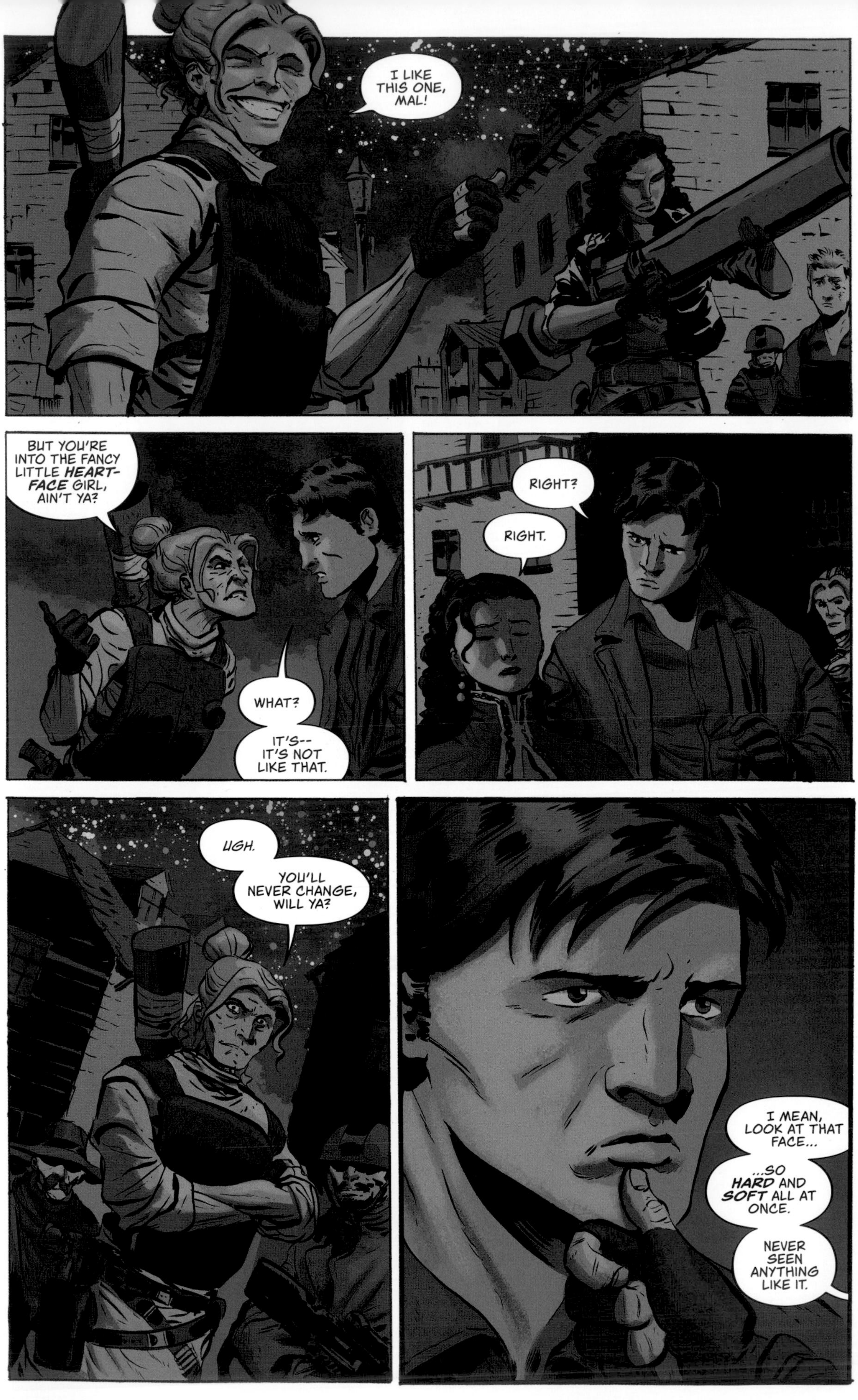

I LIKE THIS ONE, MAL!
BUT YOU'RE INTO THE FANCY LITTLE HEART-FACE GIRL, AIN'T YA?
WHAT?
IT'S-- IT'S NOT LIKE THAT.
RIGHT?
RIGHT.
UGH.
YOU'LL NEVER CHANGE, WILL YA?
I MEAN, LOOK AT THAT FACE...
...SO HARD AND SOFT ALL AT ONCE.
NEVER SEEN ANYTHING LIKE IT.

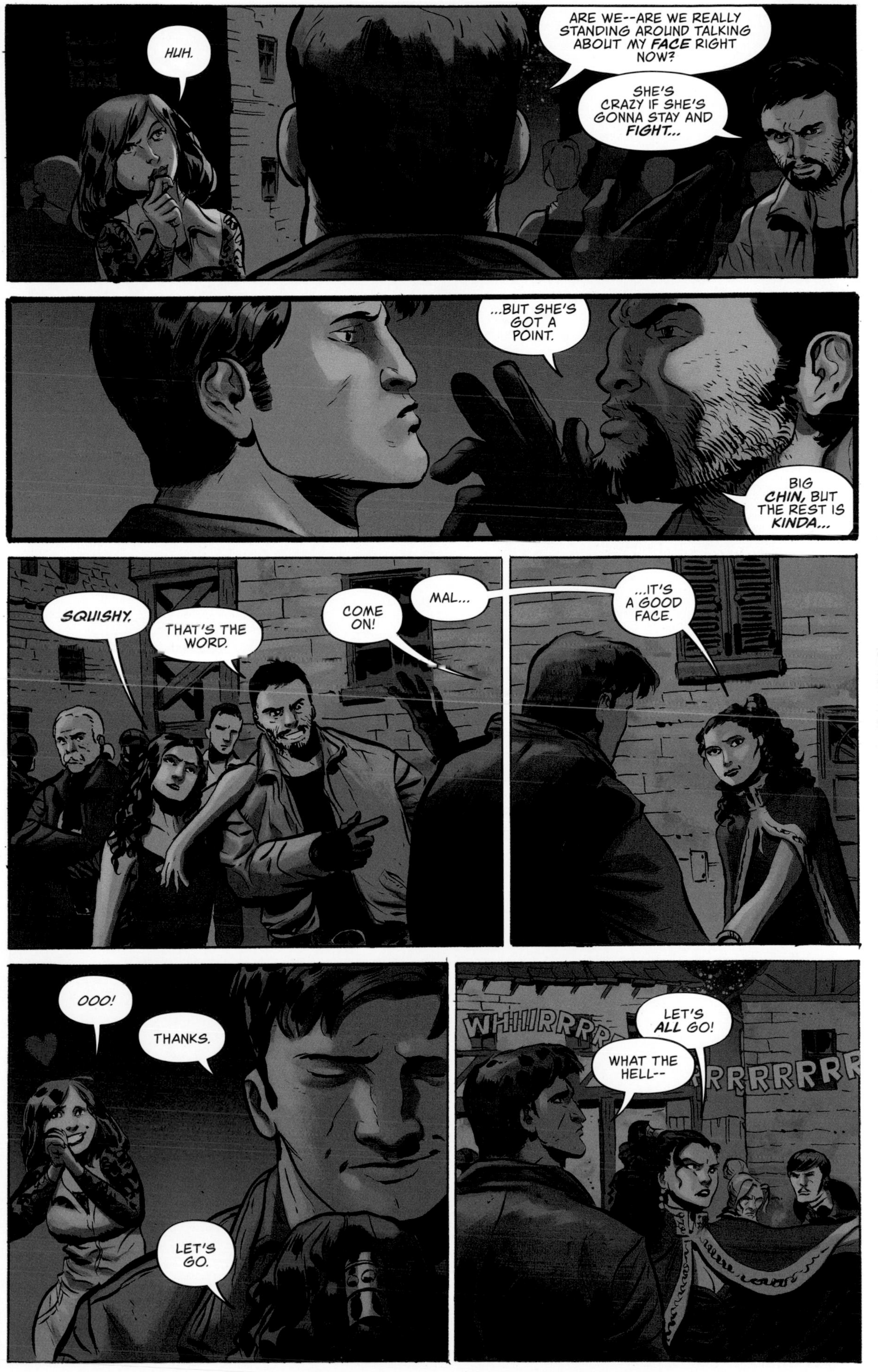
HUH.
ARE WE--ARE WE REALLY STANDING AROUND TALKING ABOUT MY FACE RIGHT NOW?
SHE'S CRAZY IF SHE'S GONNA STAY AND FIGHT...
...BUT SHE'S GOT A POINT.
BIG CHIN, BUT THE REST IS KINDA...
SQUISHY.
THAT'S THE WORD.
COME ON!
MAL...
...IT'S A GOOD FACE.
OOO!
THANKS.
LET'S GO.
WHIIIRRRR
RRRRRRRR
LET'S ALL GO!
WHAT THE HELL--

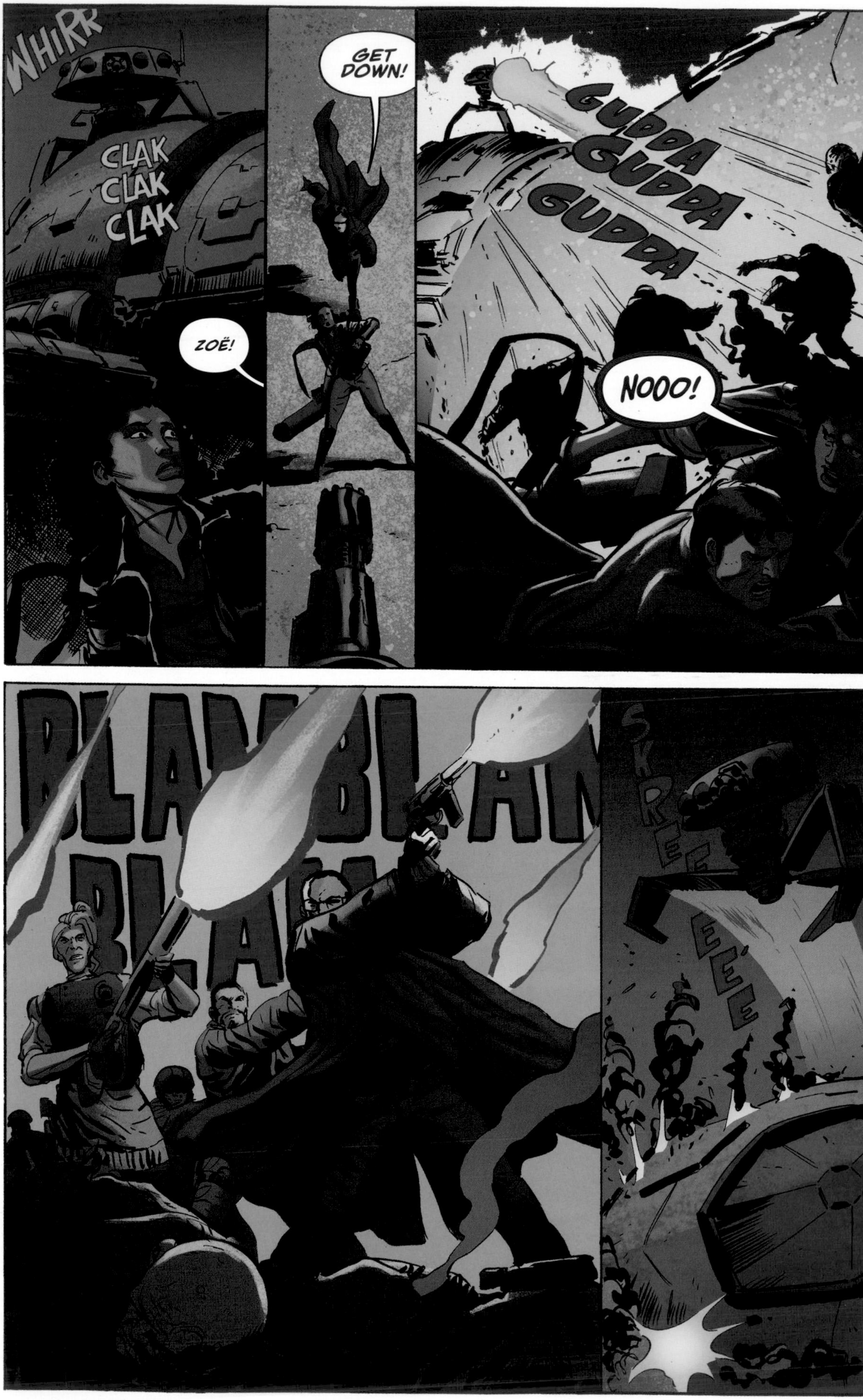
WHIRR
CLAK CLAK CLAK
ZOË!
GET DOWN!
GUDDA GUDDA GUDDA GUDDA
NOOO!
SKREEEEEEE

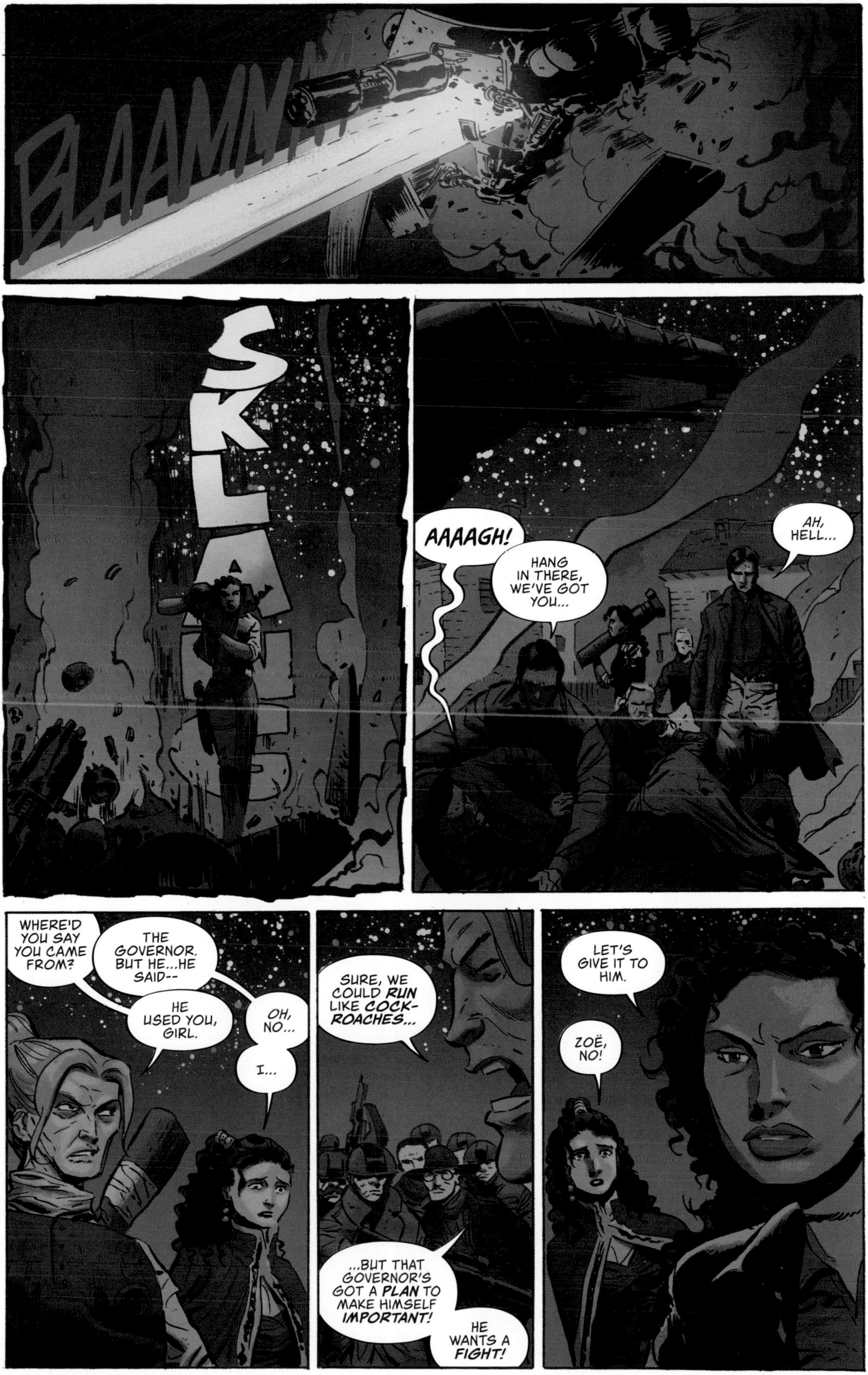
BLAAMM
SKLAM
AAAAGH!
HANG IN THERE, WE'VE GOT YOU...
AH, HELL...
WHERE'D YOU SAY YOU CAME FROM?
THE GOVERNOR. BUT HE...HE SAID--
HE USED YOU, GIRL.
OH, NO...
I...
SURE, WE COULD RUN LIKE COCK-ROACHES...
...BUT THAT GOVERNOR'S GOT A PLAN TO MAKE HIMSELF IMPORTANT!
HE WANTS A FIGHT!
LET'S GIVE IT TO HIM.
ZOË, NO!

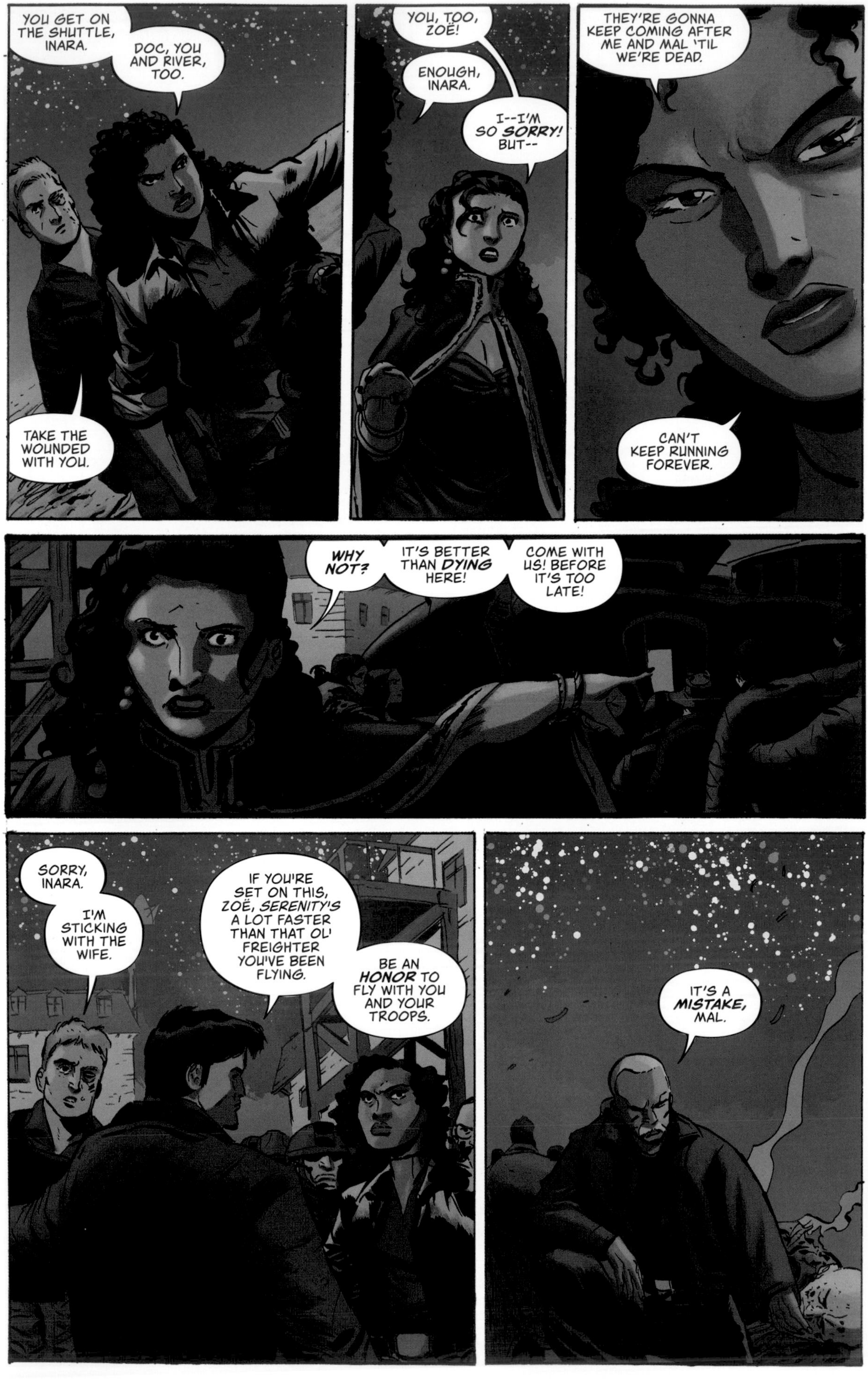
YOU GET ON THE SHUTTLE, INARA.
DOC, YOU AND RIVER, TOO.
TAKE THE WOUNDED WITH YOU.
YOU, TOO, ZOË!
ENOUGH, INARA.
I--I'M SO **SORRY!** BUT--
THEY'RE GONNA KEEP COMING AFTER ME AND MAL 'TIL WE'RE DEAD.
CAN'T KEEP RUNNING FOREVER.
WHY NOT?
IT'S BETTER THAN ***DYING*** HERE!
COME WITH US! BEFORE IT'S TOO LATE!
SORRY, INARA.
I'M STICKING WITH THE WIFE.
IF YOU'RE SET ON THIS, ZOË, *SERENITY'S* A LOT FASTER THAN THAT OL' FREIGHTER YOU'VE BEEN FLYING.
BE AN ***HONOR*** TO FLY WITH YOU AND YOUR TROOPS.
IT'S A ***MISTAKE,*** MAL.

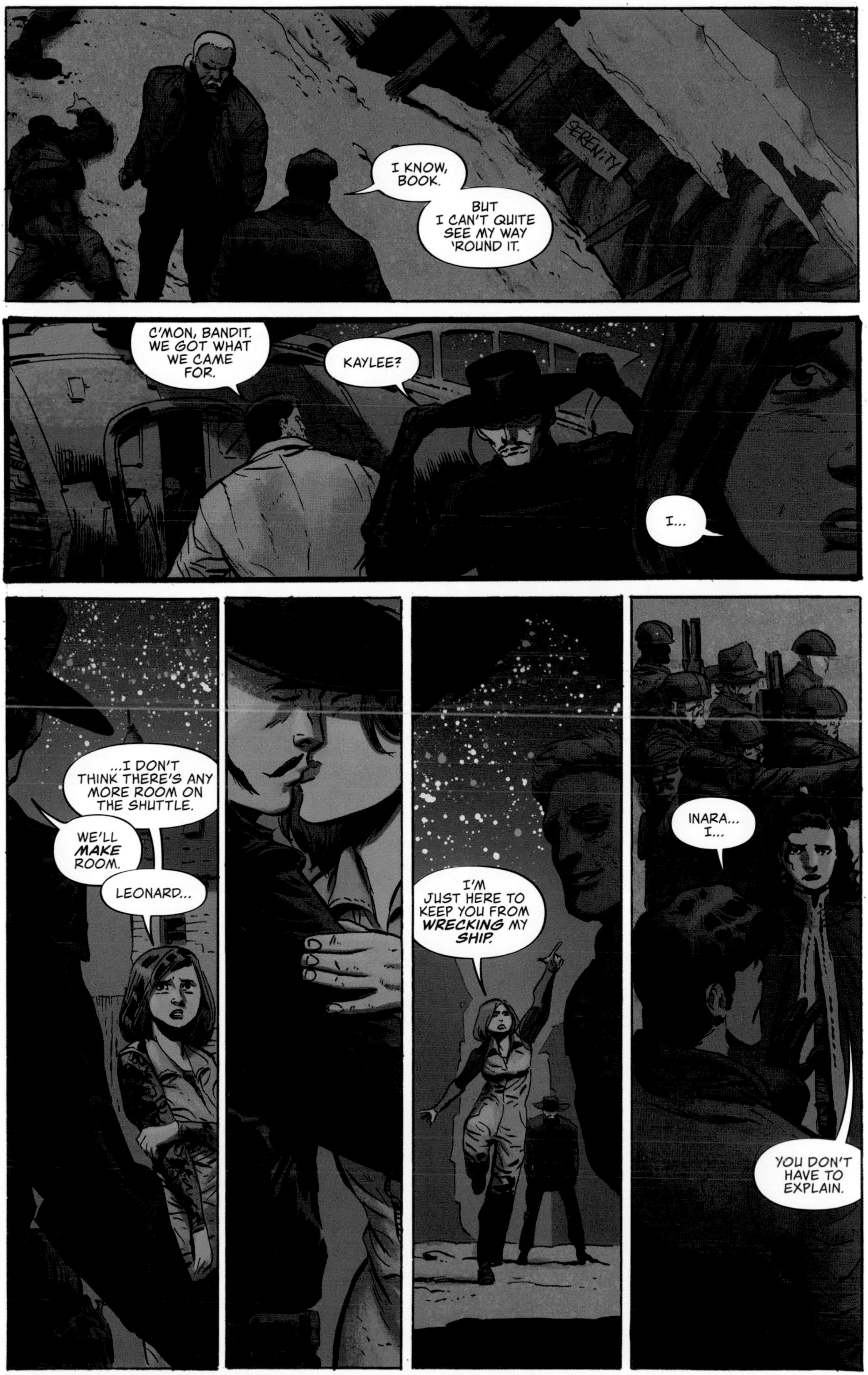
I KNOW, BOOK.
BUT I CAN'T QUITE SEE MY WAY 'ROUND IT.
SERENITY
C'MON, BANDIT. WE GOT WHAT WE CAME FOR.
KAYLEE?
I...
...I DON'T THINK THERE'S ANY MORE ROOM ON THE SHUTTLE.
WE'LL MAKE ROOM.
LEONARD...
I'M JUST HERE TO KEEP YOU FROM WRECKING MY SHIP.
INARA... I...
YOU DON'T HAVE TO EXPLAIN.

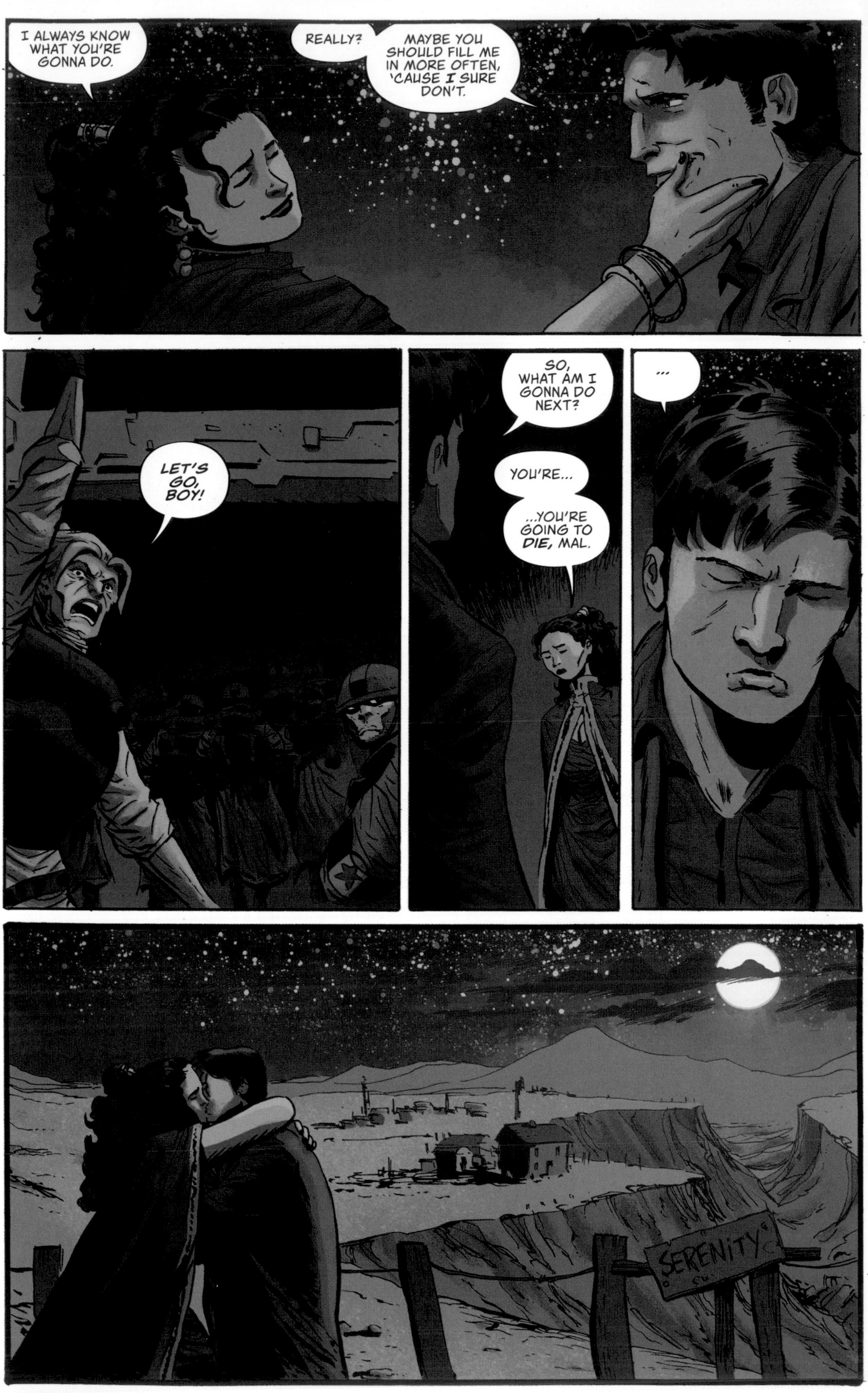
I ALWAYS KNOW WHAT YOU'RE GONNA DO.
REALLY?
MAYBE YOU SHOULD FILL ME IN MORE OFTEN, 'CAUSE I SURE DON'T.
LET'S GO, BOY!
SO, WHAT AM I GONNA DO NEXT?
YOU'RE...
...YOU'RE GOING TO DIE, MAL.
...
SERENITY

WHAT MAKES US SPECIAL

WE'VE GOT US SOME CRIME TO BE DONE.

wood spot, sir. She still has the adva...

know why? Because we are so very pretty. We are just too pretty for God to let us die.

I don't believe there's a power in the 'Verse can stop Kaylee from being cheerful. Sometimes you jus...

And I'm thinking you weren't burdened with an overabundance of schooling. So why don't we ju...

Ship like this will be with you ti... the day you die. That's 'cause it's a death trap.

Sir, I think you have a problem with your brain being missing.

YOU'RE LO...

WE ALL A...

喧闹 起来

INEVITABLE BETRAYAL.

WE'D BE DEAD.

Curse your sudden but...

Can't ge... paid if you're dead.

This is why... lost. you k...

SUP...

AWFUL

ED IN MY SKY.

It's a real burden

BEING RIGHT SO OFTEN

ty bar!

Fruity oaty bar!

Seems to me the last time there was a chance for a little palaver we were all manner of...
This ain't bad. There's a trick to it. Wood alcohol. Now we're favored guests treated t...

FINEST IN BEVERAGES THAT MAKE YO...

喧闹 起来

I brought you some supper. But if you'd prefer a lecture I have a few very catchy ones prepped.

What did I say to you about barging into my shuttle? Th...

MAN OF HO...

DEN OF THI...

SIN AND HELLFIRE. ONE HAS...

EEPERS. 旅

MANLY AND IMPULSIV...

Preacher, don't... pretty specific... Quite specific...

BLUE SUN 蓝日

青日

Sergeant Ma... Now I... Big tough veteran. Now I... Only I think you're still a sergeant. Y...

CA... HA... YS

CHAPTER TWELVE

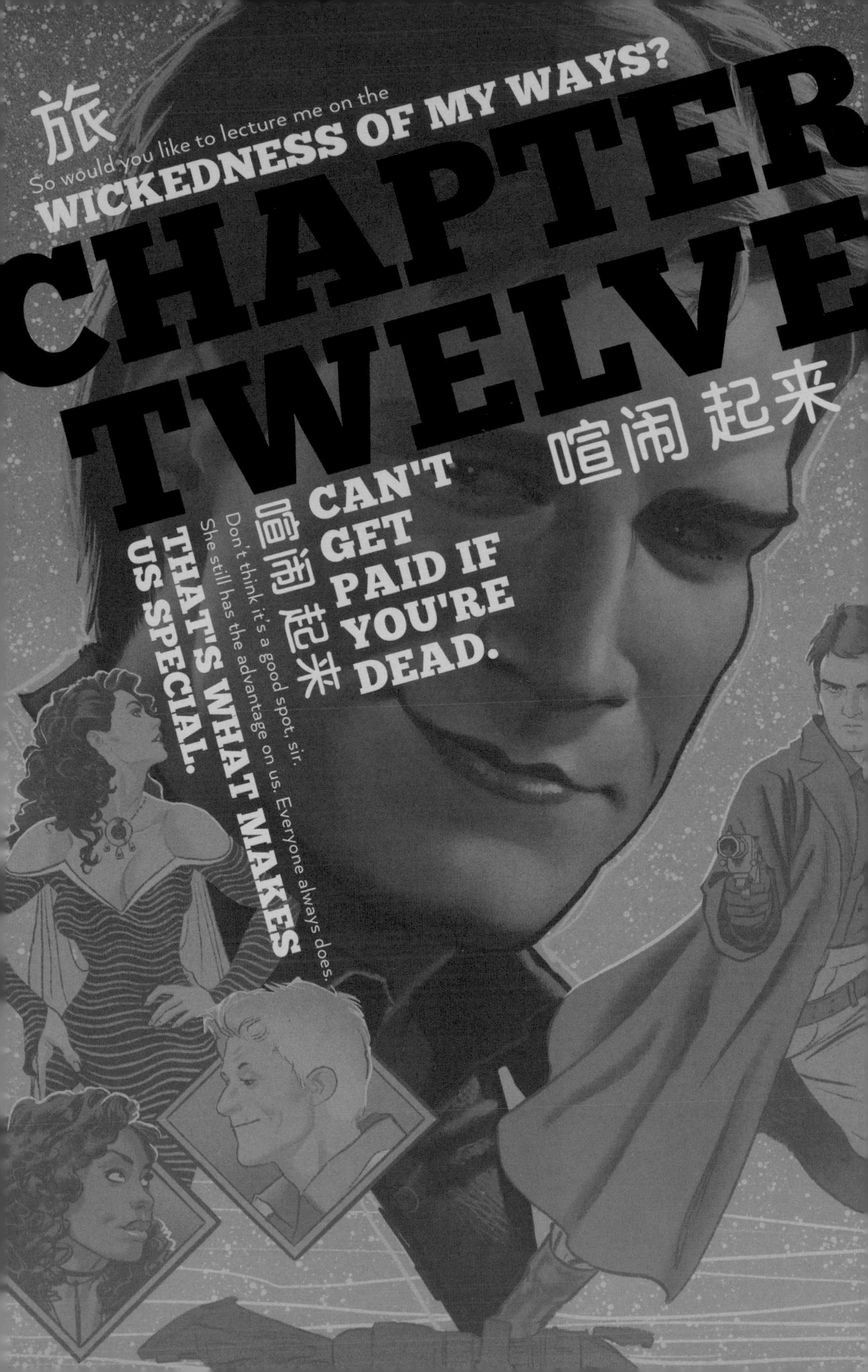

旅
So would you like to lecture me on the
WICKEDNESS OF MY WAYS?
喧闹起来
CAN'T GET PAID IF YOU'RE DEAD.
喧闹起来
Don't think it's a good spot, sir.
She still has the advantage on us. Everyone always does.
THAT'S WHAT MAKES US SPECIAL.

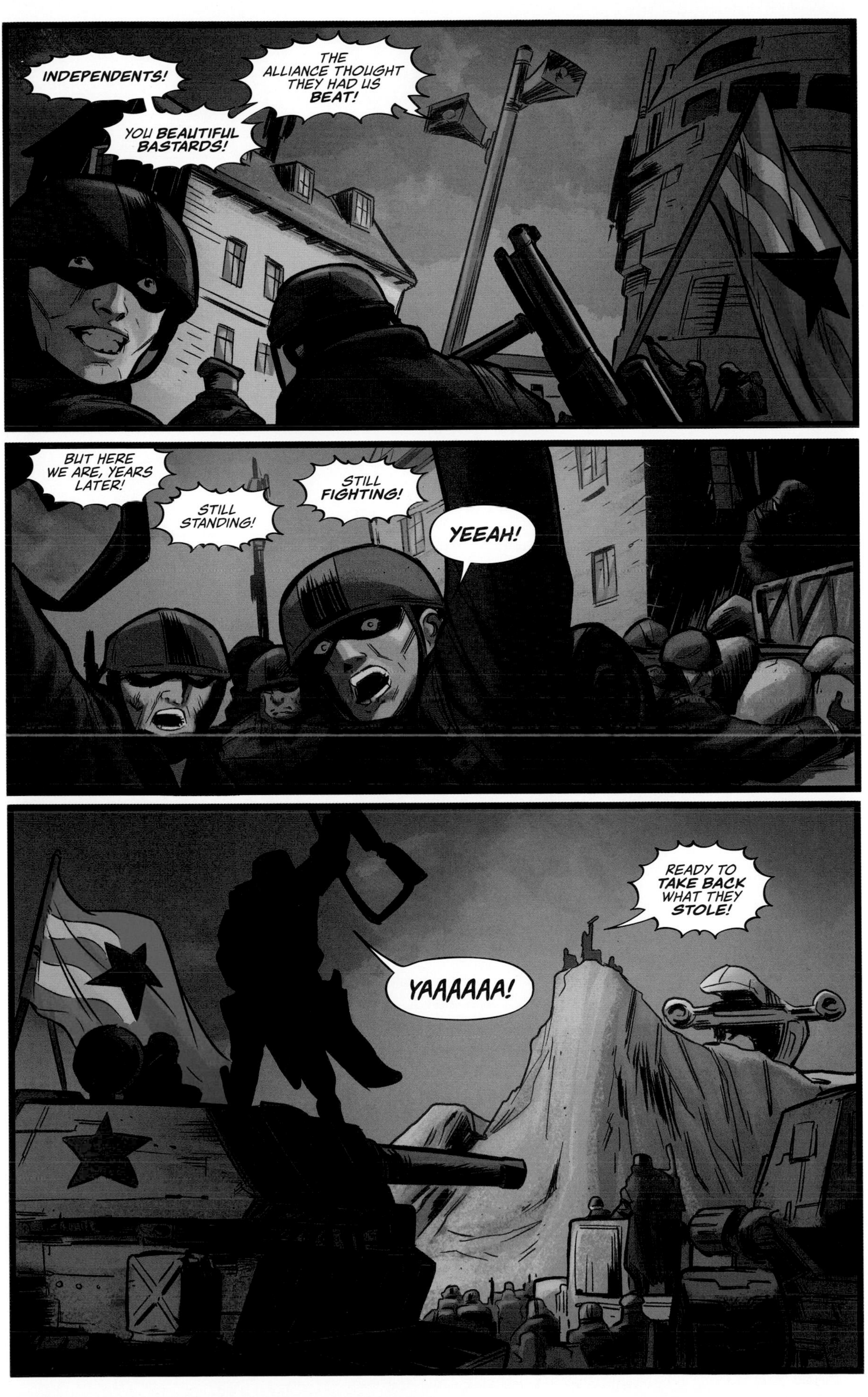
INDEPENDENTS!
THE ALLIANCE THOUGHT THEY HAD US BEAT!
YOU BEAUTIFUL BASTARDS!
BUT HERE WE ARE, YEARS LATER!
STILL STANDING!
STILL FIGHTING!
YEEAH!
READY TO TAKE BACK WHAT THEY STOLE!
YAAAAAA!

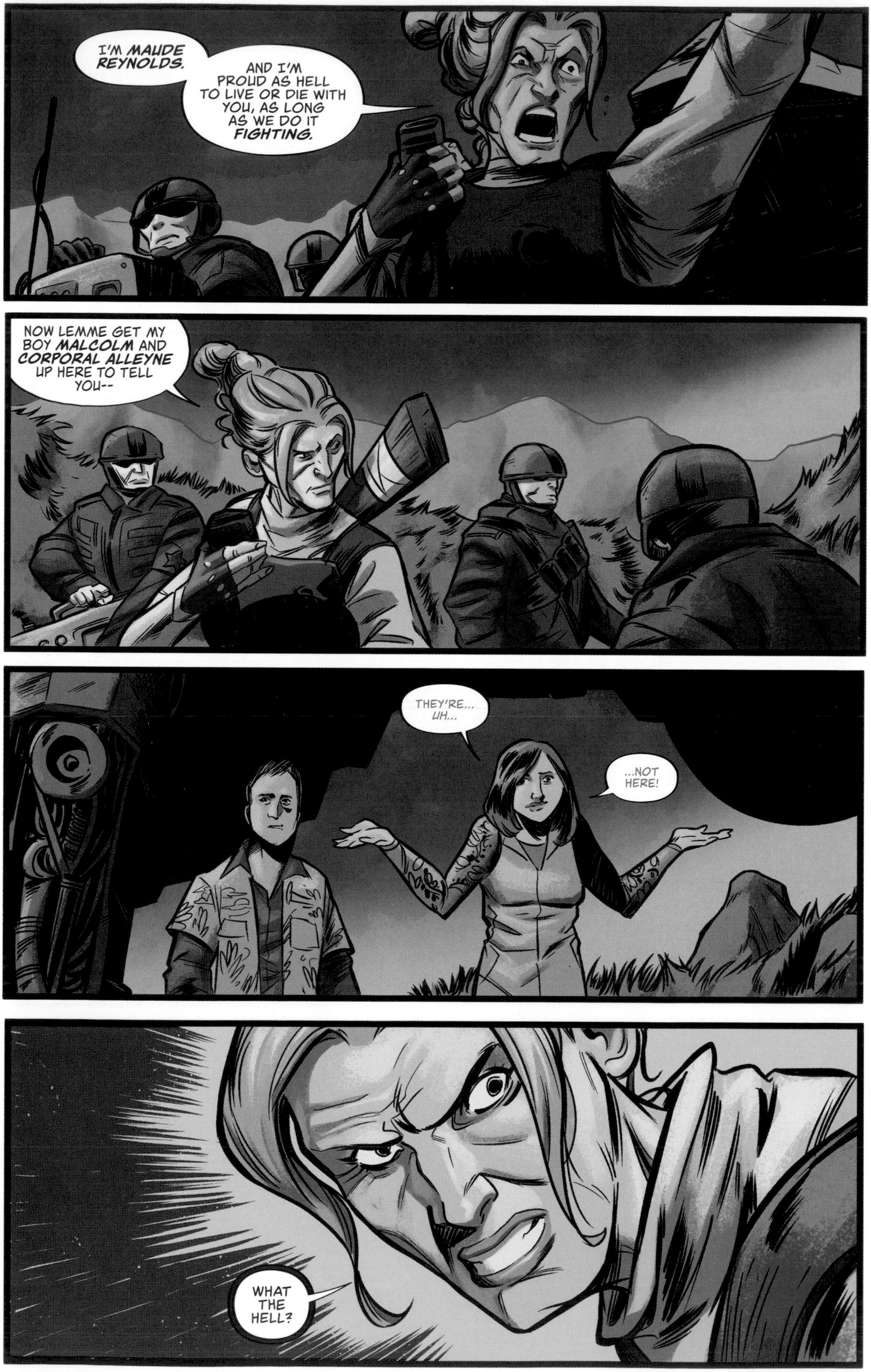
I'M MAUDE REYNOLDS.
AND I'M PROUD AS HELL TO LIVE OR DIE WITH YOU, AS LONG AS WE DO IT FIGHTING.
NOW LEMME GET MY BOY MALCOLM AND CORPORAL ALLEYNE UP HERE TO TELL YOU--
THEY'RE... UH...
...NOT HERE!
WHAT THE HELL?

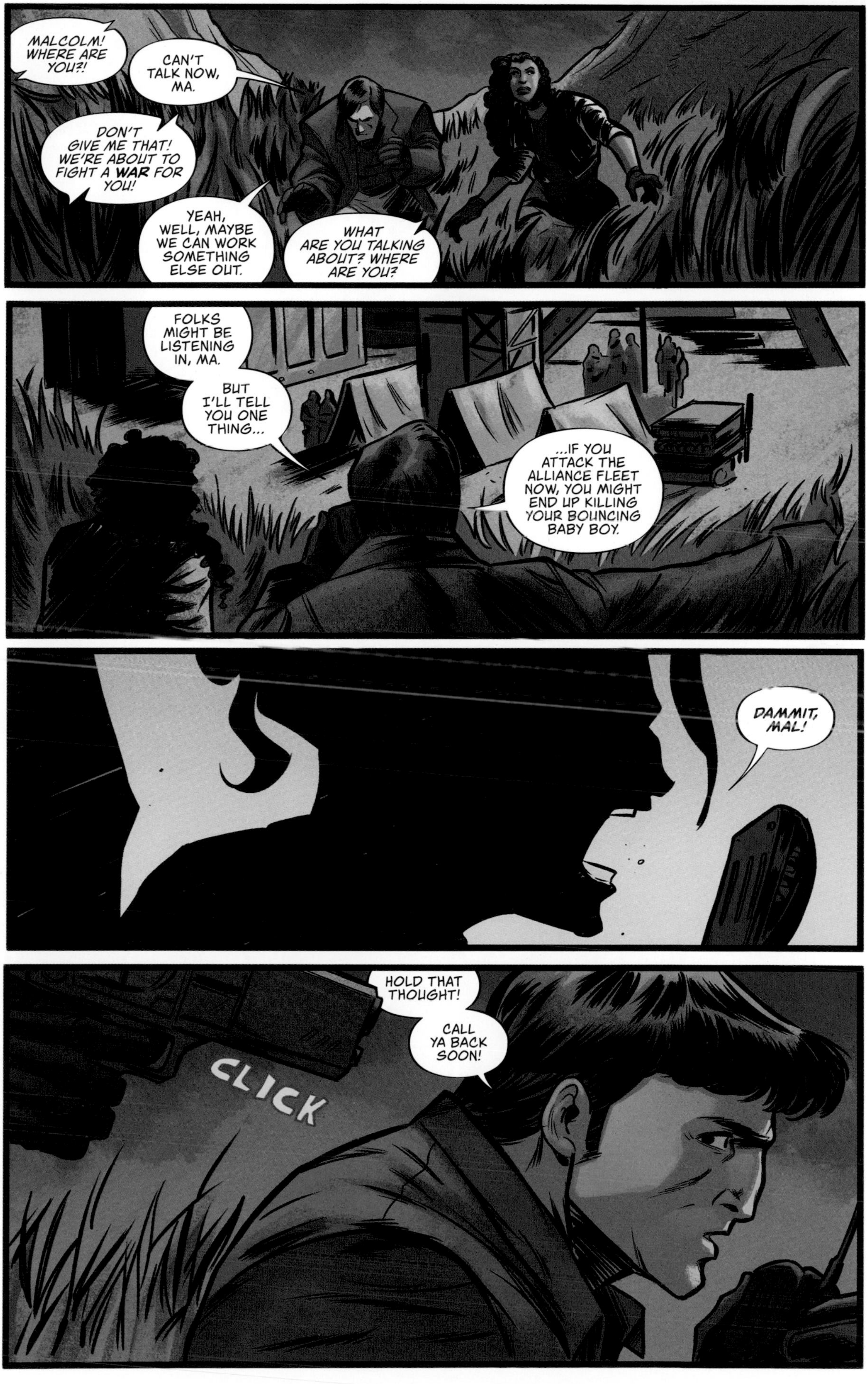
MALCOLM! WHERE ARE YOU?!
CAN'T TALK NOW, MA.
DON'T GIVE ME THAT! WE'RE ABOUT TO FIGHT A **WAR** FOR YOU!
YEAH, WELL, MAYBE WE CAN WORK SOMETHING ELSE OUT.
WHAT ARE YOU TALKING ABOUT? WHERE ARE YOU?
FOLKS MIGHT BE LISTENING IN, MA.
BUT I'LL TELL YOU ONE THING...
...IF YOU ATTACK THE ALLIANCE FLEET NOW, YOU MIGHT END UP KILLING YOUR BOUNCING BABY BOY.
DAMMIT, MAL!
HOLD THAT THOUGHT!
CALL YA BACK SOON!
CLICK

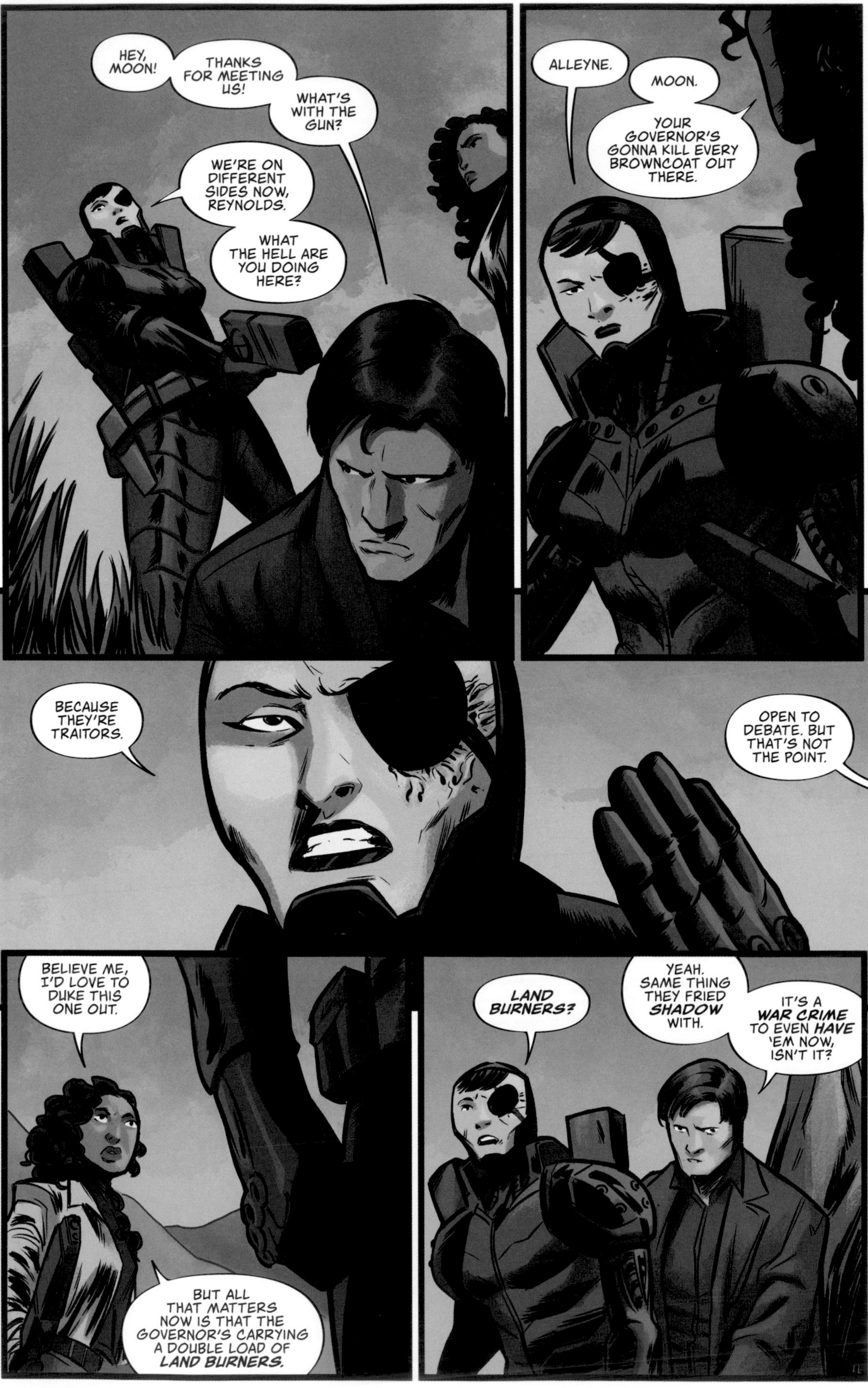
HEY, MOON!
THANKS FOR MEETING US!
WHAT'S WITH THE GUN?
WE'RE ON DIFFERENT SIDES NOW, REYNOLDS.
WHAT THE HELL ARE YOU DOING HERE?
ALLEYNE.
MOON.
YOUR GOVERNOR'S GONNA KILL EVERY BROWNCOAT OUT THERE.
BECAUSE THEY'RE TRAITORS.
OPEN TO DEBATE. BUT THAT'S NOT THE POINT.
BELIEVE ME, I'D LOVE TO DUKE THIS ONE OUT.
BUT ALL THAT MATTERS NOW IS THAT THE GOVERNOR'S CARRYING A DOUBLE LOAD OF LAND BURNERS.
LAND BURNERS?
YEAH. SAME THING THEY FRIED SHADOW WITH.
IT'S A WAR CRIME TO EVEN HAVE 'EM NOW, ISN'T IT?

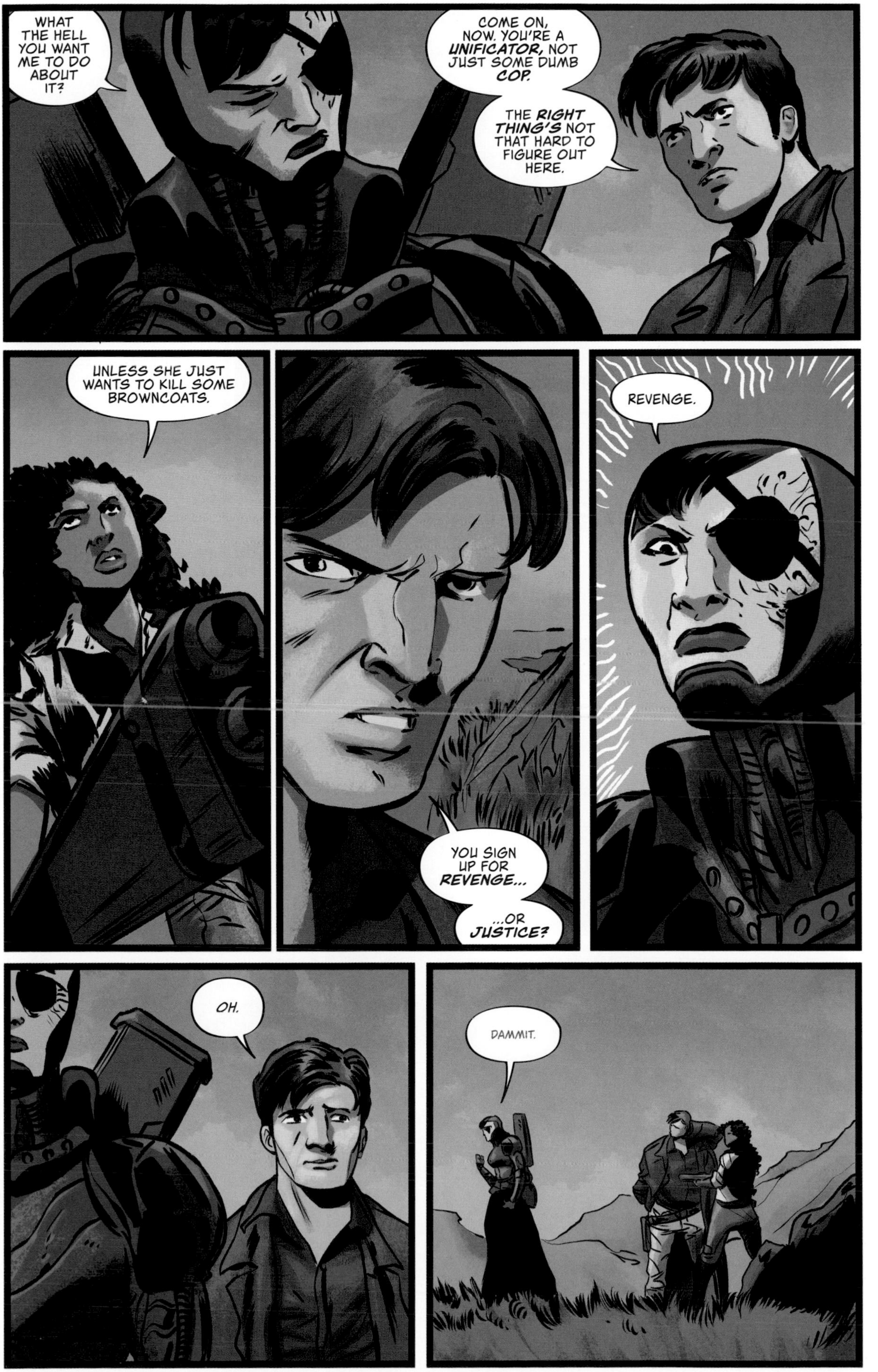

WHAT THE HELL YOU WANT ME TO DO ABOUT IT?
COME ON, NOW. YOU'RE A UNIFICATOR, NOT JUST SOME DUMB COP.
THE RIGHT THING'S NOT THAT HARD TO FIGURE OUT HERE.
UNLESS SHE JUST WANTS TO KILL SOME BROWNCOATS.
YOU SIGN UP FOR REVENGE...
...OR JUSTICE?
REVENGE.
OH.
DAMMIT.

NINETEEN MINUTES LATER...

UFF.

WHAT?

NOTHING. IT'S JUST A LITTLE *TIGHT...*

...IN THE *HINDER* REGIONS.

YOU MEAN YOU'RE A LITTLE *BROAD* IN THE HINDER--

SHHH.

HOW'S IT LOOKING, SOLDIER?

WHO WANTS TO KNOW?

BOSS MOON. UNIFICATOR I.D. 44454.

CHECKING ON THE STATUS OF THE *LAND BURNERS.*

OH, THEY'RE ALREADY LOADED, BOSS.

GREAT. WHICH SHIP?

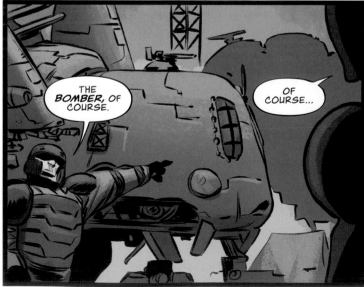

THE *BOMBER,* OF COURSE.

OF COURSE...

SO...WHAT DO YOU UNIFICATORS HAVE TO DO WITH--

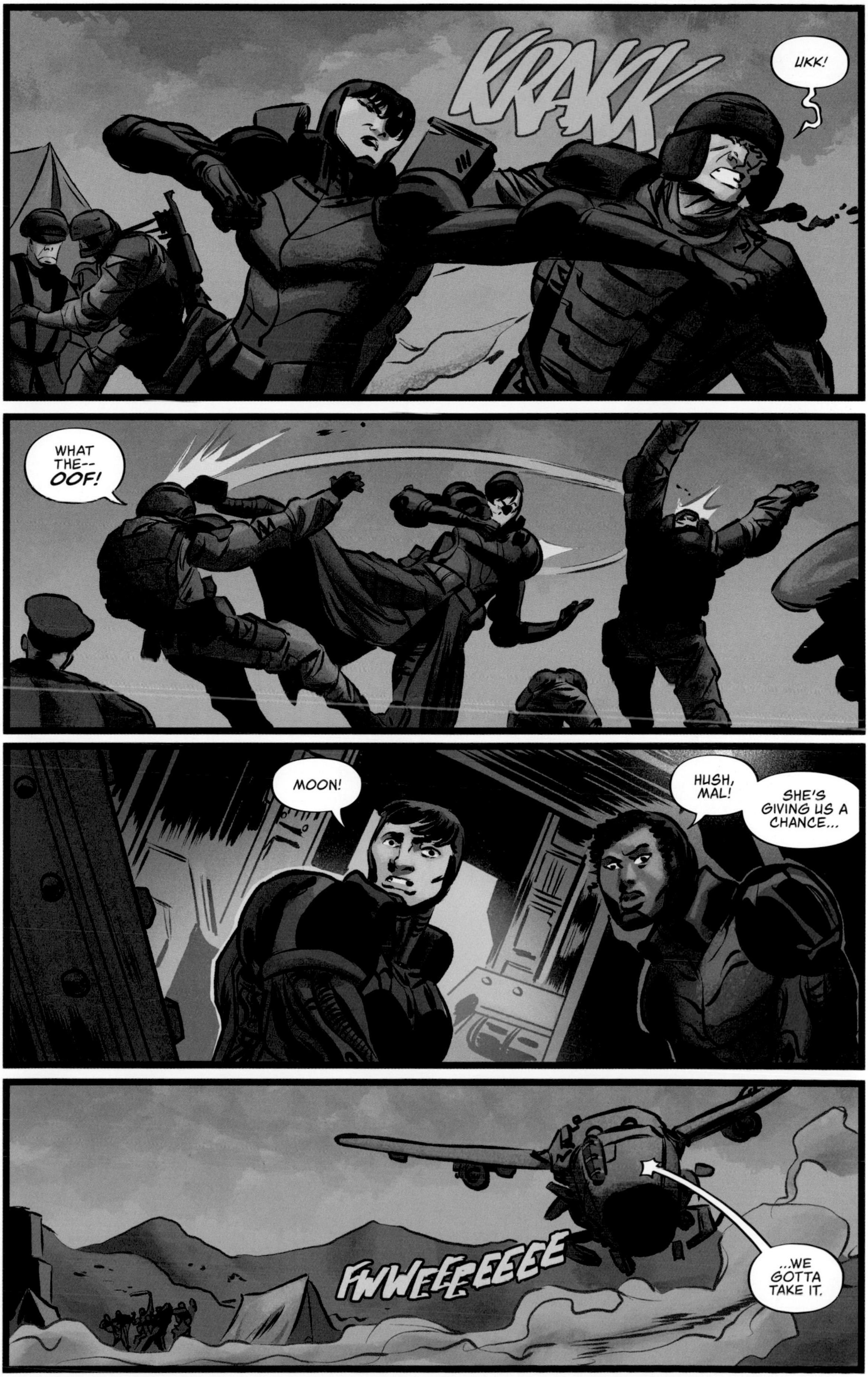
KRAKK
UKK!
WHAT THE-- OOF!
MOON!
HUSH, MAL!
SHE'S GIVING US A CHANCE...
FWWEEEEEEE
...WE GOTTA TAKE IT.

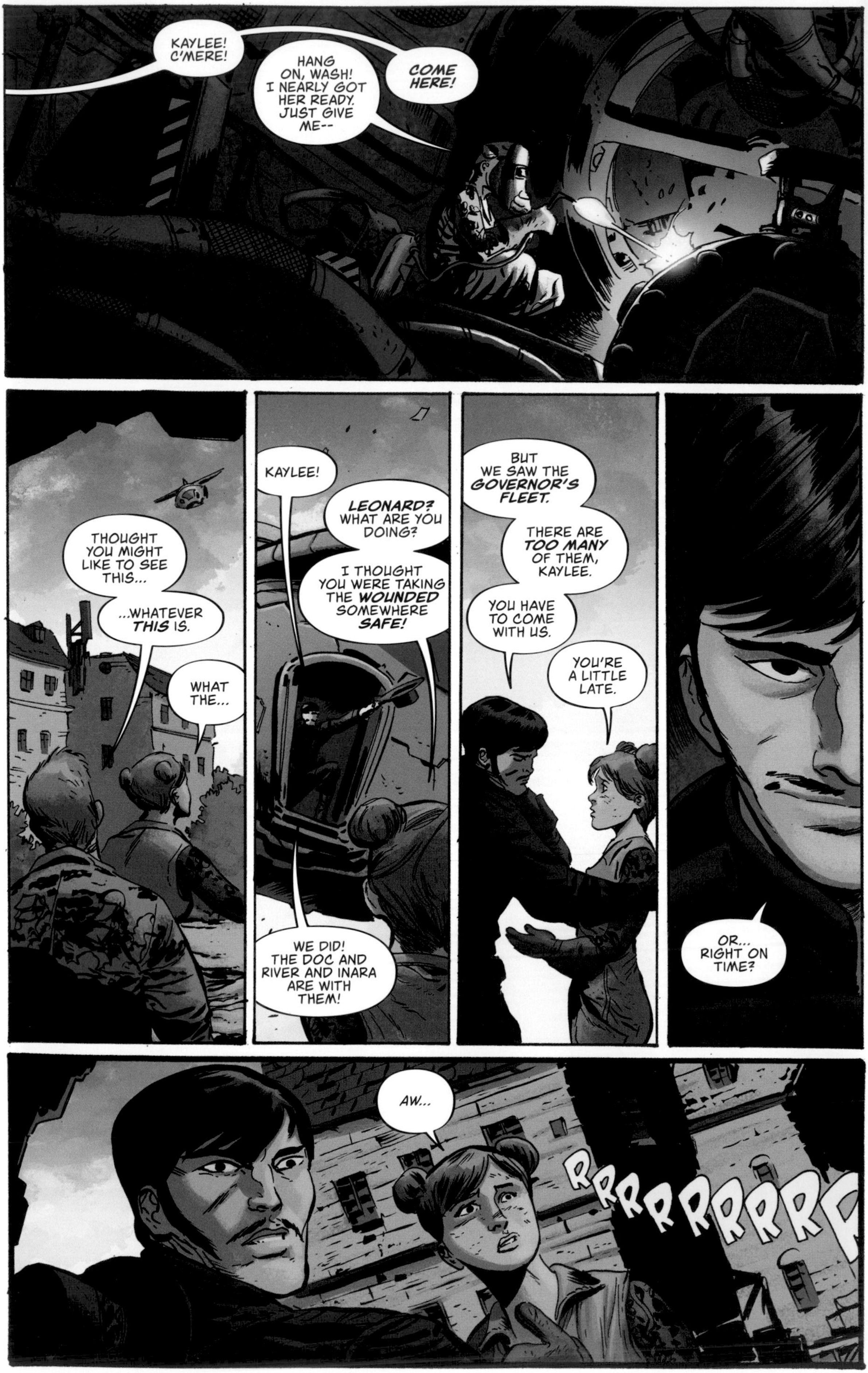
KAYLEE! C'MERE!
HANG ON, WASH! I NEARLY GOT HER READY. JUST GIVE ME--
COME HERE!
THOUGHT YOU MIGHT LIKE TO SEE THIS...
...WHATEVER THIS IS.
WHAT THE...
KAYLEE!
LEONARD? WHAT ARE YOU DOING?
I THOUGHT YOU WERE TAKING THE WOUNDED SOMEWHERE SAFE!
WE DID! THE DOC AND RIVER AND INARA ARE WITH THEM!
BUT WE SAW THE GOVERNOR'S FLEET.
THERE ARE TOO MANY OF THEM, KAYLEE.
YOU HAVE TO COME WITH US.
YOU'RE A LITTLE LATE.
OR... RIGHT ON TIME?
AW...
RRRRRRRRRR

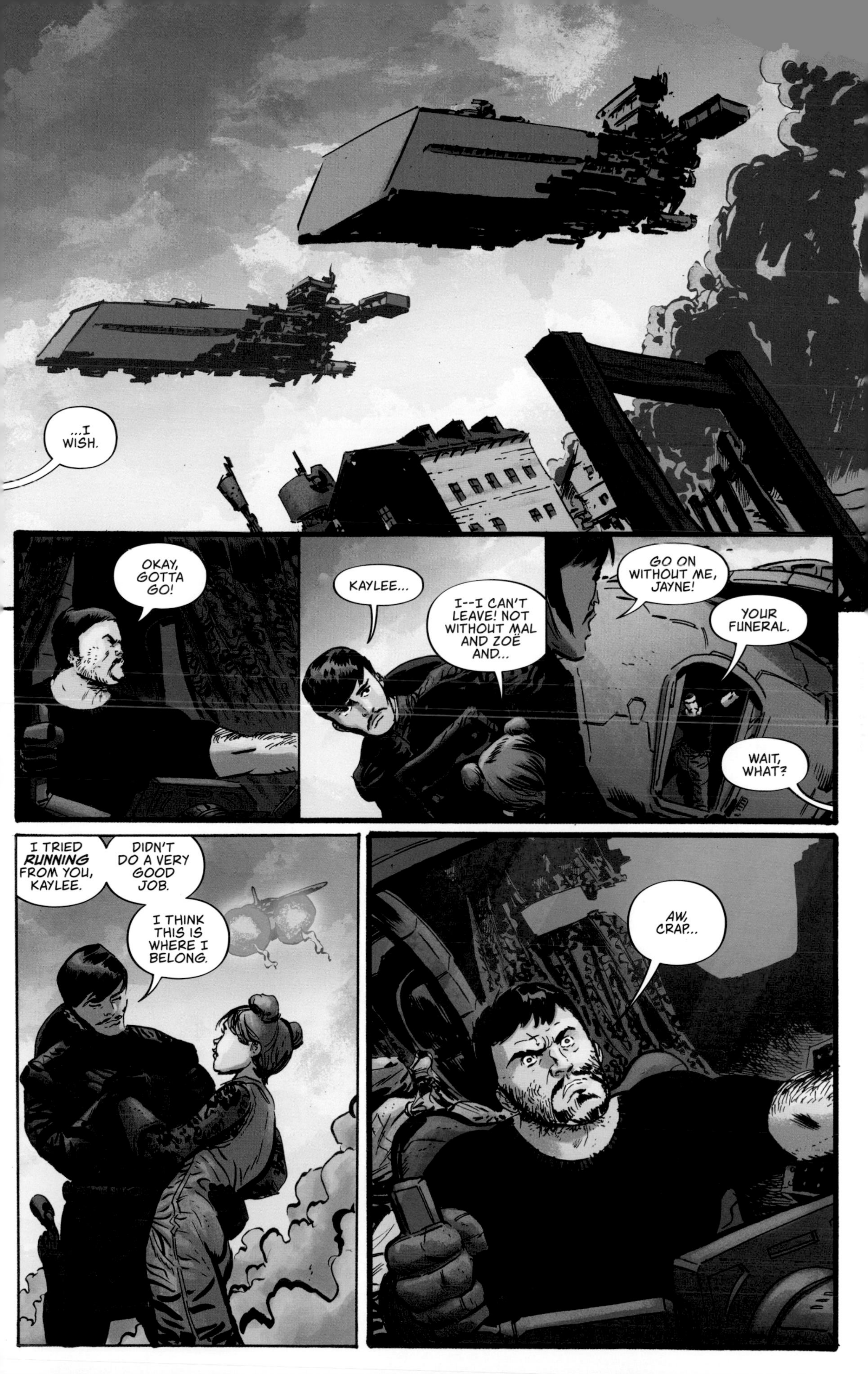
...I WISH.
OKAY, GOTTA GO!
KAYLEE...
I--I CAN'T LEAVE! NOT WITHOUT MAL AND ZOË AND...
GO ON WITHOUT ME, JAYNE!
YOUR FUNERAL.
WAIT, WHAT?
I TRIED RUNNING FROM YOU, KAYLEE.
DIDN'T DO A VERY GOOD JOB.
I THINK THIS IS WHERE I BELONG.
AW, CRAP...

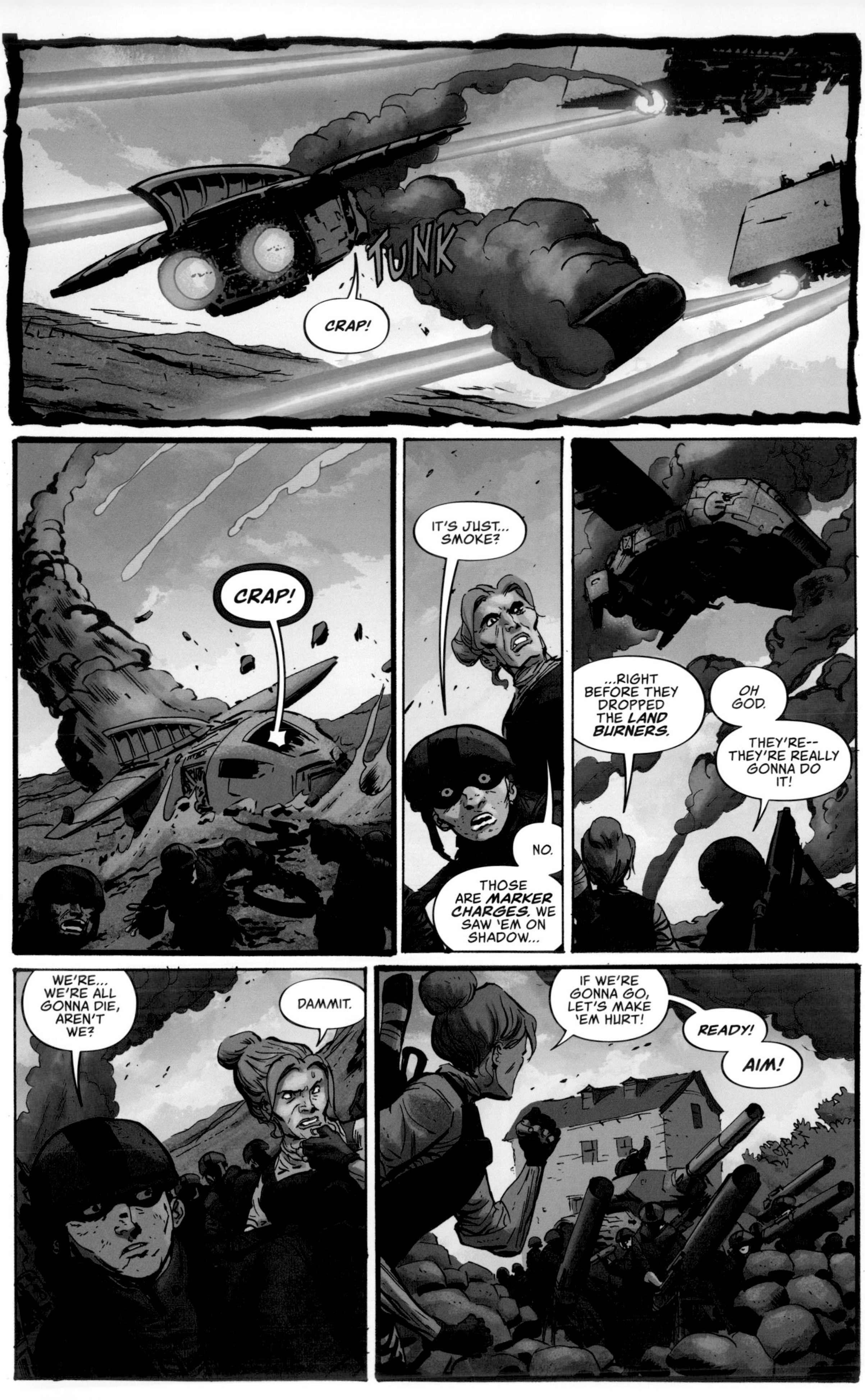
TUNK
CRAP!
CRAP!
IT'S JUST... SMOKE?
NO.
THOSE ARE MARKER CHARGES. WE SAW 'EM ON SHADOW...
...RIGHT BEFORE THEY DROPPED THE LAND BURNERS.
OH GOD.
THEY'RE-- THEY'RE REALLY GONNA DO IT!
WE'RE... WE'RE ALL GONNA DIE, AREN'T WE?
DAMMIT.
IF WE'RE GONNA GO, LET'S MAKE 'EM HURT!
READY!
AIM!

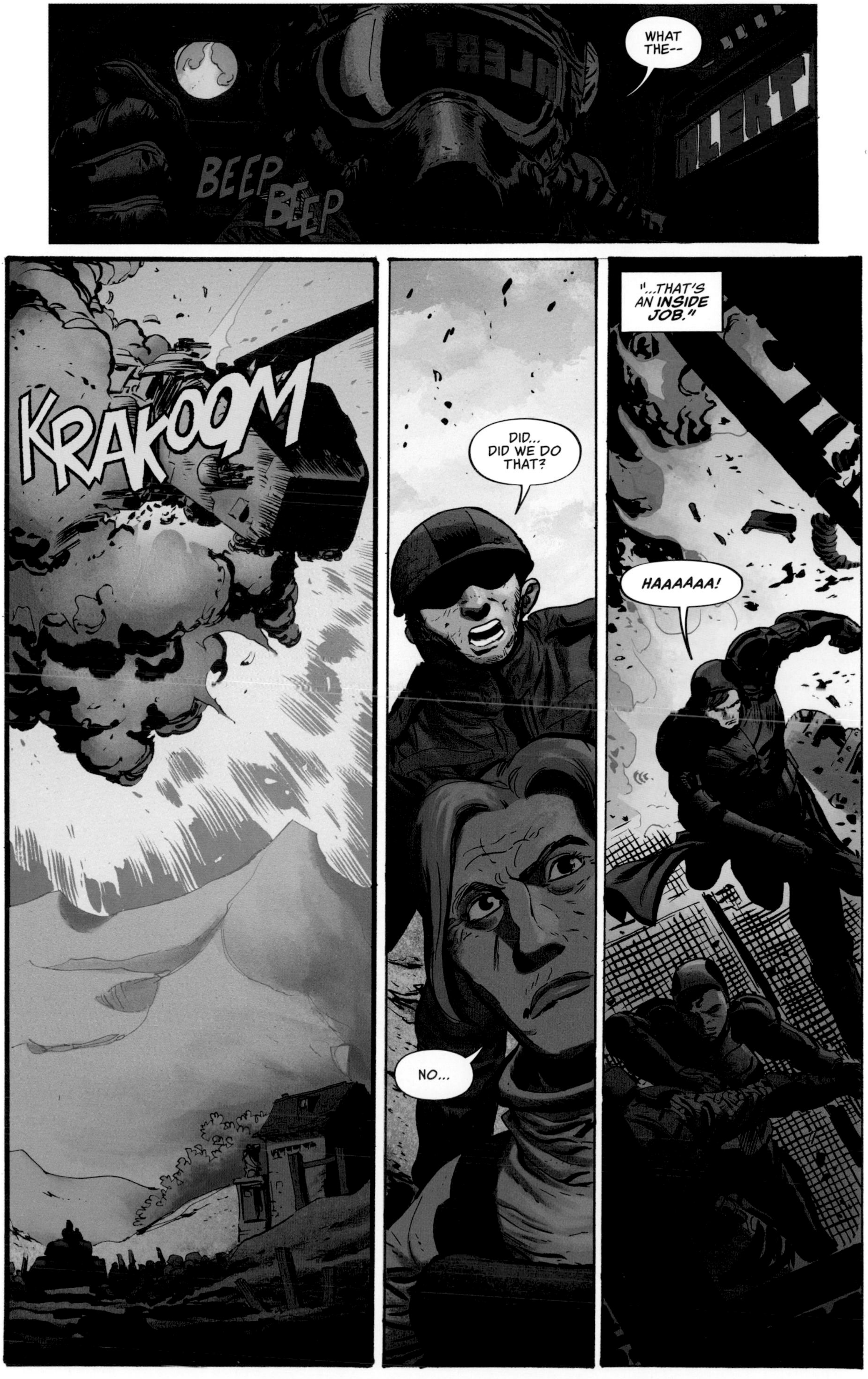
ALERT
WHAT THE--
BEEP
BEEP
ALERT
KRAKOOM
DID... DID WE DO THAT?
NO...
"...THAT'S AN INSIDE JOB."
HAAAAAA!

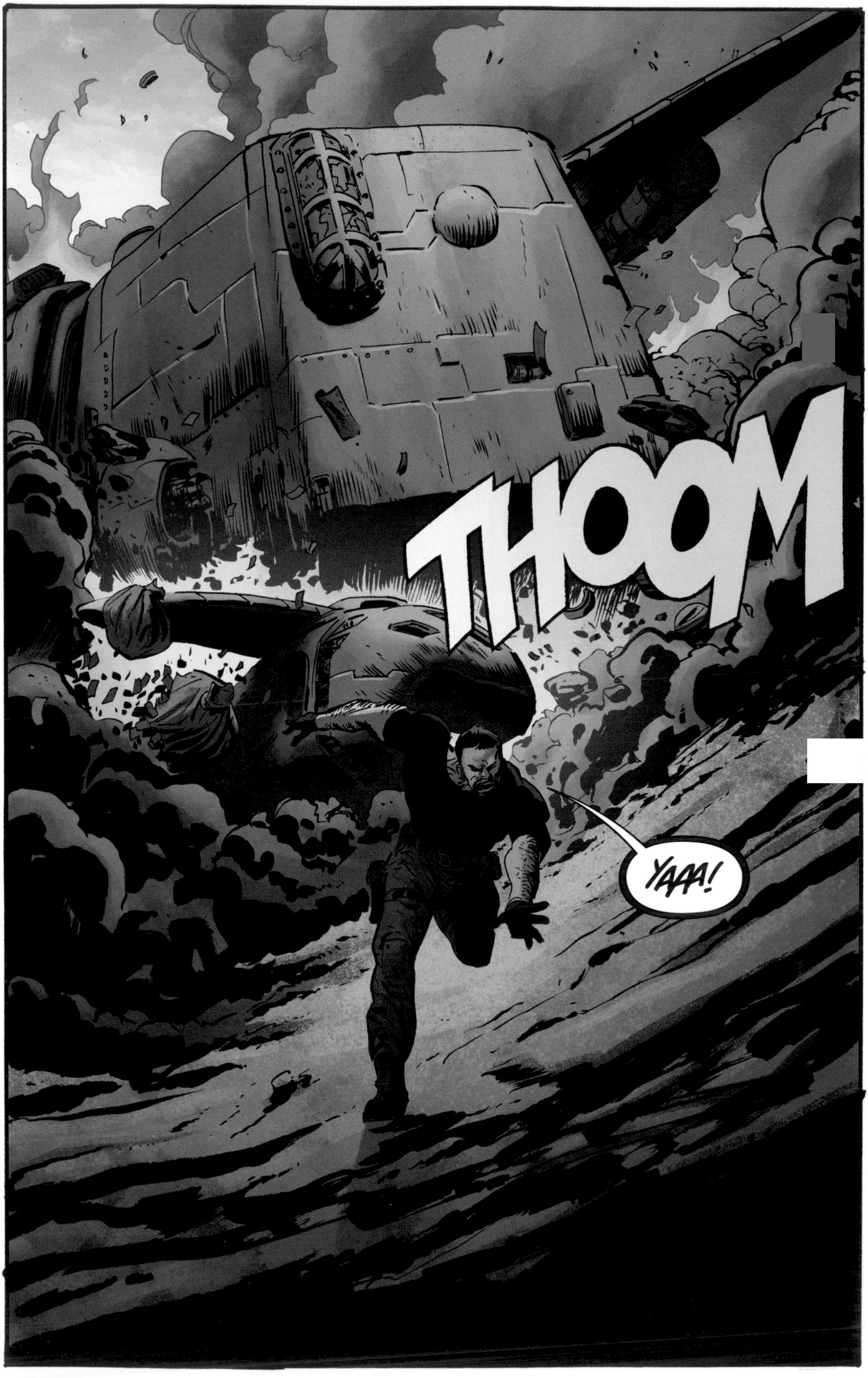
THOOM
YAAA!

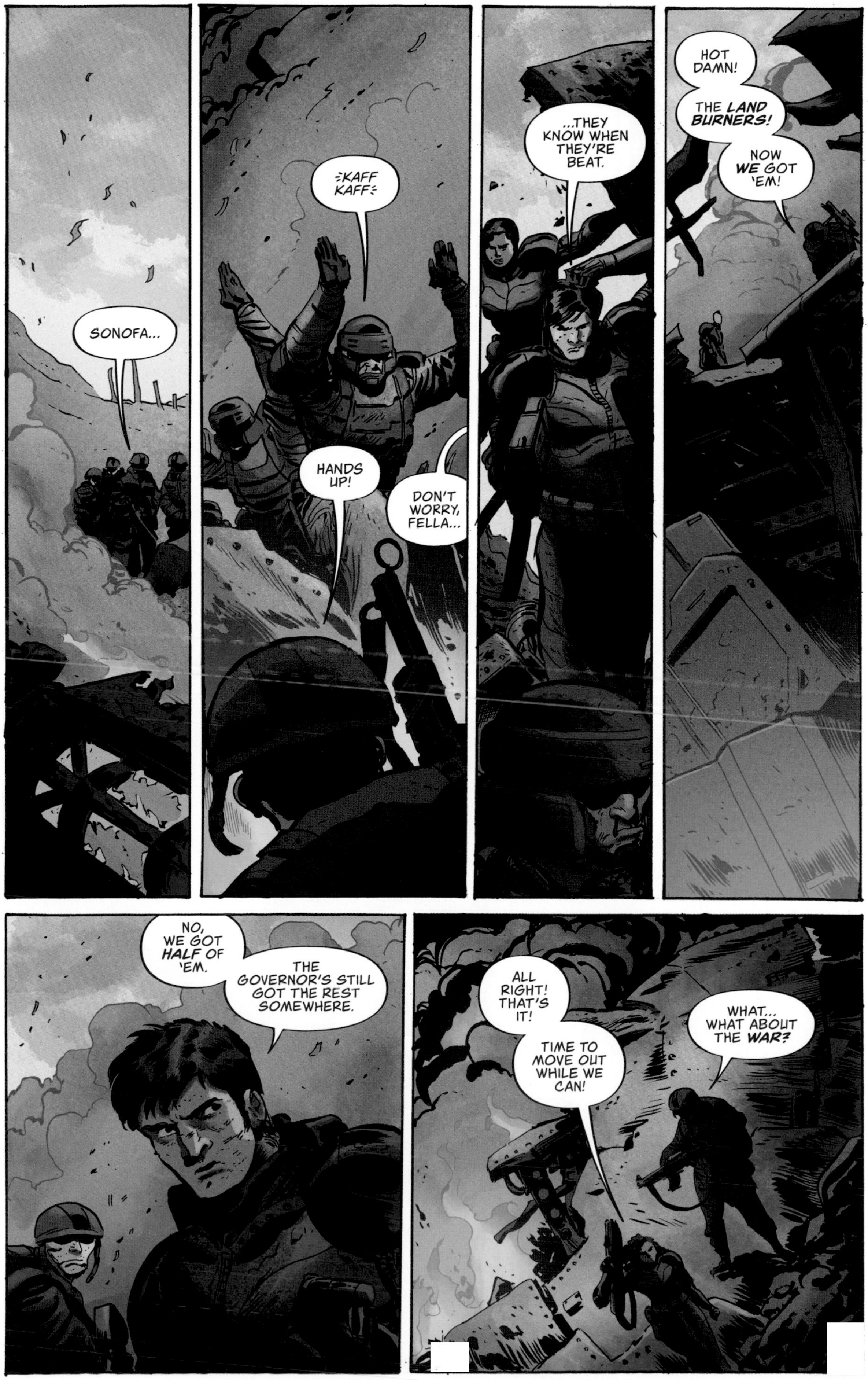
SONOFA...
KAFF KAFF
HANDS UP!
DON'T WORRY, FELLA...
...THEY KNOW WHEN THEY'RE BEAT.
HOT DAMN!
THE LAND BURNERS!
NOW WE GOT 'EM!
NO, WE GOT HALF OF 'EM.
THE GOVERNOR'S STILL GOT THE REST SOMEWHERE.
ALL RIGHT! THAT'S IT!
TIME TO MOVE OUT WHILE WE CAN!
WHAT... WHAT ABOUT THE WAR?

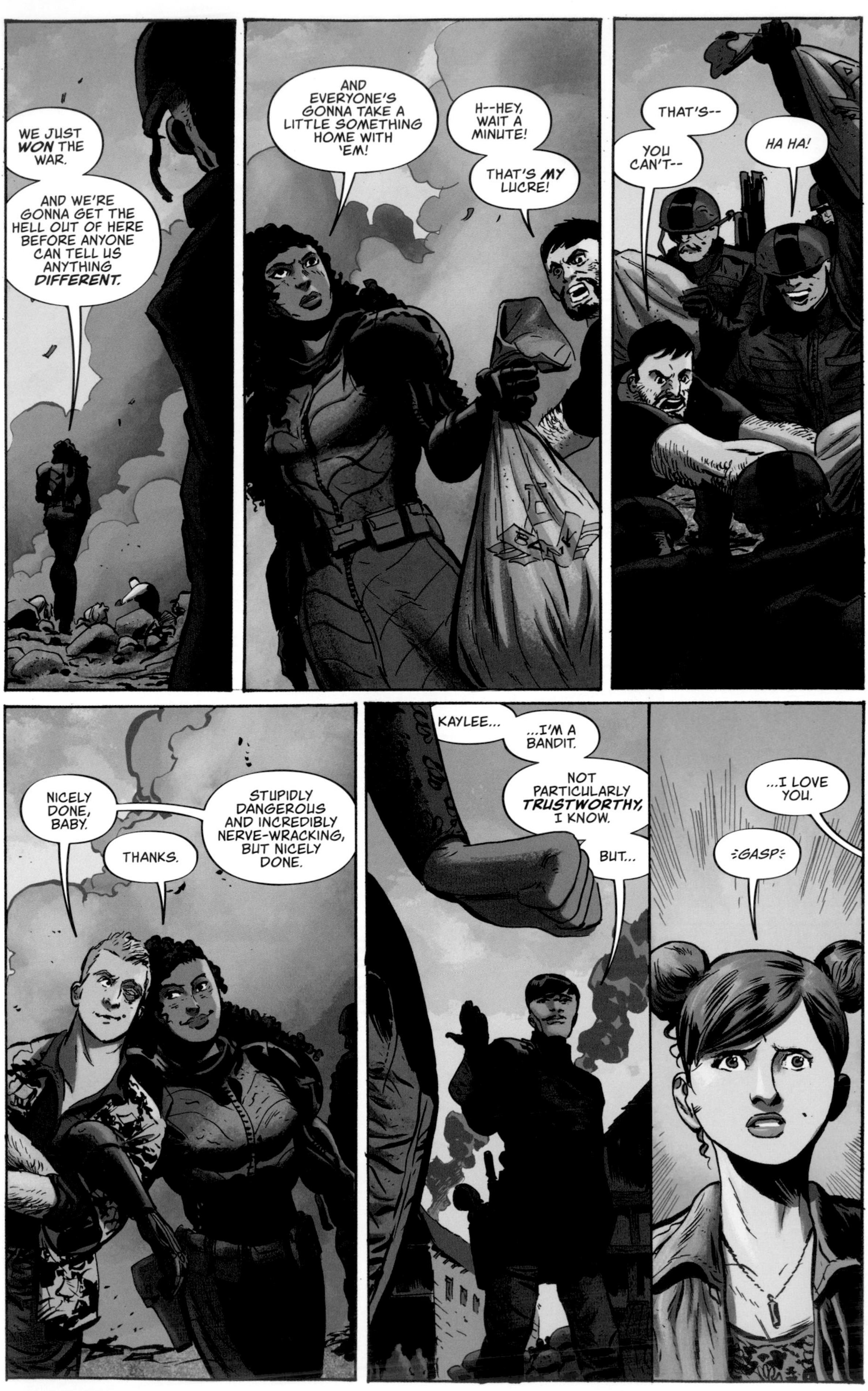

WE JUST WON THE WAR.
AND WE'RE GONNA GET THE HELL OUT OF HERE BEFORE ANYONE CAN TELL US ANYTHING DIFFERENT.
AND EVERYONE'S GONNA TAKE A LITTLE SOMETHING HOME WITH 'EM!
H--HEY, WAIT A MINUTE!
THAT'S MY LUCRE!
THAT'S--
YOU CAN'T--
HA HA!
NICELY DONE, BABY.
THANKS.
STUPIDLY DANGEROUS AND INCREDIBLY NERVE-WRACKING, BUT NICELY DONE.
KAYLEE...
...I'M A BANDIT.
NOT PARTICULARLY TRUSTWORTHY, I KNOW.
BUT...
...I LOVE YOU.
GASP

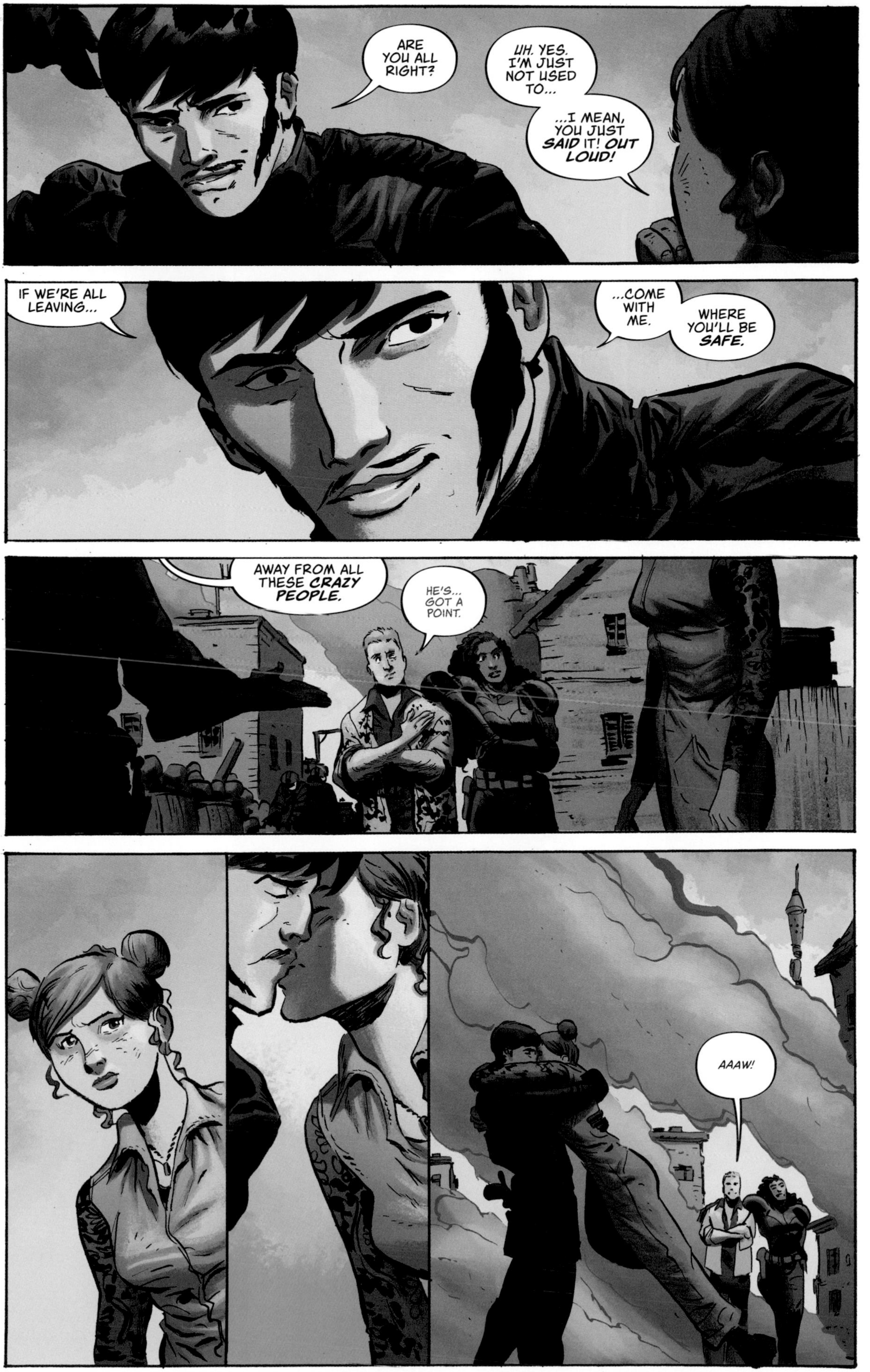
ARE YOU ALL RIGHT?
UH. YES. I'M JUST NOT USED TO...
...I MEAN, YOU JUST SAID IT! OUT LOUD!
IF WE'RE ALL LEAVING...
...COME WITH ME.
WHERE YOU'LL BE SAFE.
AWAY FROM ALL THESE CRAZY PEOPLE.
HE'S... GOT A POINT.
AAAW!

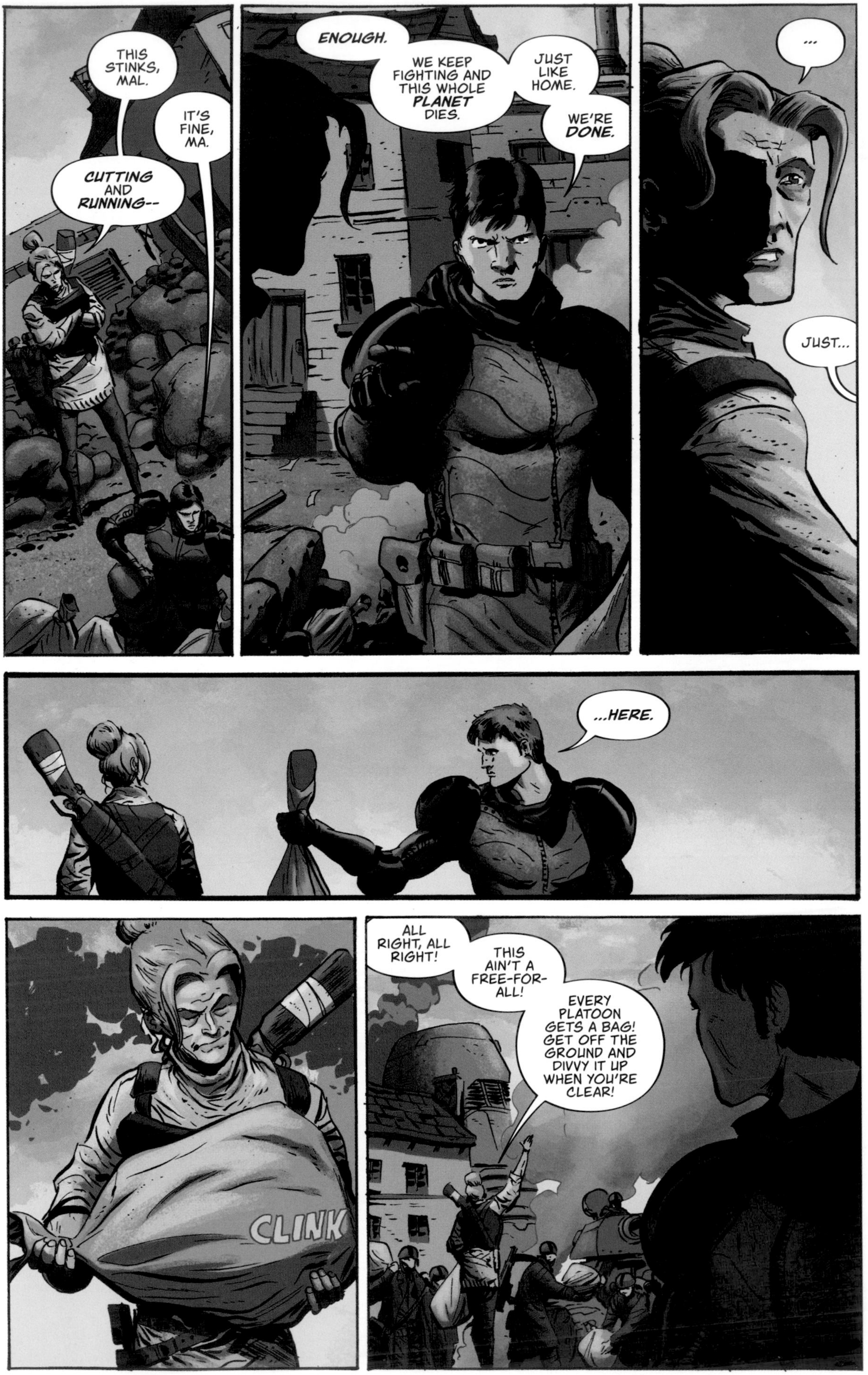
THIS STINKS, MAL.
IT'S FINE, MA.
CUTTING AND RUNNING--
ENOUGH.
WE KEEP FIGHTING AND THIS WHOLE PLANET DIES.
JUST LIKE HOME.
WE'RE DONE.
...
JUST...
...HERE.
CLINK
ALL RIGHT, ALL RIGHT!
THIS AIN'T A FREE-FOR-ALL!
EVERY PLATOON GETS A BAG! GET OFF THE GROUND AND DIVVY IT UP WHEN YOU'RE CLEAR!

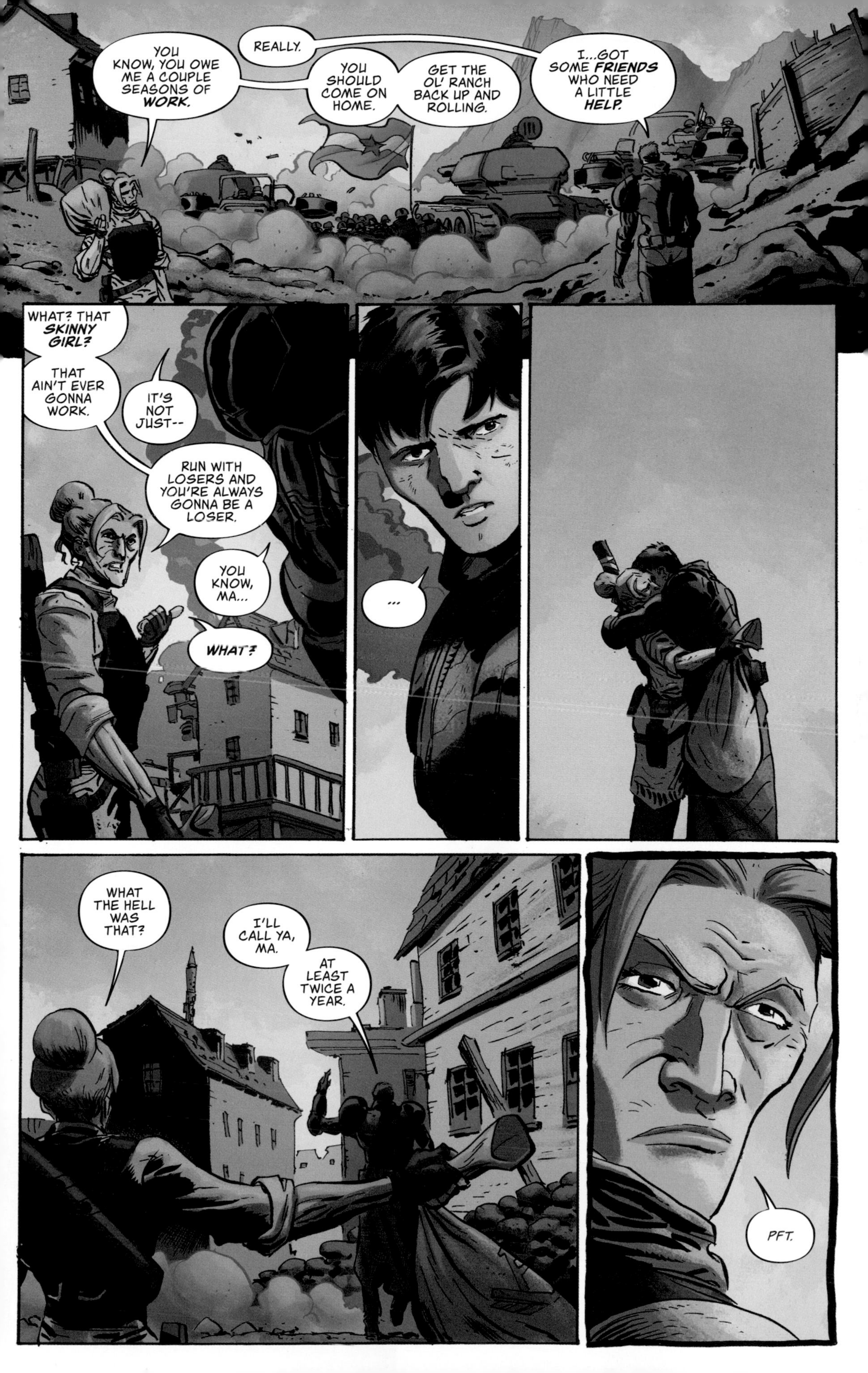
YOU KNOW, YOU OWE ME A COUPLE SEASONS OF WORK.
REALLY.
YOU SHOULD COME ON HOME.
GET THE OL' RANCH BACK UP AND ROLLING.
I...GOT SOME FRIENDS WHO NEED A LITTLE HELP.
WHAT? THAT SKINNY GIRL?
THAT AIN'T EVER GONNA WORK.
IT'S NOT JUST--
RUN WITH LOSERS AND YOU'RE ALWAYS GONNA BE A LOSER.
YOU KNOW, MA...
WHAT?
...
WHAT THE HELL WAS THAT?
I'LL CALL YA, MA.
AT LEAST TWICE A YEAR.
PFT.

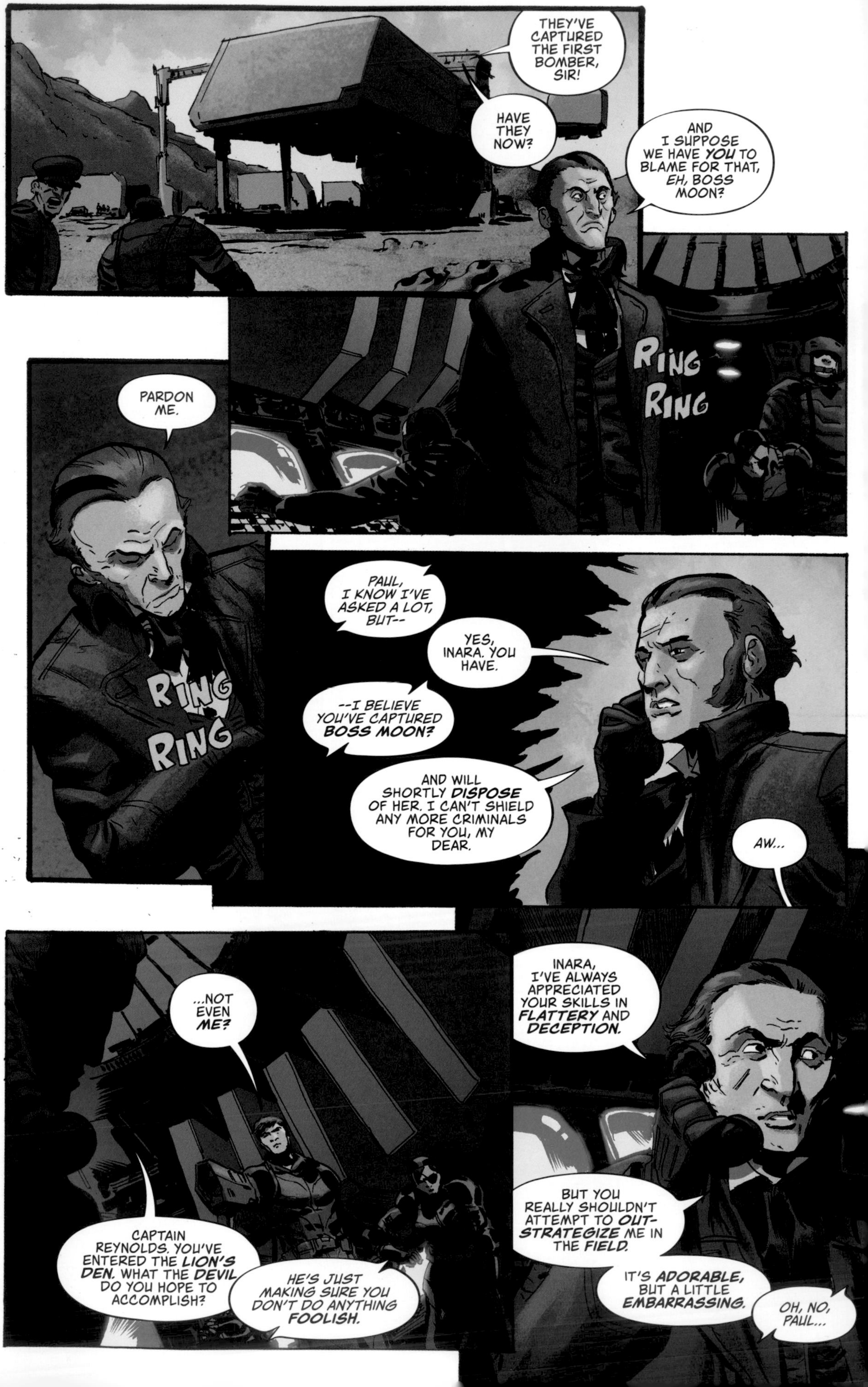
THEY'VE CAPTURED THE FIRST BOMBER, SIR!
HAVE THEY NOW?
AND I SUPPOSE WE HAVE YOU TO BLAME FOR THAT, EH, BOSS MOON?
RING RING
PARDON ME.
RING RING
PAUL, I KNOW I'VE ASKED A LOT, BUT--
YES, INARA. YOU HAVE.
--I BELIEVE YOU'VE CAPTURED BOSS MOON?
AND WILL SHORTLY DISPOSE OF HER. I CAN'T SHIELD ANY MORE CRIMINALS FOR YOU, MY DEAR.
AW...
...NOT EVEN ME?
INARA, I'VE ALWAYS APPRECIATED YOUR SKILLS IN FLATTERY AND DECEPTION.
CAPTAIN REYNOLDS. YOU'VE ENTERED THE LION'S DEN. WHAT THE DEVIL DO YOU HOPE TO ACCOMPLISH?
HE'S JUST MAKING SURE YOU DON'T DO ANYTHING FOOLISH.
BUT YOU REALLY SHOULDN'T ATTEMPT TO OUT-STRATEGIZE ME IN THE FIELD.
IT'S ADORABLE, BUT A LITTLE EMBARRASSING.
OH, NO, PAUL...

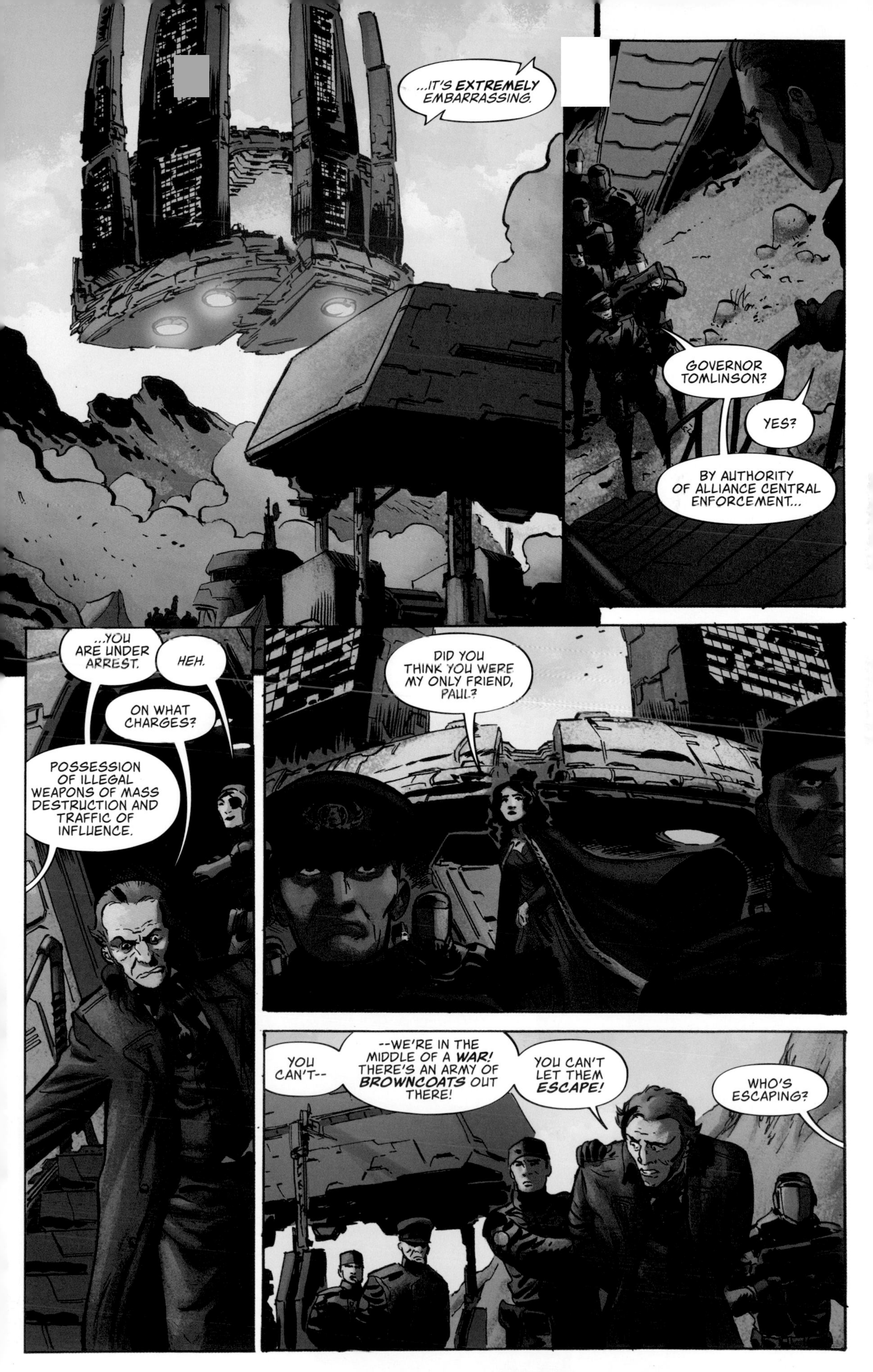
...IT'S EXTREMELY EMBARRASSING.
GOVERNOR TOMLINSON?
YES?
BY AUTHORITY OF ALLIANCE CENTRAL ENFORCEMENT...
...YOU ARE UNDER ARREST.
HEH.
ON WHAT CHARGES?
POSSESSION OF ILLEGAL WEAPONS OF MASS DESTRUCTION AND TRAFFIC OF INFLUENCE.
DID YOU THINK YOU WERE MY ONLY FRIEND, PAUL?
YOU CAN'T--
--WE'RE IN THE MIDDLE OF A WAR! THERE'S AN ARMY OF BROWNCOATS OUT THERE!
YOU CAN'T LET THEM ESCAPE!
WHO'S ESCAPING?

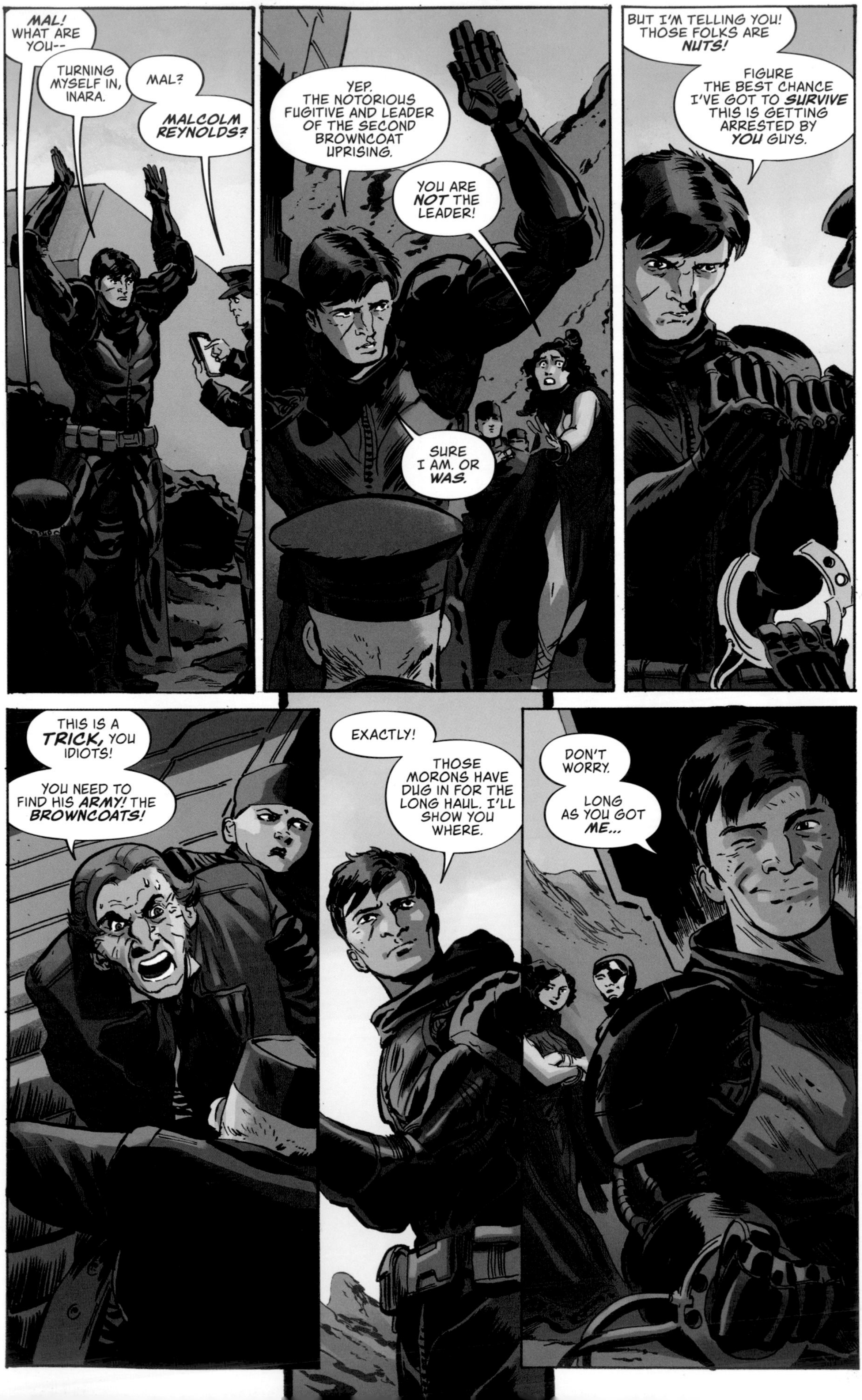
MAL! WHAT ARE YOU--
TURNING MYSELF IN, INARA.
MAL?
MALCOLM REYNOLDS?
YEP. THE NOTORIOUS FUGITIVE AND LEADER OF THE SECOND BROWNCOAT UPRISING.
YOU ARE NOT THE LEADER!
SURE I AM. OR WAS.
BUT I'M TELLING YOU! THOSE FOLKS ARE NUTS!
FIGURE THE BEST CHANCE I'VE GOT TO SURVIVE THIS IS GETTING ARRESTED BY YOU GUYS.
THIS IS A TRICK, YOU IDIOTS!
YOU NEED TO FIND HIS ARMY! THE BROWNCOATS!
EXACTLY!
THOSE MORONS HAVE DUG IN FOR THE LONG HAUL. I'LL SHOW YOU WHERE.
DON'T WORRY.
LONG AS YOU GOT ME...

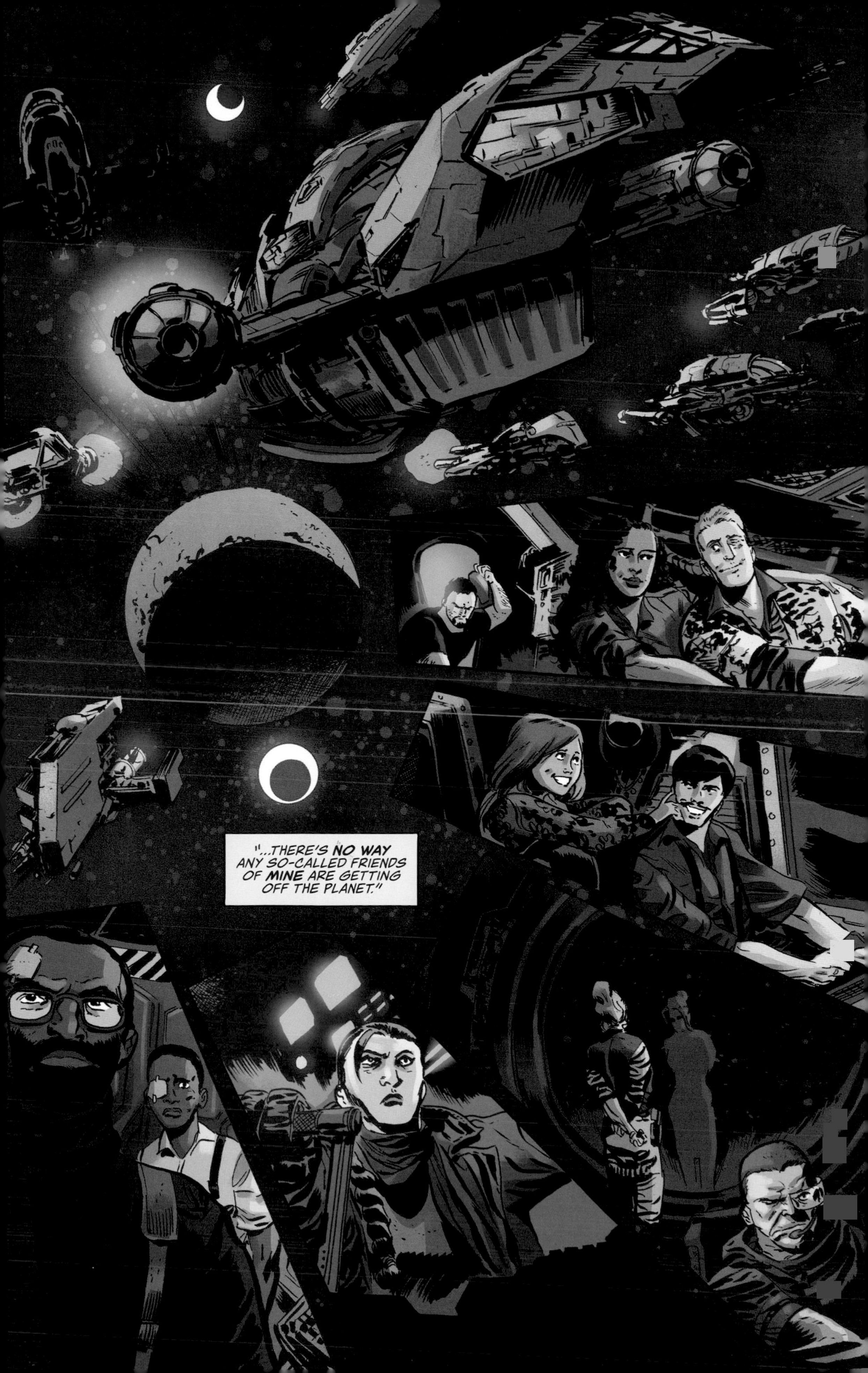
"...THERE'S NO WAY ANY SO-CALLED FRIENDS OF MINE ARE GETTING OFF THE PLANET."

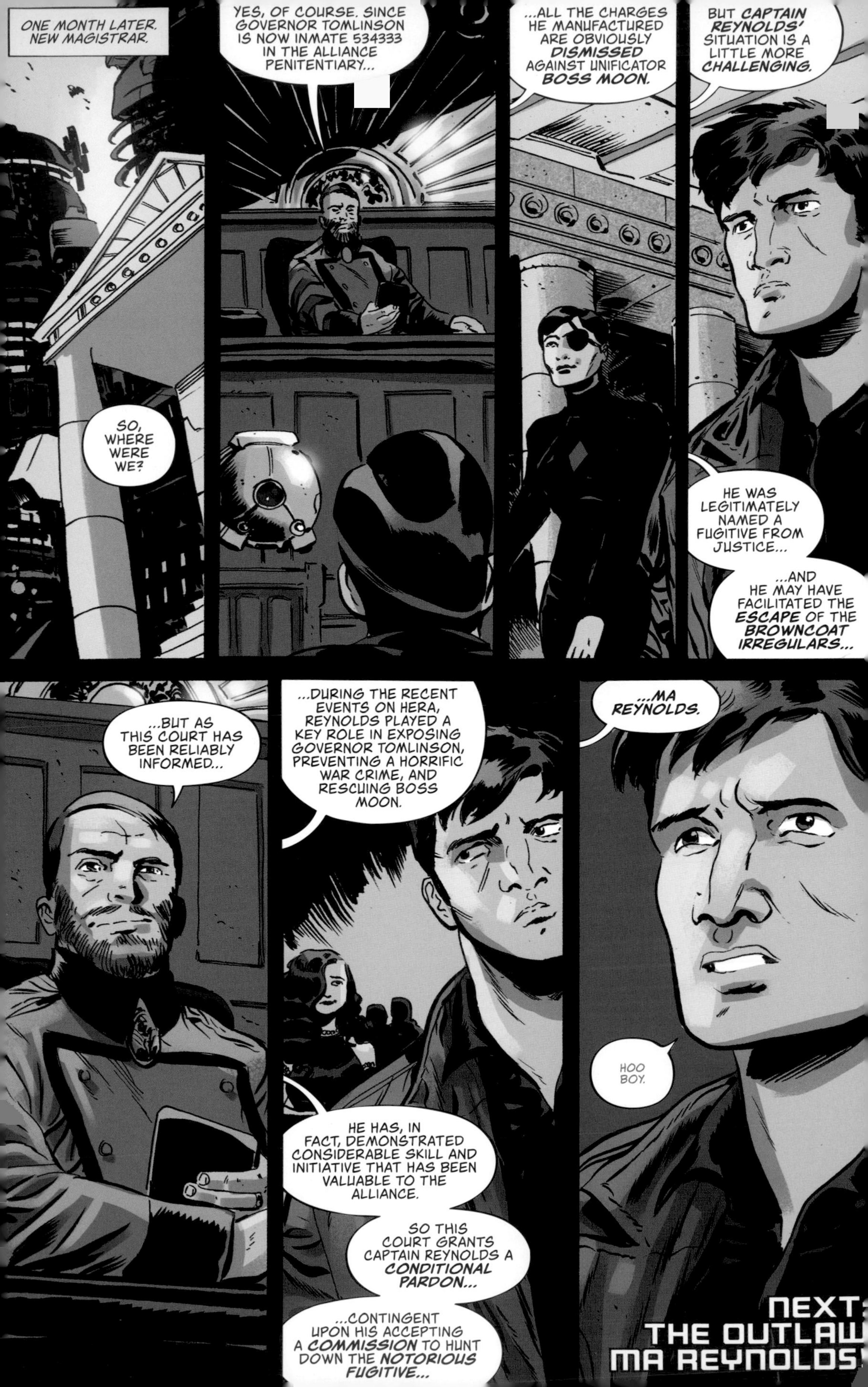
ONE MONTH LATER. NEW MAGISTRAR.
SO, WHERE WERE WE?
YES, OF COURSE. SINCE GOVERNOR TOMLINSON IS NOW INMATE 534333 IN THE ALLIANCE PENITENTIARY...
...ALL THE CHARGES HE MANUFACTURED ARE OBVIOUSLY DISMISSED AGAINST UNIFICATOR BOSS MOON.
BUT CAPTAIN REYNOLDS' SITUATION IS A LITTLE MORE CHALLENGING.
HE WAS LEGITIMATELY NAMED A FUGITIVE FROM JUSTICE...
...AND HE MAY HAVE FACILITATED THE ESCAPE OF THE BROWNCOAT IRREGULARS...
...BUT AS THIS COURT HAS BEEN RELIABLY INFORMED...
...DURING THE RECENT EVENTS ON HERA, REYNOLDS PLAYED A KEY ROLE IN EXPOSING GOVERNOR TOMLINSON, PREVENTING A HORRIFIC WAR CRIME, AND RESCUING BOSS MOON.
HE HAS, IN FACT, DEMONSTRATED CONSIDERABLE SKILL AND INITIATIVE THAT HAS BEEN VALUABLE TO THE ALLIANCE.
SO THIS COURT GRANTS CAPTAIN REYNOLDS A CONDITIONAL PARDON...
...CONTINGENT UPON HIS ACCEPTING A COMMISSION TO HUNT DOWN THE NOTORIOUS FUGITIVE...
...MA REYNOLDS.
HOO BOY.
NEXT: THE OUTLAW MA REYNOLDS!

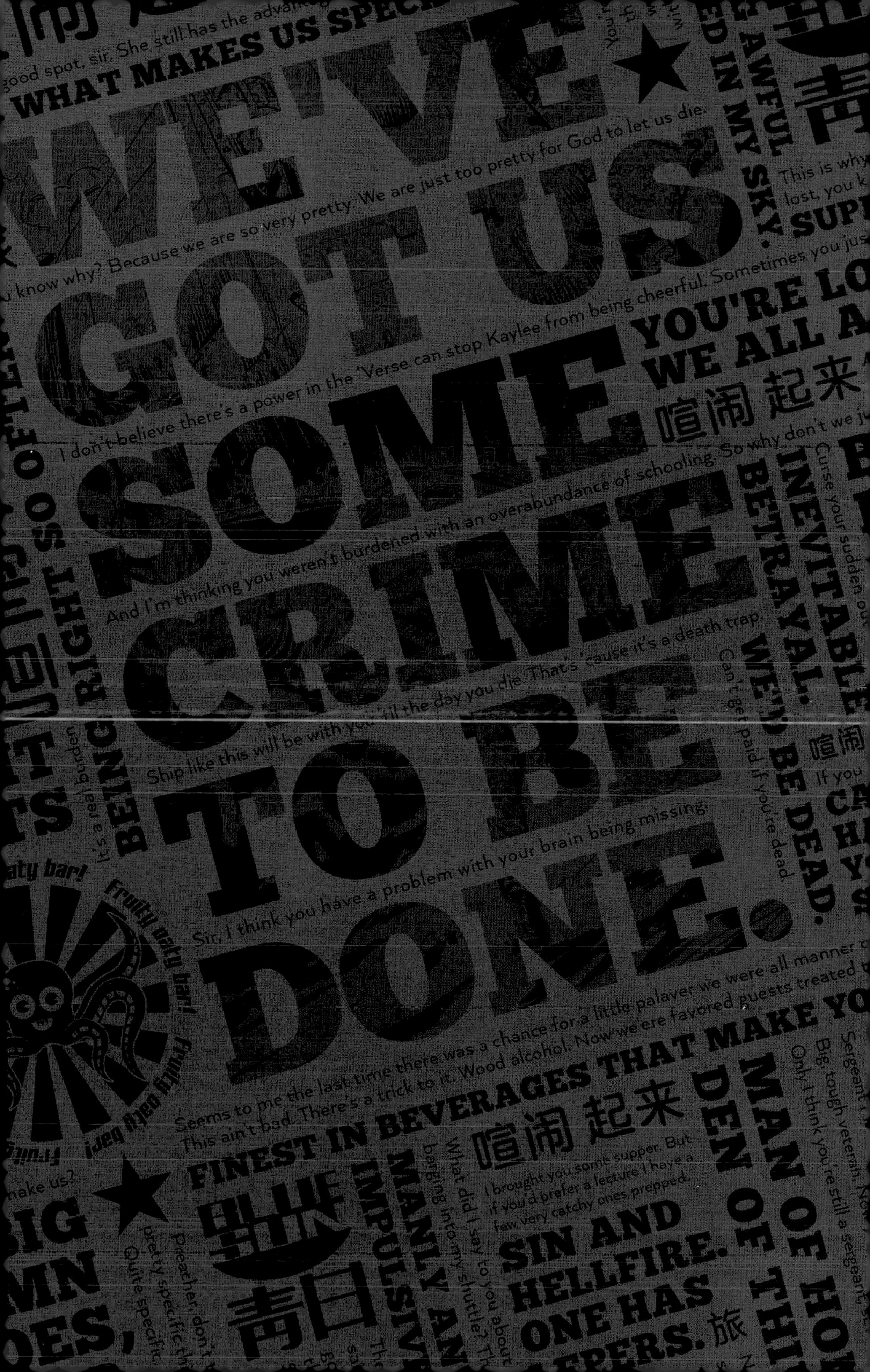

WE'VE GOT US SOME CRIME TO BE DONE.
WHAT MAKES US SPECI
good spot, sir. She still has the advantag
know why? Because we are so very pretty. We are just too pretty for God to let us die.
I don't believe there's a power in the 'Verse can stop Kaylee from being cheerful. Sometimes you jus
And I'm thinking you weren't burdened with an overabundance of schooling. So why don't we j
Ship like this will be with you 'til the day you die. That's 'cause it's a death trap.
Sir, I think you have a problem with your brain being missing.
Seems to me the last time there was a chance for a little palaver we were all manner o
This ain't bad. There's a trick to it. Wood alcohol. Now we're favored guests treated t
FINEST IN BEVERAGES THAT MAKE YO
喧闹 起来
I brought you some supper. But if you'd prefer a lecture I have a few very catchy ones prepped.
SIN AND HELLFIRE.
ONE HAS
YOU'RE LO
WE ALL A
喧闹 起来
INEVITABLE
BETRAYAL.
WE'D BE DEAD.
Curse your sudden but
Can't get paid if you're dead.
AWFUL
IN MY SKY.
This is why
lost, you k
BEING RIGHT SO OFTEN
It's a real burden
Fruity oaty bar!
MAN OF THE
DEN OF THI
Big, tough veteran.
Only I think you're still a sergeant,
IMPULSIVE
MANLY AN
What did I say to you about barging into my shuttle?
Preacher, don't
pretty specific
Quite specific
make us?

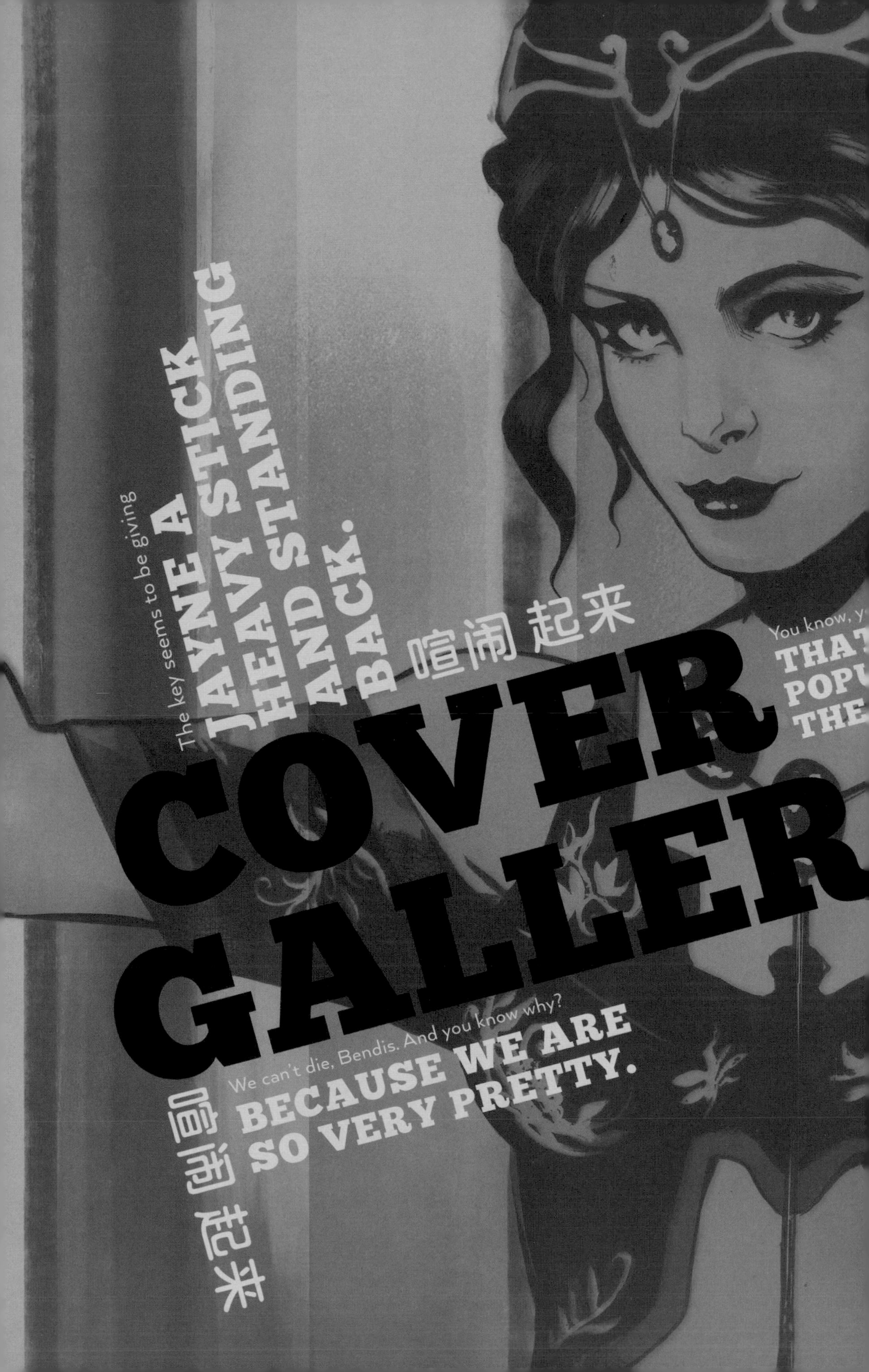

The key seems to be giving
JAYNE A STICK
HEAVY STANDING
AND STAND
BACK.
喧闹 起来
COVER
GALLER
You know, y
THA
POPU
THE
We can't die, Bendis. And you know why?
BECAUSE WE ARE
SO VERY PRETTY.
喧闹 起来

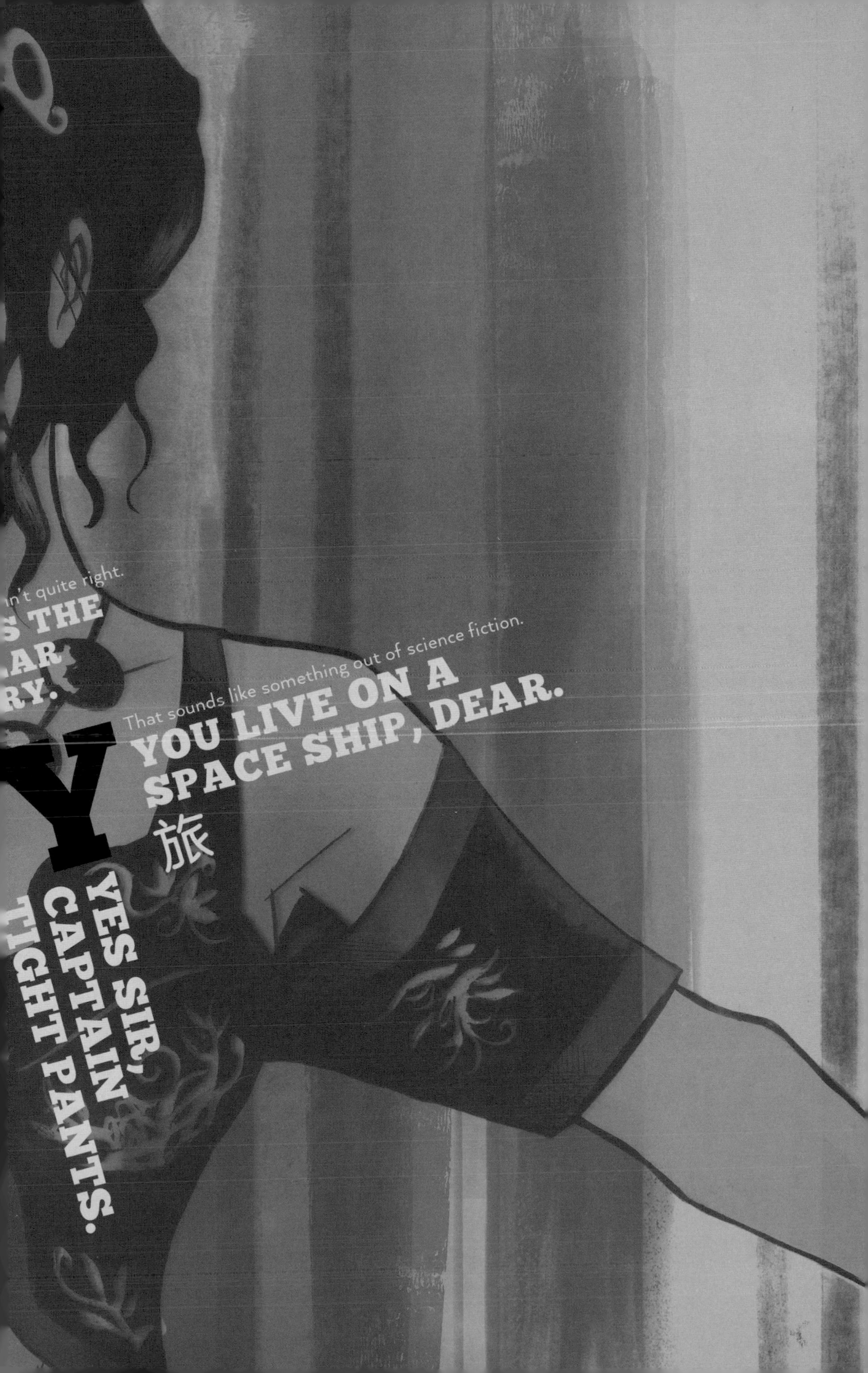
quite right.
THE
That sounds like something out of science fiction.
YOU LIVE ON A SPACE SHIP, DEAR.
旅
YES SIR, CAPTAIN TIGHT PANTS.

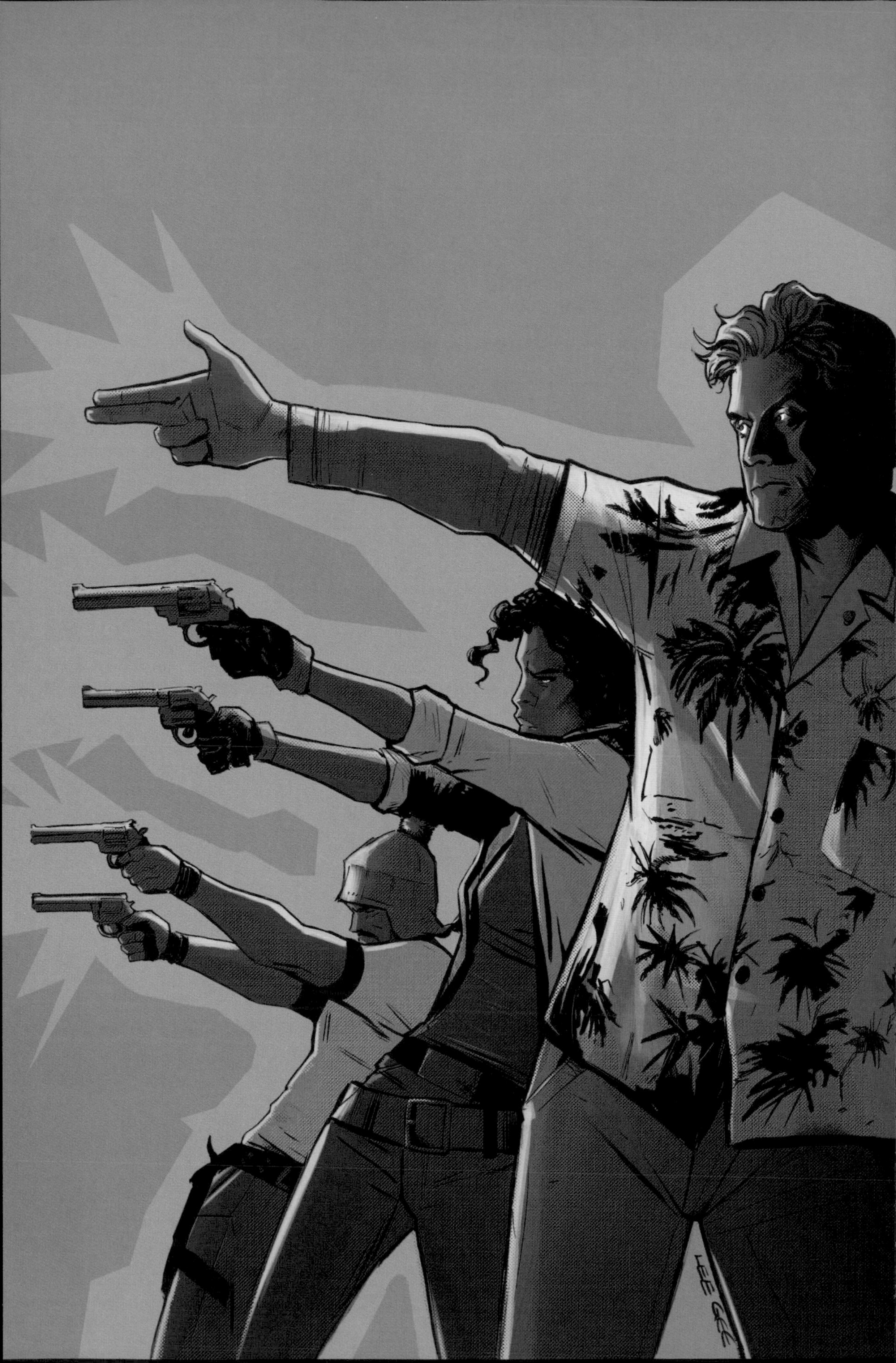

Firefly #9 Cover by **Lee Garbett**

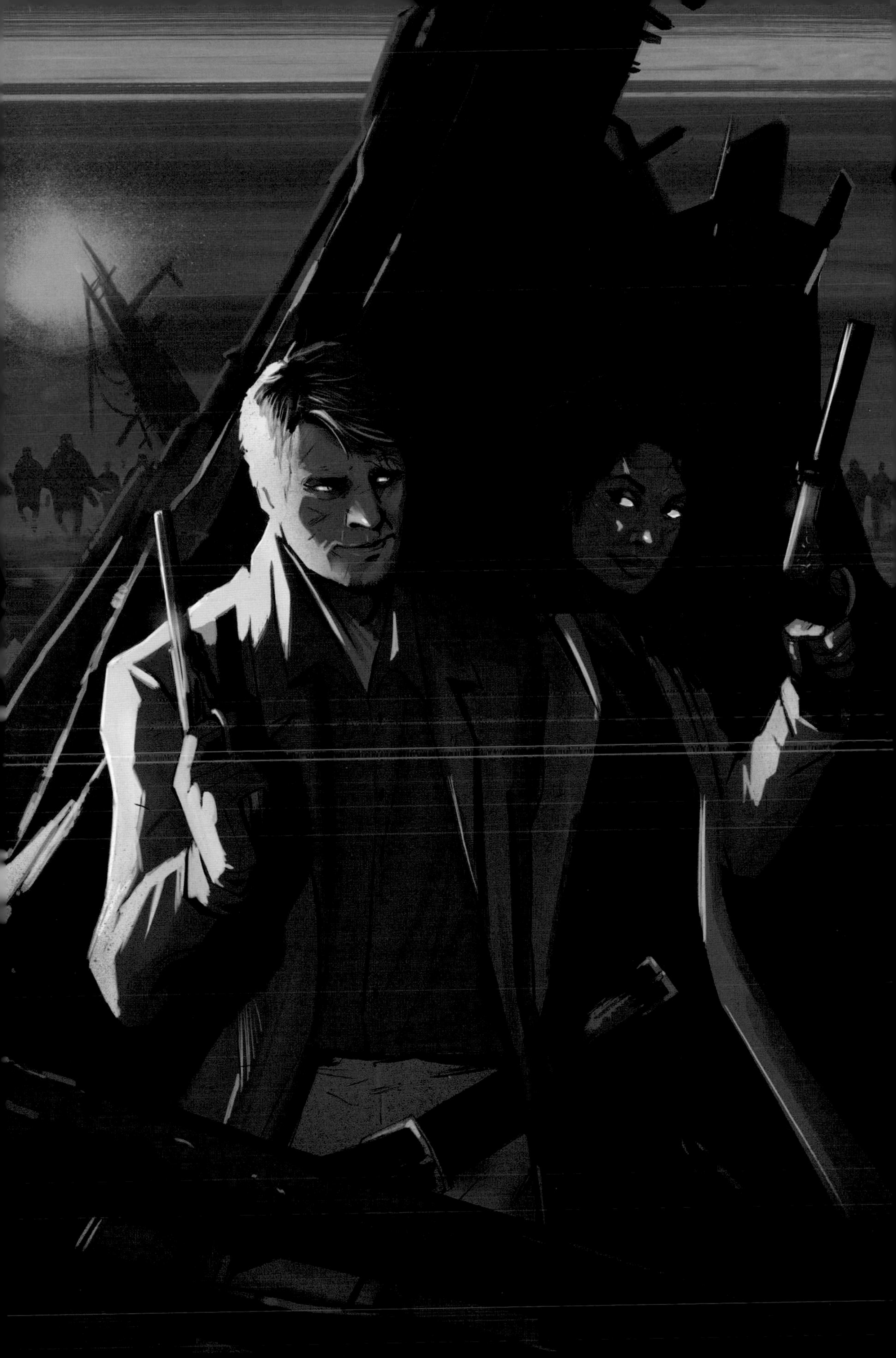

Firefly #10 Cover by **Lee Garbett**

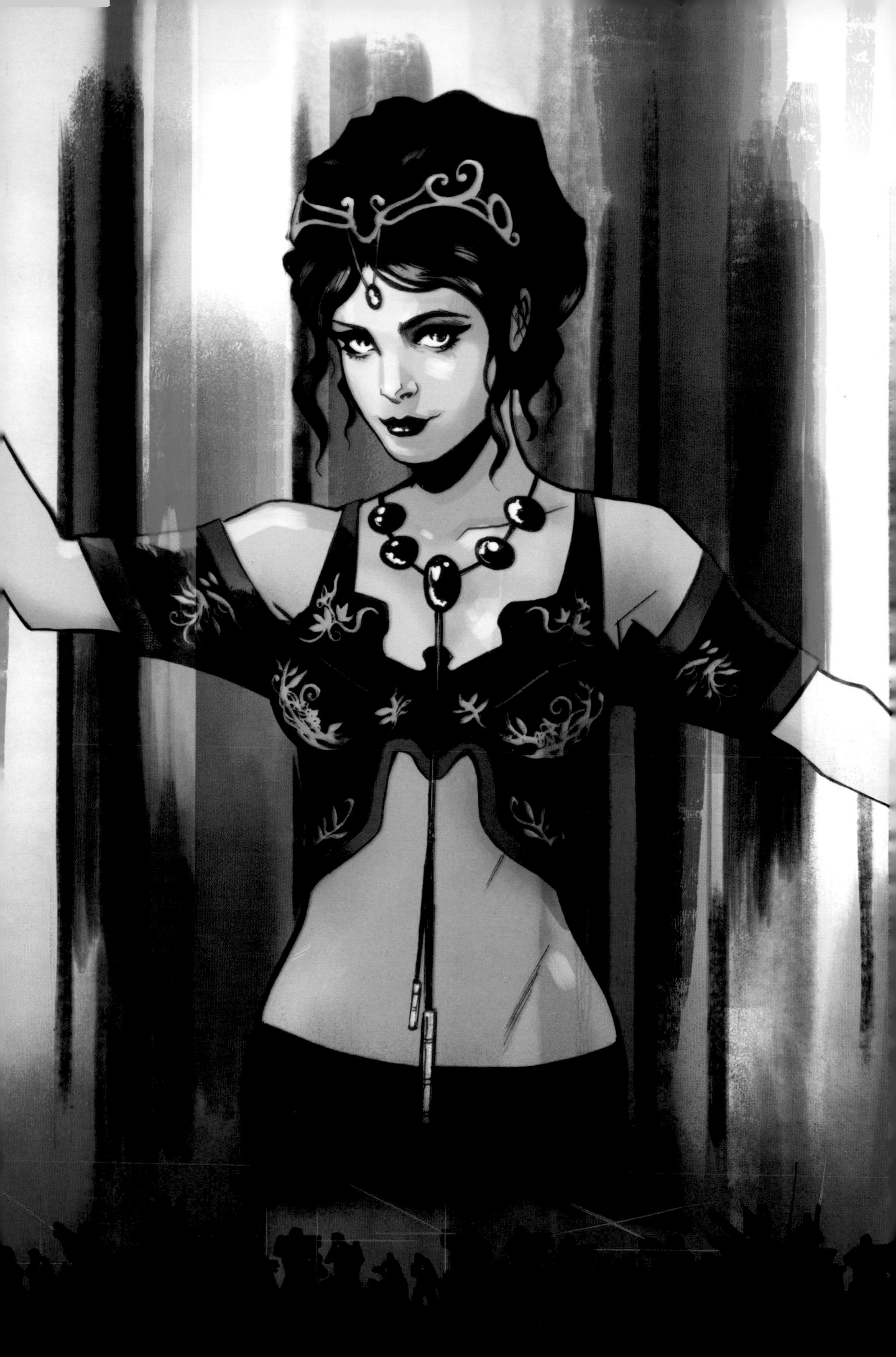

Firefly #11 Cover by **Lee Garbett**

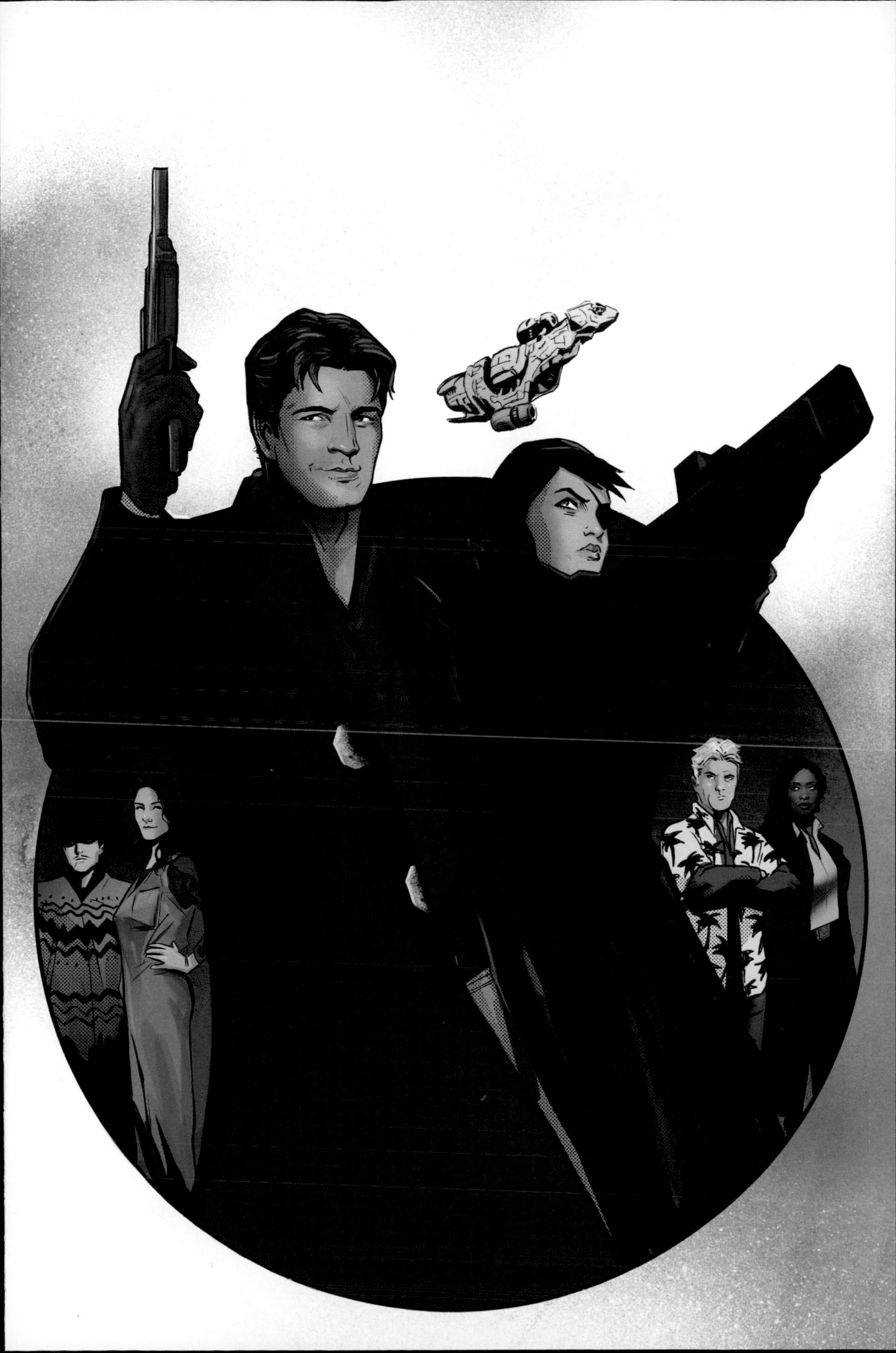

Firefly #12 Cover by **Lee Garbett**

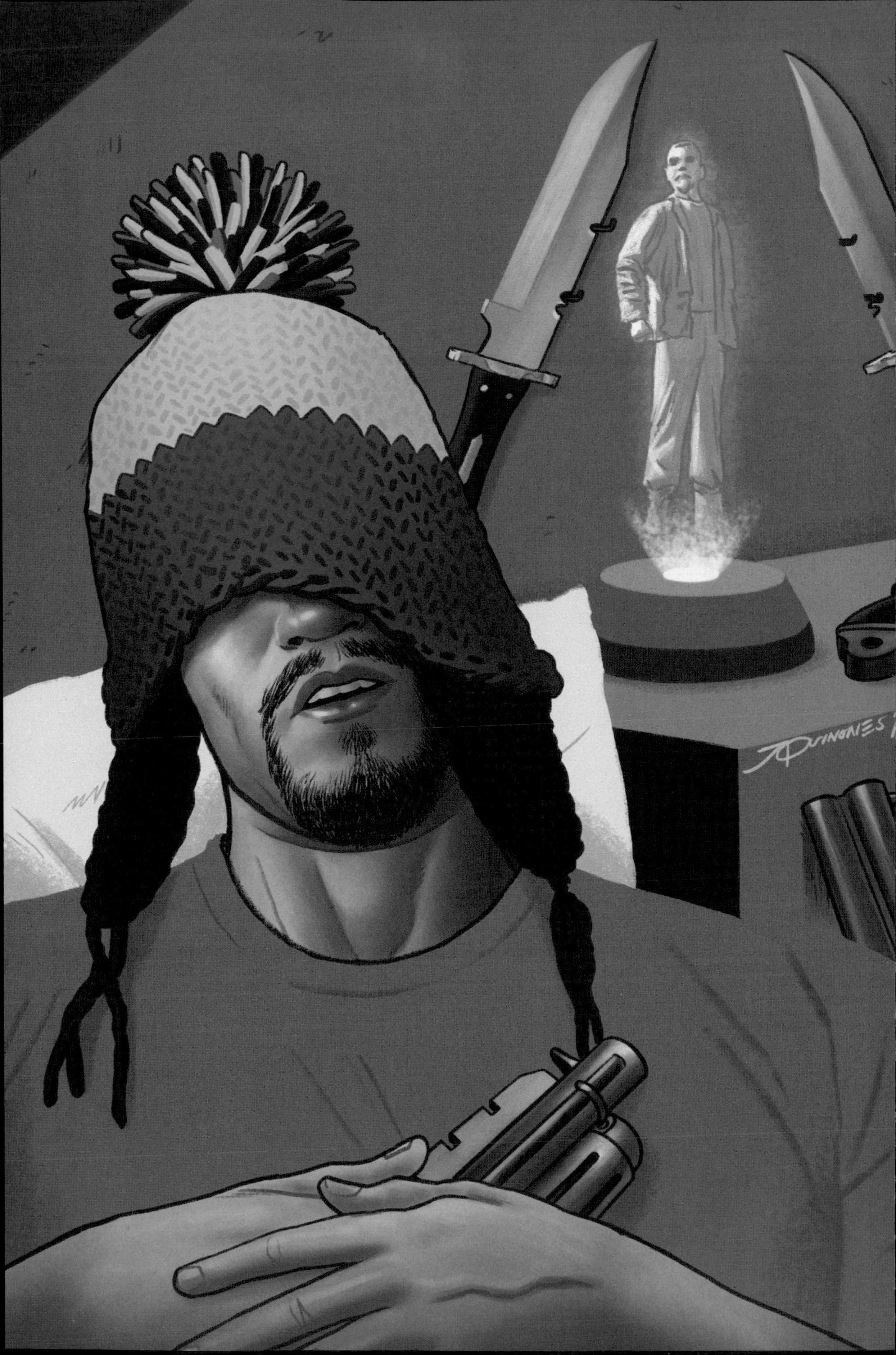
JQUINONES

Firefly #9 Preorder Cover by **Joe Quinones**

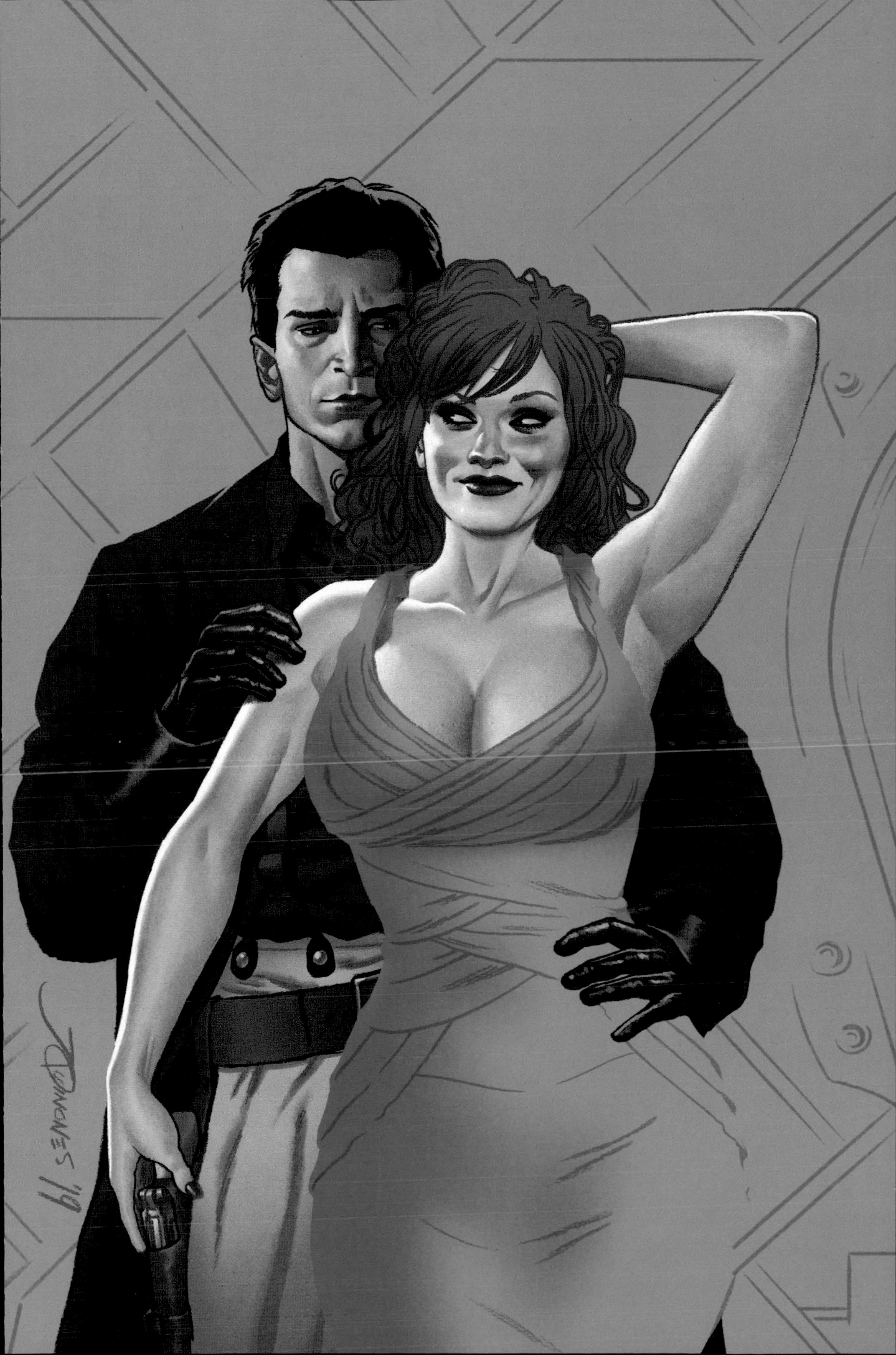

Firefly #10 Preorder Cover by **Joe Quinones**

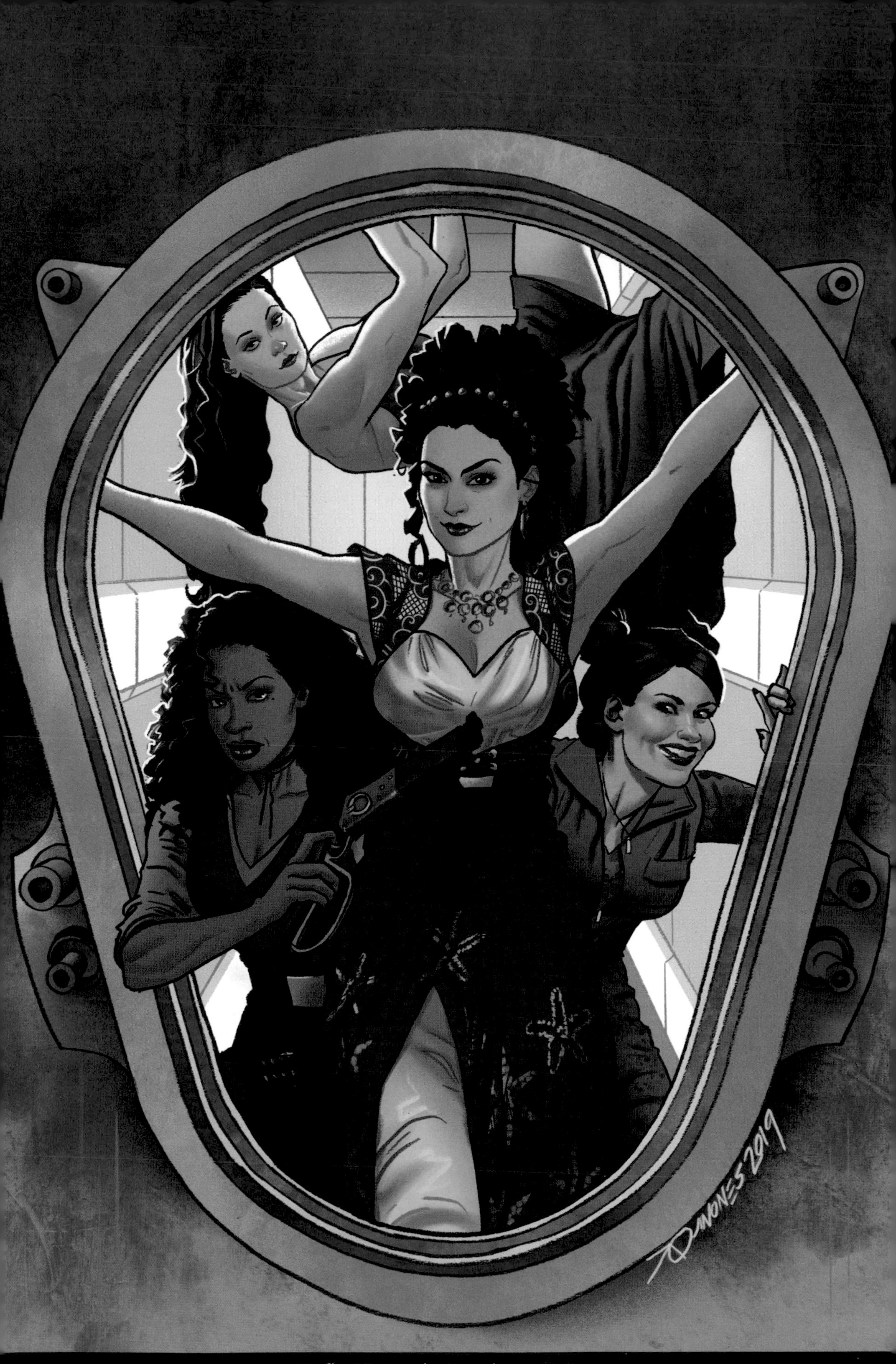
QUINONES 2019

Firefly #11 Preorder Cover by **Joe Quinones**

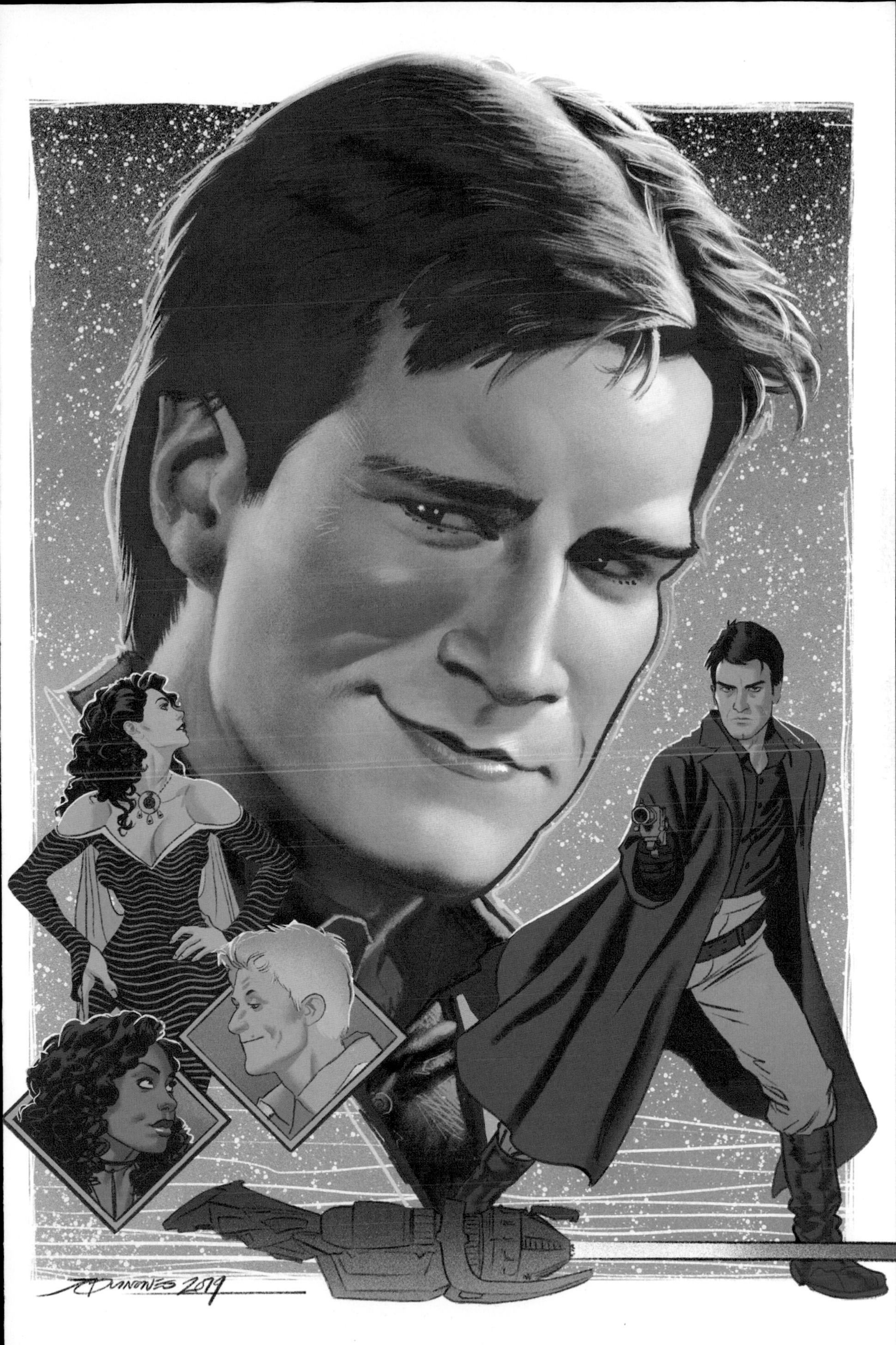
QUINONES 2019

Firefly #12 Preorder Cover by **Joe Quinones**

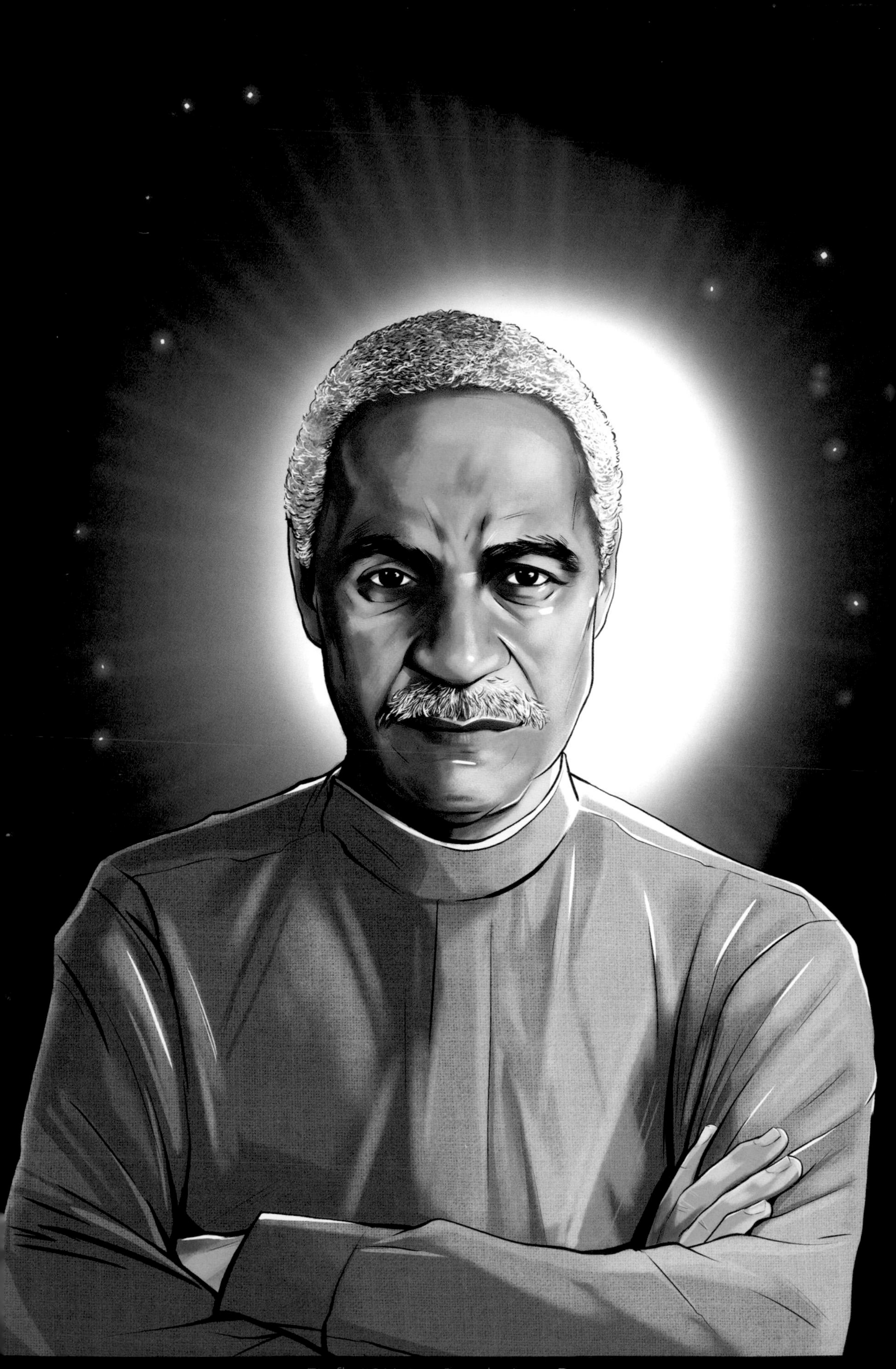

Firefly #9 Variant Cover by **Aaron Dana**

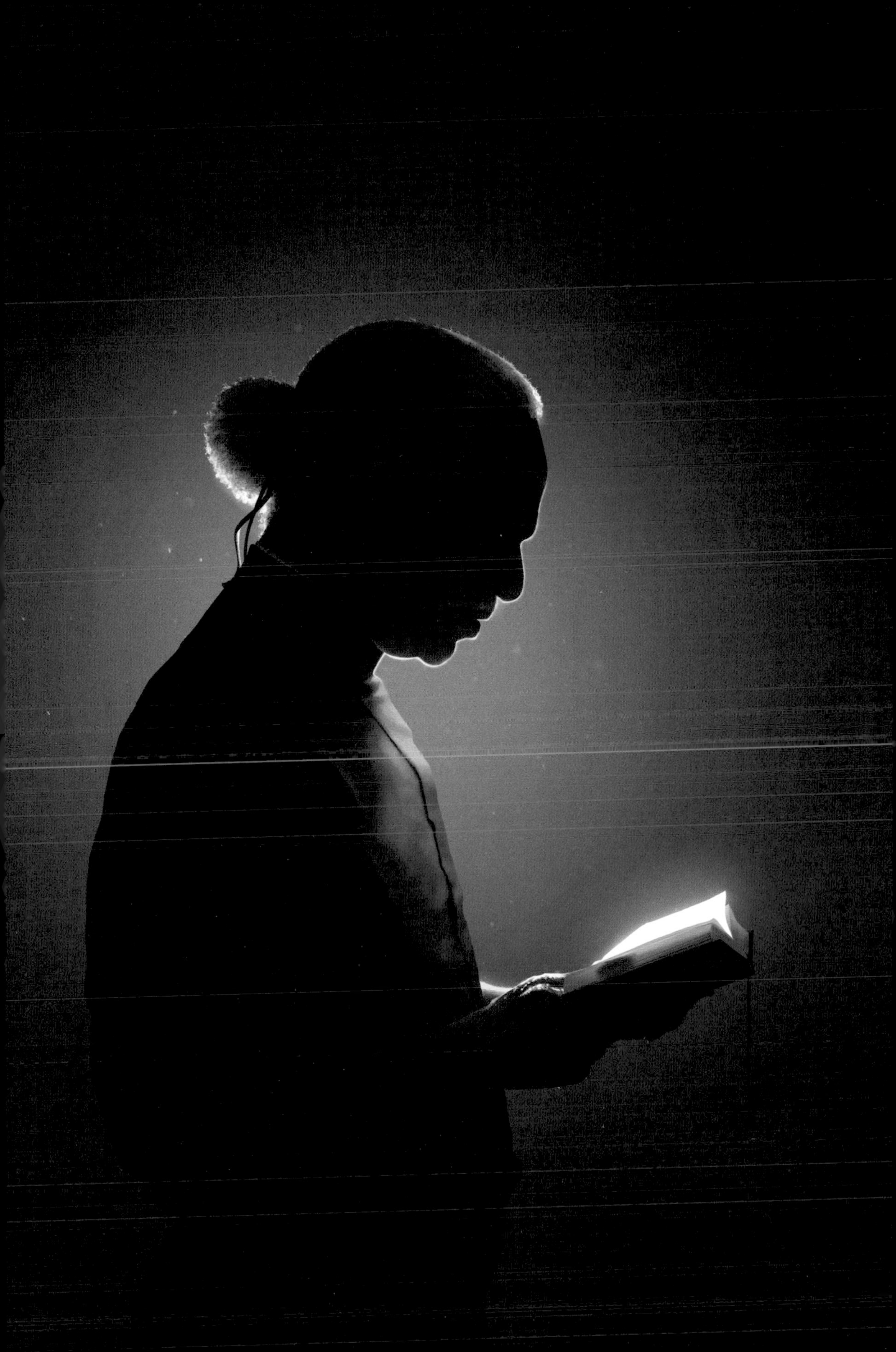

Firefly #10 Variant Cover by **Rahzzah**

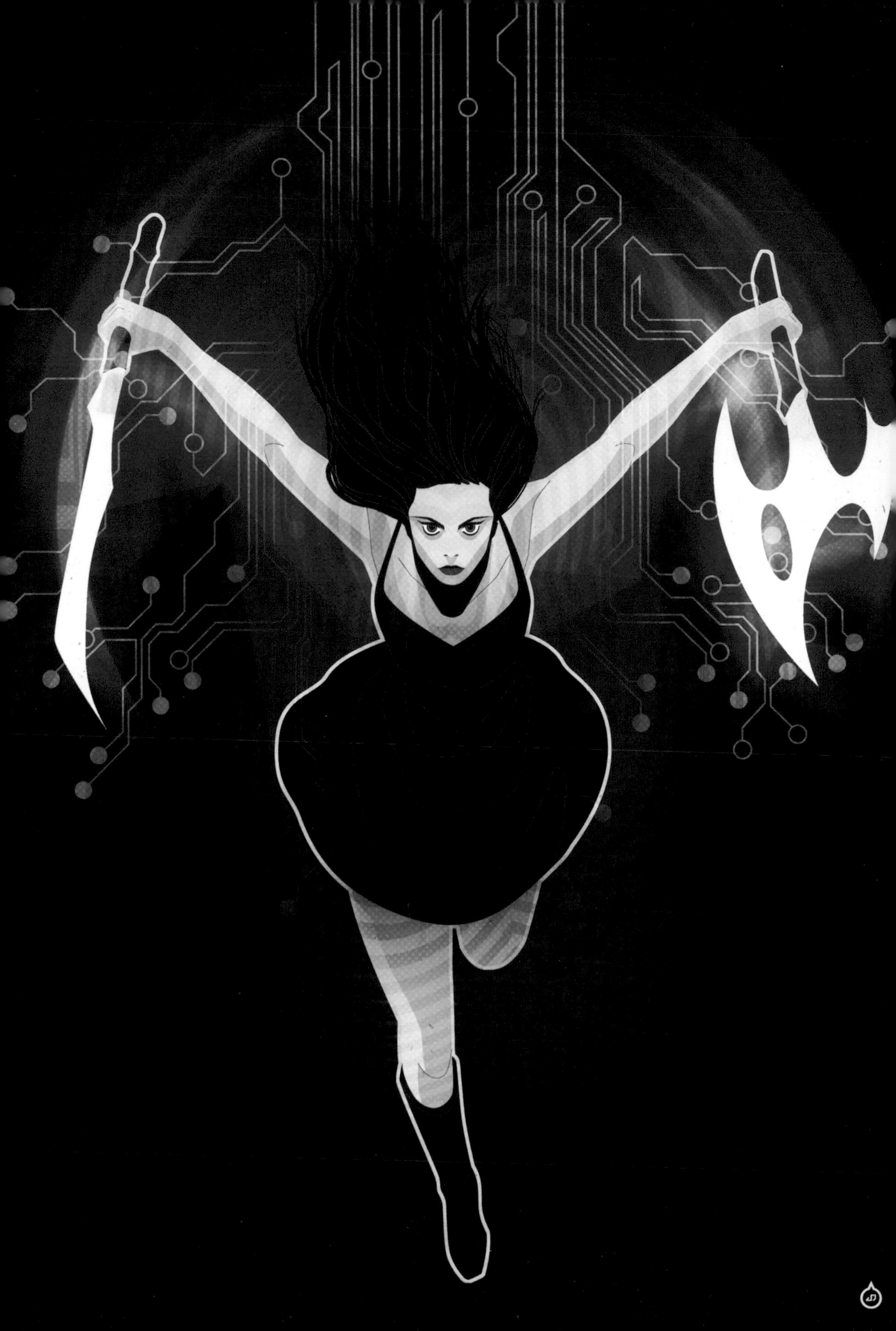

Firefly #11 Variant Cover by **Juan Doe**

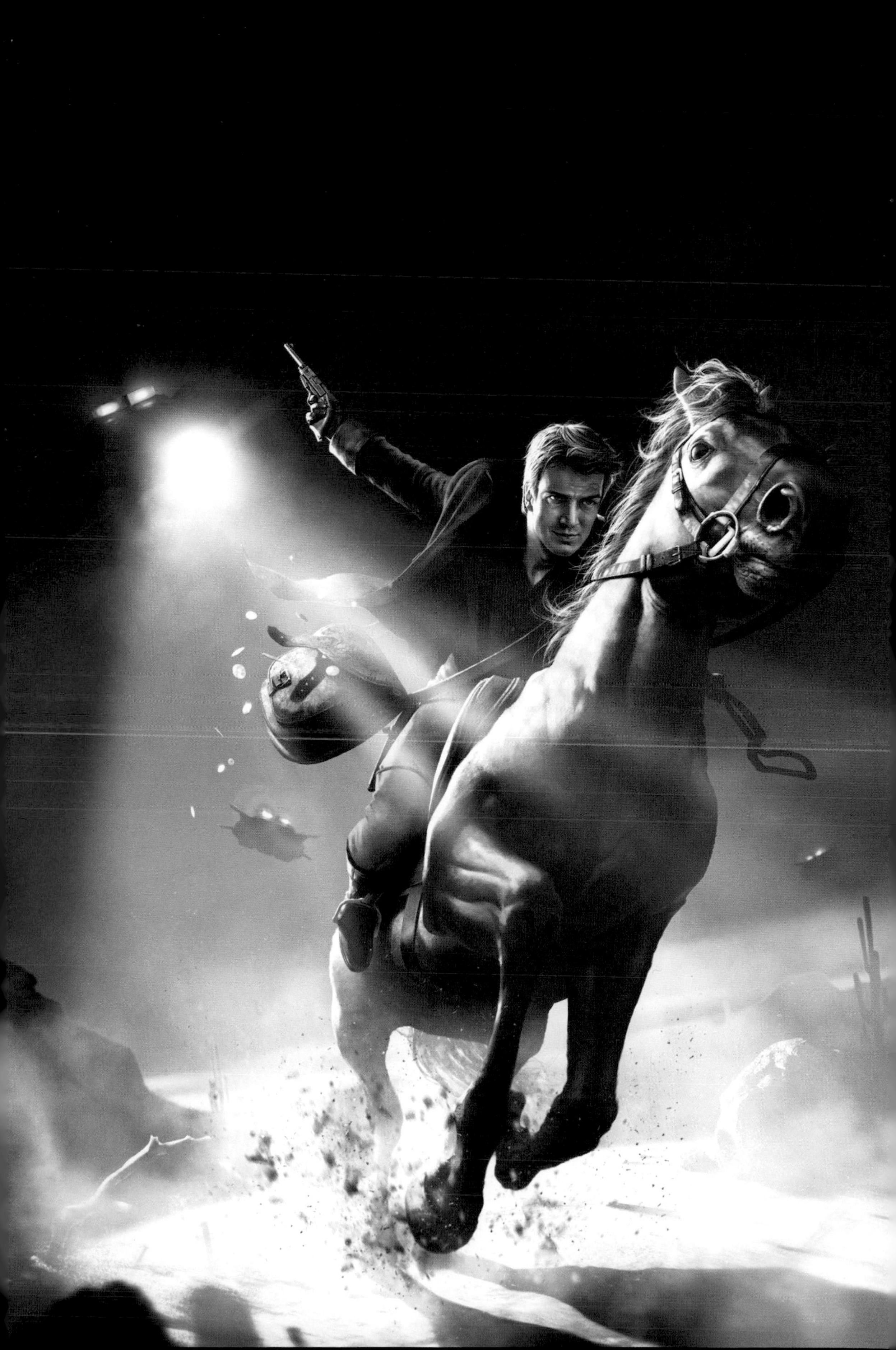

Firefly #12 Variant Cover by **Rahzzah**

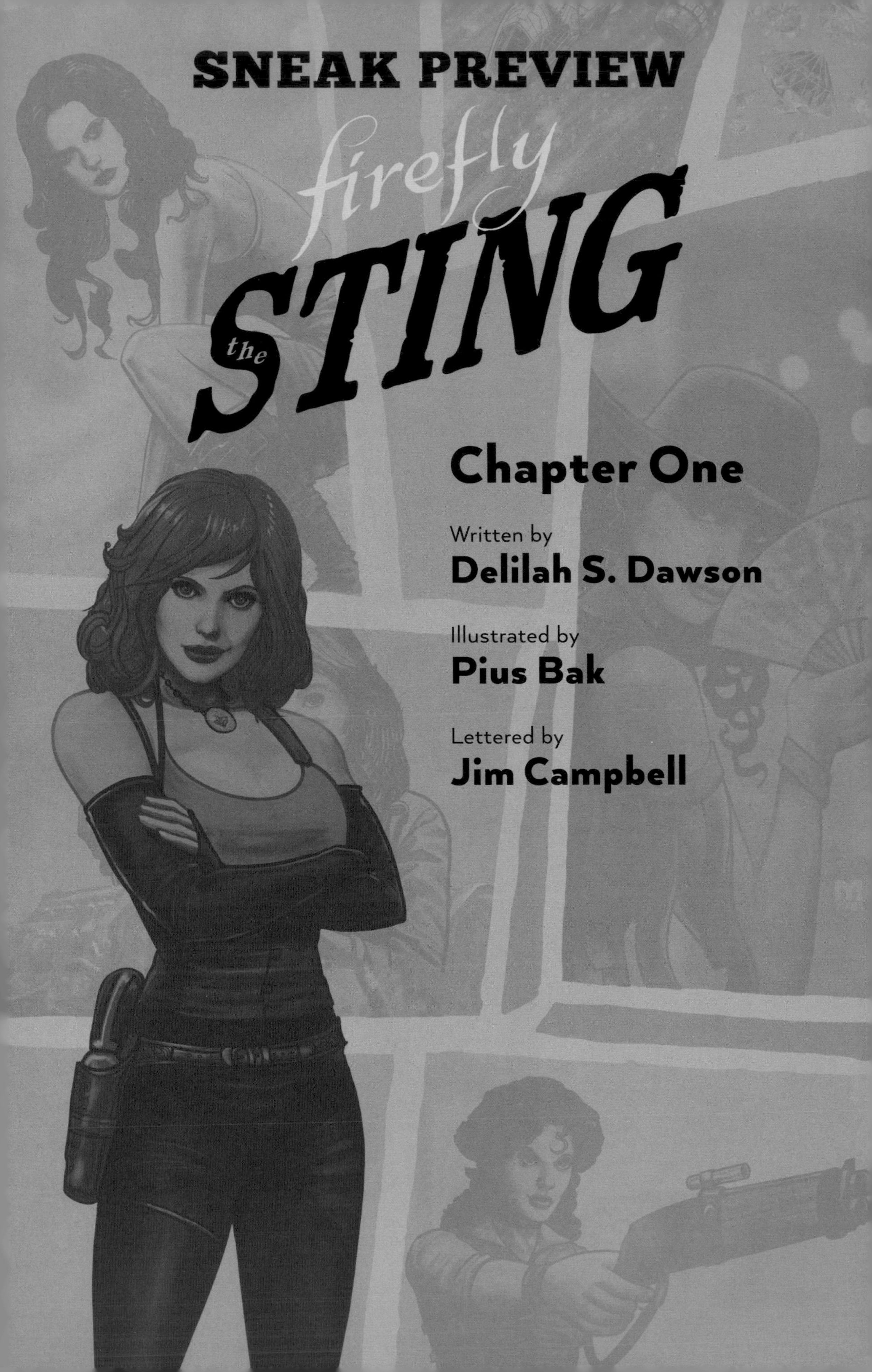

SNEAK PREVIEW

firefly
the STING

Chapter One

Written by
Delilah S. Dawson

Illustrated by
Pius Bak

Lettered by
Jim Campbell

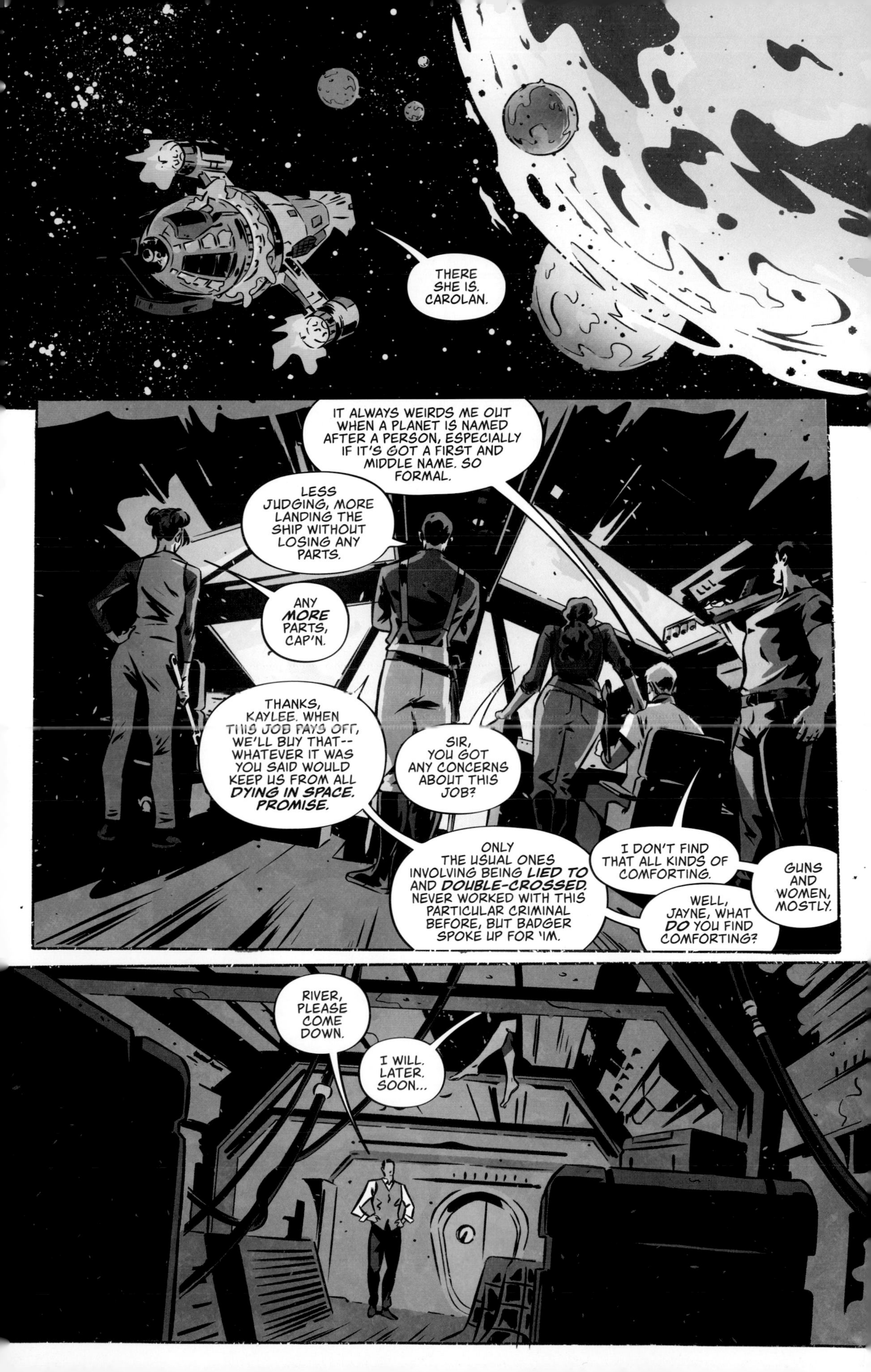
THERE SHE IS. CAROLAN.
IT ALWAYS WEIRDS ME OUT WHEN A PLANET IS NAMED AFTER A PERSON, ESPECIALLY IF IT'S GOT A FIRST AND MIDDLE NAME. SO FORMAL.
LESS JUDGING, MORE LANDING THE SHIP WITHOUT LOSING ANY PARTS.
ANY *MORE* PARTS, CAP'N.
THANKS, KAYLEE. WHEN THIS JOB PAYS OFF, WE'LL BUY THAT--WHATEVER IT WAS YOU SAID WOULD KEEP US FROM ALL *DYING IN SPACE. PROMISE.*
SIR, YOU GOT ANY CONCERNS ABOUT THIS JOB?
ONLY THE USUAL ONES INVOLVING BEING *LIED TO* AND *DOUBLE-CROSSED.* NEVER WORKED WITH THIS PARTICULAR CRIMINAL BEFORE, BUT BADGER SPOKE UP FOR 'IM.
I DON'T FIND THAT ALL KINDS OF COMFORTING.
WELL, JAYNE, WHAT *DO* YOU FIND COMFORTING?
GUNS AND WOMEN, MOSTLY.
RIVER, PLEASE COME DOWN.
I WILL. LATER. SOON...

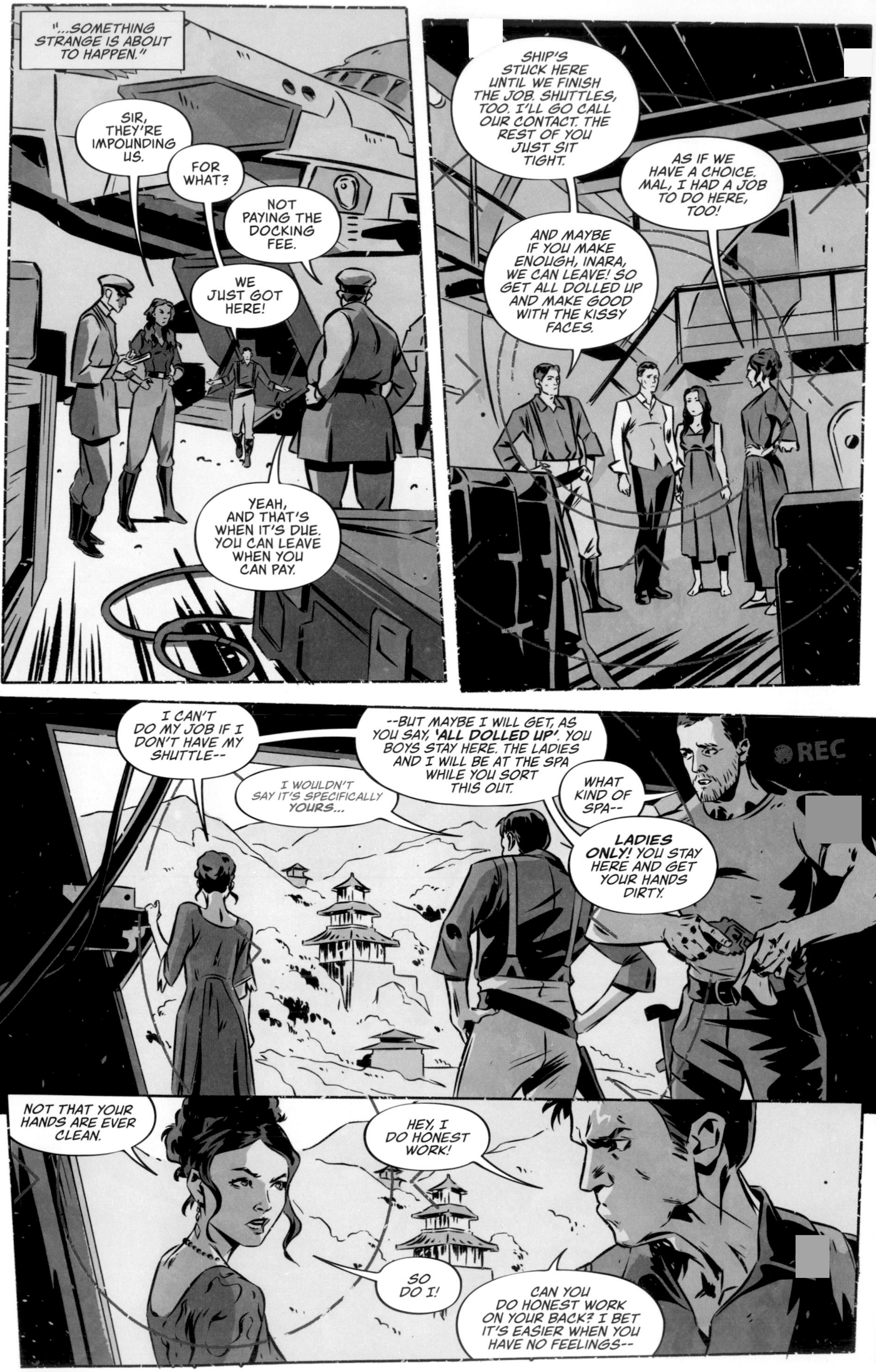
"...SOMETHING STRANGE IS ABOUT TO HAPPEN."
SIR, THEY'RE IMPOUNDING US.
FOR WHAT?
NOT PAYING THE DOCKING FEE.
WE JUST GOT HERE!
YEAH, AND THAT'S WHEN IT'S DUE. YOU CAN LEAVE WHEN YOU CAN PAY.
SHIP'S STUCK HERE UNTIL WE FINISH THE JOB. SHUTTLES, TOO. I'LL GO CALL OUR CONTACT. THE REST OF YOU JUST SIT TIGHT.
AS IF WE HAVE A CHOICE. MAL, I HAD A JOB TO DO HERE, TOO!
AND MAYBE IF YOU MAKE ENOUGH, INARA, WE CAN LEAVE! SO GET ALL DOLLED UP AND MAKE GOOD WITH THE KISSY FACES.
REC
I CAN'T DO MY JOB IF I DON'T HAVE MY SHUTTLE--
I WOULDN'T SAY IT'S SPECIFICALLY YOURS...
--BUT MAYBE I WILL GET, AS YOU SAY, 'ALL DOLLED UP'. YOU BOYS STAY HERE. THE LADIES AND I WILL BE AT THE SPA WHILE YOU SORT THIS OUT.
WHAT KIND OF SPA--
LADIES ONLY! YOU STAY HERE AND GET YOUR HANDS DIRTY.
NOT THAT YOUR HANDS ARE EVER CLEAN.
HEY, I DO HONEST WORK!
SO DO I!
CAN YOU DO HONEST WORK ON YOUR BACK? I BET IT'S EASIER WHEN YOU HAVE NO FEELINGS--

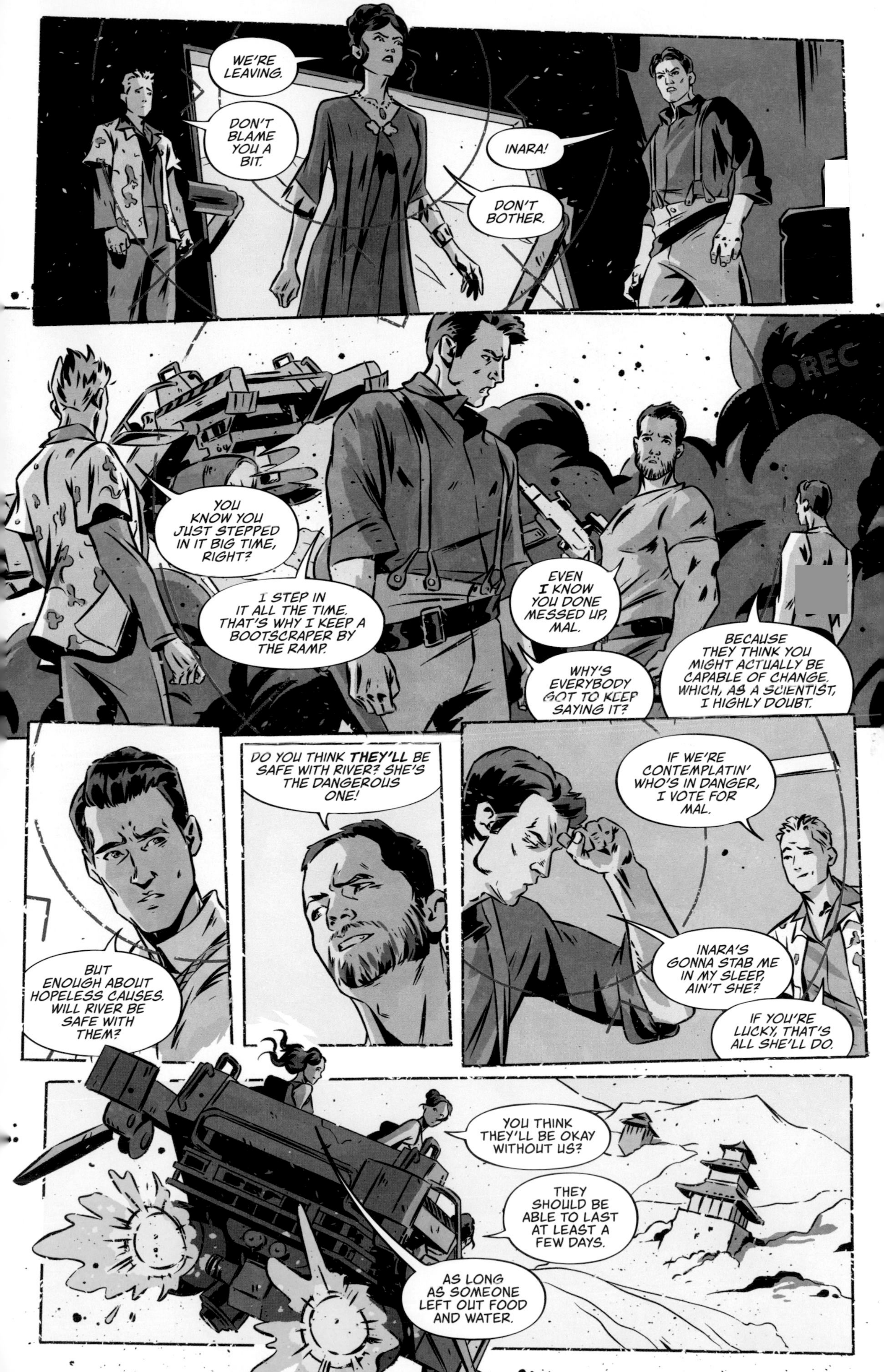
WE'RE LEAVING.
DON'T BLAME YOU A BIT.
INARA!
DON'T BOTHER.
REC
YOU KNOW YOU JUST STEPPED IN IT BIG TIME, RIGHT?
I STEP IN IT ALL THE TIME. THAT'S WHY I KEEP A BOOTSCRAPER BY THE RAMP.
EVEN I KNOW YOU DONE MESSED UP, MAL.
WHY'S EVERYBODY GOT TO KEEP SAYING IT?
BECAUSE THEY THINK YOU MIGHT ACTUALLY BE CAPABLE OF CHANGE. WHICH, AS A SCIENTIST, I HIGHLY DOUBT.
BUT ENOUGH ABOUT HOPELESS CAUSES. WILL RIVER BE SAFE WITH THEM?
DO YOU THINK THEY'LL BE SAFE WITH RIVER? SHE'S THE DANGEROUS ONE!
IF WE'RE CONTEMPLATIN' WHO'S IN DANGER, I VOTE FOR MAL.
INARA'S GONNA STAB ME IN MY SLEEP, AIN'T SHE?
IF YOU'RE LUCKY, THAT'S ALL SHE'LL DO.
YOU THINK THEY'LL BE OKAY WITHOUT US?
THEY SHOULD BE ABLE TO LAST AT LEAST A FEW DAYS.
AS LONG AS SOMEONE LEFT OUT FOOD AND WATER.

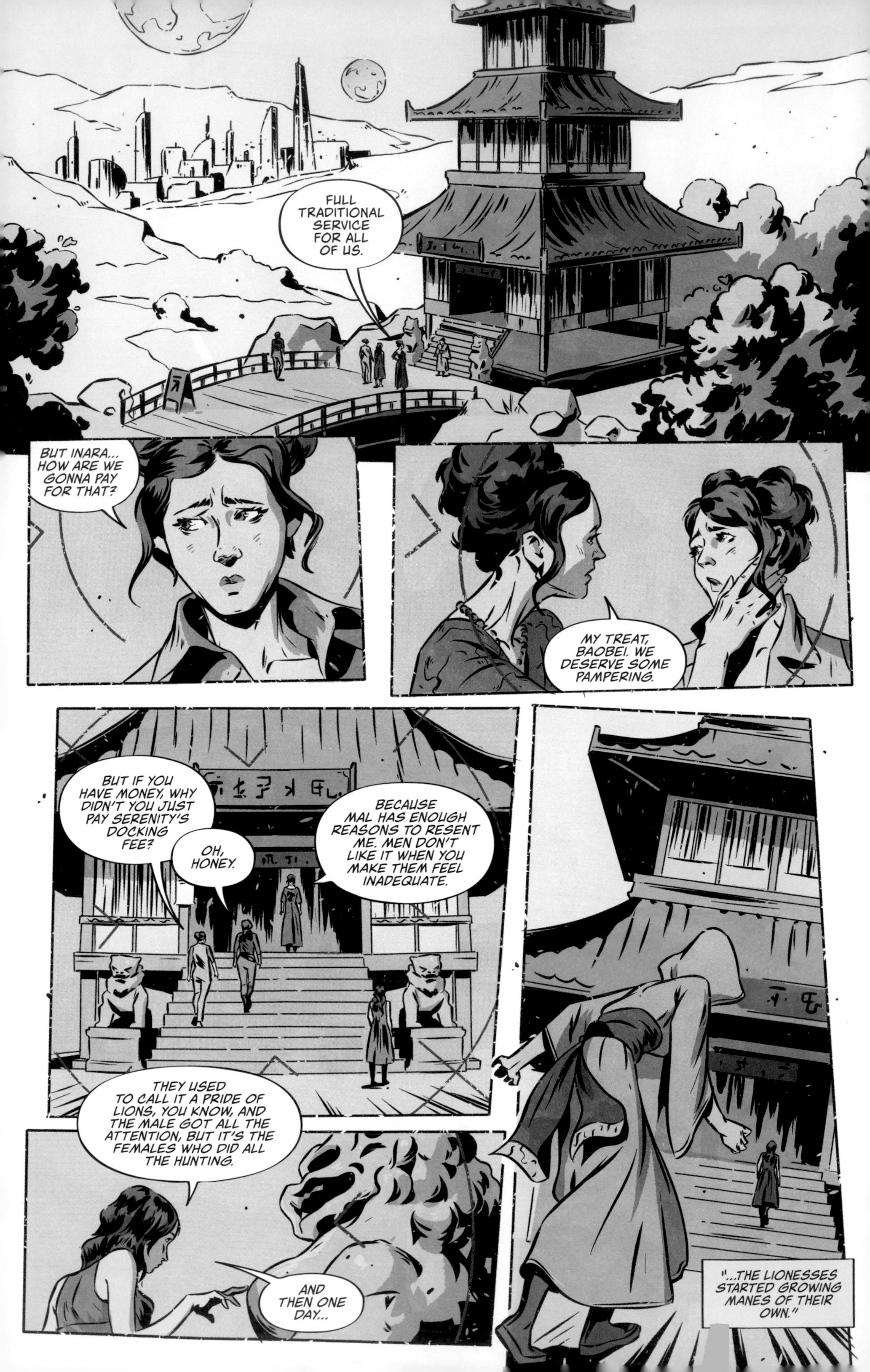
FULL TRADITIONAL SERVICE FOR ALL OF US.
BUT INARA... HOW ARE WE GONNA PAY FOR THAT?
MY TREAT, BAOBEI. WE DESERVE SOME PAMPERING.
BUT IF YOU HAVE MONEY, WHY DIDN'T YOU JUST PAY SERENITY'S DOCKING FEE?
OH, HONEY.
BECAUSE MAL HAS ENOUGH REASONS TO RESENT ME. MEN DON'T LIKE IT WHEN YOU MAKE THEM FEEL INADEQUATE.
THEY USED TO CALL IT A PRIDE OF LIONS, YOU KNOW, AND THE MALE GOT ALL THE ATTENTION, BUT IT'S THE FEMALES WHO DID ALL THE HUNTING.
AND THEN ONE DAY...
"...THE LIONESSES STARTED GROWING MANES OF THEIR OWN."

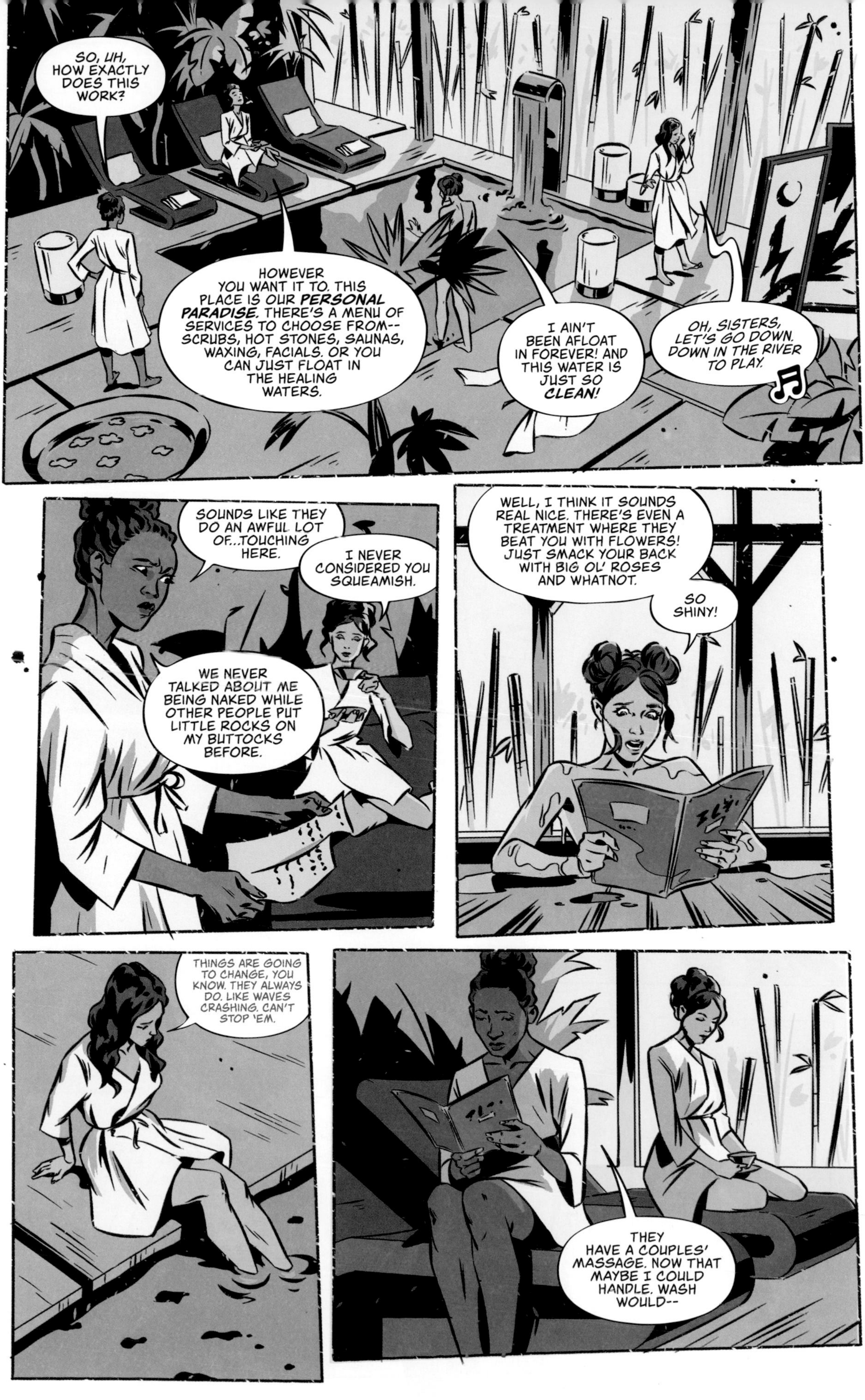
SO, UH, HOW EXACTLY DOES THIS WORK?
HOWEVER YOU WANT IT TO. THIS PLACE IS OUR PERSONAL PARADISE. THERE'S A MENU OF SERVICES TO CHOOSE FROM-- SCRUBS, HOT STONES, SAUNAS, WAXING, FACIALS. OR YOU CAN JUST FLOAT IN THE HEALING WATERS.
I AIN'T BEEN AFLOAT IN FOREVER! AND THIS WATER IS JUST SO CLEAN!
OH, SISTERS, LET'S GO DOWN. DOWN IN THE RIVER TO PLAY.
SOUNDS LIKE THEY DO AN AWFUL LOT OF...TOUCHING HERE.
I NEVER CONSIDERED YOU SQUEAMISH.
WE NEVER TALKED ABOUT ME BEING NAKED WHILE OTHER PEOPLE PUT LITTLE ROCKS ON MY BUTTOCKS BEFORE.
WELL, I THINK IT SOUNDS REAL NICE. THERE'S EVEN A TREATMENT WHERE THEY BEAT YOU WITH FLOWERS! JUST SMACK YOUR BACK WITH BIG OL' ROSES AND WHATNOT.
SO SHINY!
THINGS ARE GOING TO CHANGE, YOU KNOW. THEY ALWAYS DO. LIKE WAVES CRASHING. CAN'T STOP 'EM.
THEY HAVE A COUPLES' MASSAGE. NOW THAT MAYBE I COULD HANDLE. WASH WOULD--

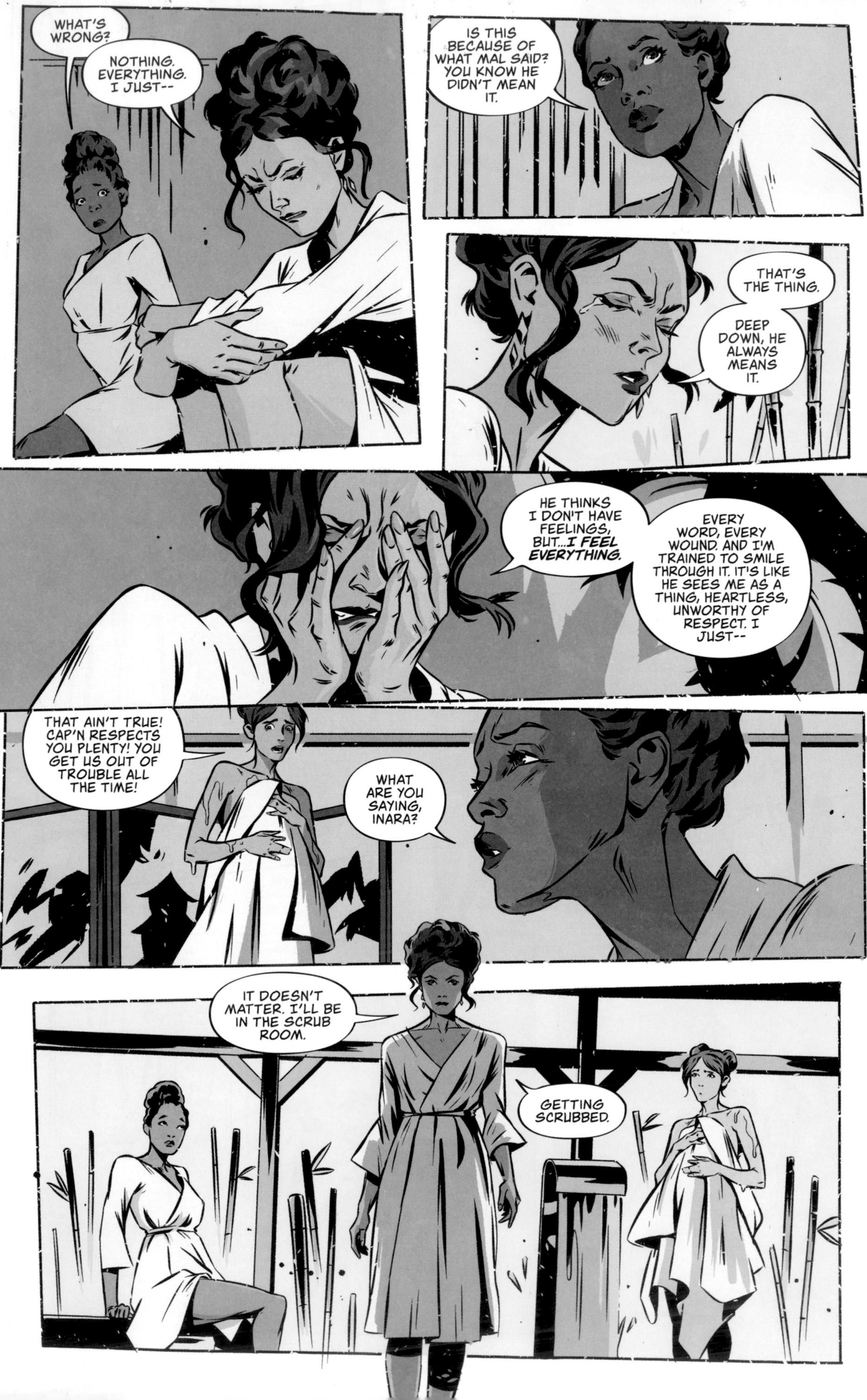
WHAT'S WRONG?
NOTHING. EVERYTHING. I JUST--
IS THIS BECAUSE OF WHAT MAL SAID? YOU KNOW HE DIDN'T MEAN IT.
THAT'S THE THING.
DEEP DOWN, HE ALWAYS MEANS IT.
HE THINKS I DON'T HAVE FEELINGS, BUT...I FEEL EVERYTHING.
EVERY WORD, EVERY WOUND. AND I'M TRAINED TO SMILE THROUGH IT. IT'S LIKE HE SEES ME AS A THING, HEARTLESS, UNWORTHY OF RESPECT. I JUST--
THAT AIN'T TRUE! CAP'N RESPECTS YOU PLENTY! YOU GET US OUT OF TROUBLE ALL THE TIME!
WHAT ARE YOU SAYING, INARA?
IT DOESN'T MATTER. I'LL BE IN THE SCRUB ROOM.
GETTING SCRUBBED.

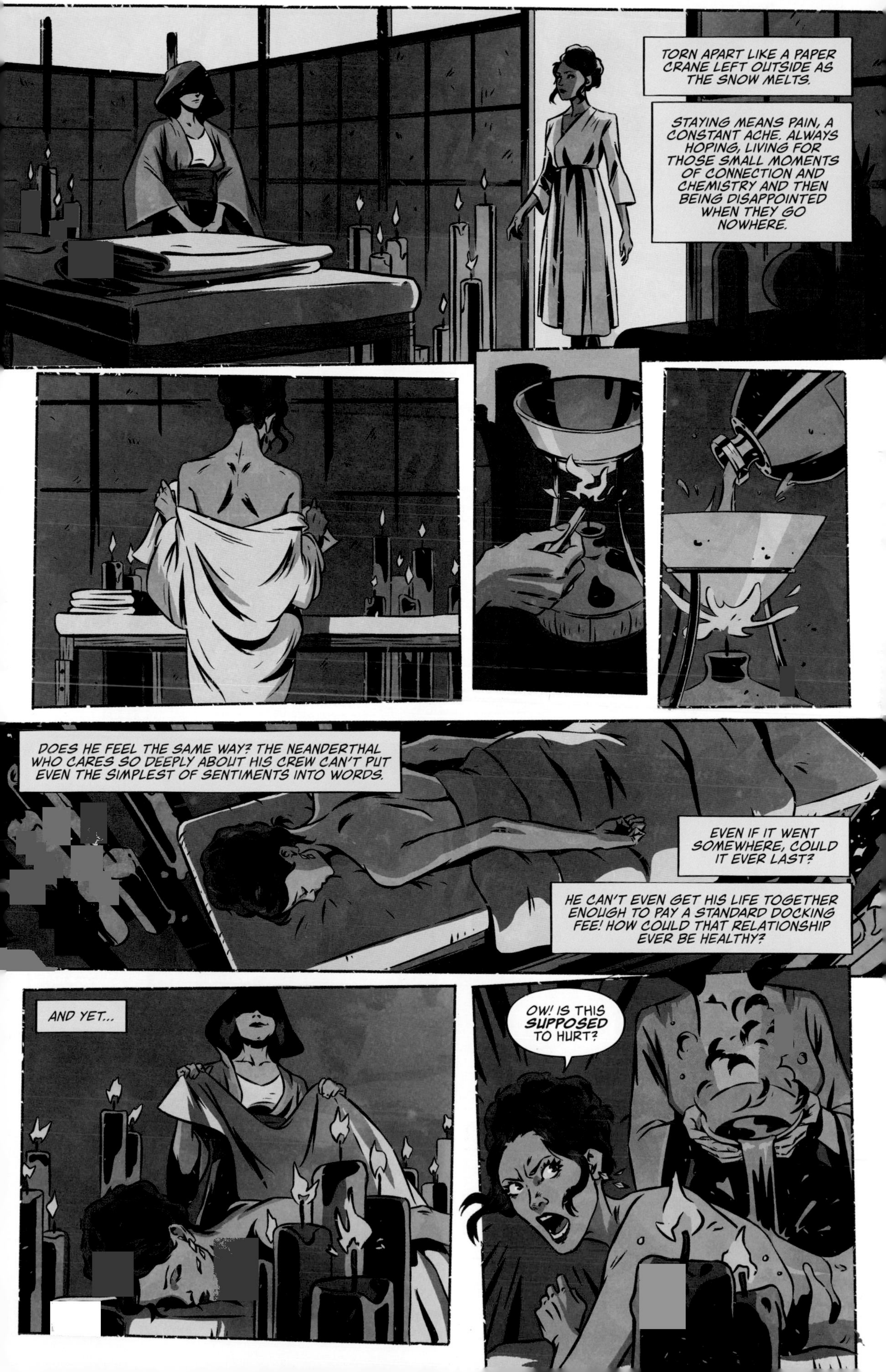
TORN APART LIKE A PAPER CRANE LEFT OUTSIDE AS THE SNOW MELTS.
STAYING MEANS PAIN, A CONSTANT ACHE. ALWAYS HOPING, LIVING FOR THOSE SMALL MOMENTS OF CONNECTION AND CHEMISTRY AND THEN BEING DISAPPOINTED WHEN THEY GO NOWHERE.
DOES HE FEEL THE SAME WAY? THE NEANDERTHAL WHO CARES SO DEEPLY ABOUT HIS CREW CAN'T PUT EVEN THE SIMPLEST OF SENTIMENTS INTO WORDS.
EVEN IF IT WENT SOMEWHERE, COULD IT EVER LAST?
HE CAN'T EVEN GET HIS LIFE TOGETHER ENOUGH TO PAY A STANDARD DOCKING FEE! HOW COULD THAT RELATIONSHIP EVER BE HEALTHY?
AND YET...
OW! IS THIS SUPPOSED TO HURT?

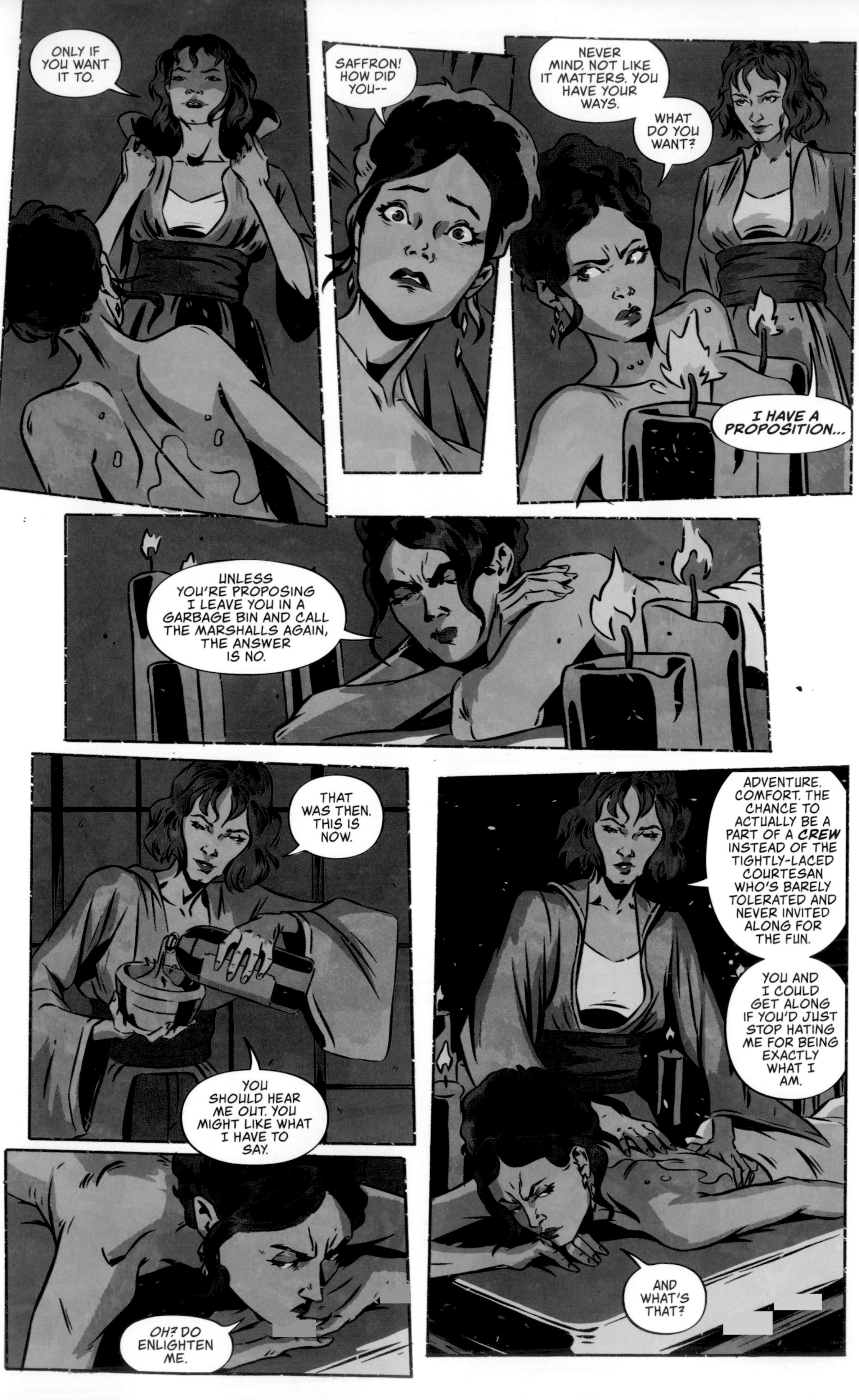
ONLY IF YOU WANT IT TO.
SAFFRON! HOW DID YOU--
NEVER MIND. NOT LIKE IT MATTERS. YOU HAVE YOUR WAYS.
WHAT DO YOU WANT?
I HAVE A PROPOSITION...
UNLESS YOU'RE PROPOSING I LEAVE YOU IN A GARBAGE BIN AND CALL THE MARSHALLS AGAIN, THE ANSWER IS NO.
THAT WAS THEN. THIS IS NOW.
YOU SHOULD HEAR ME OUT. YOU MIGHT LIKE WHAT I HAVE TO SAY.
OH? DO ENLIGHTEN ME.
ADVENTURE. COMFORT. THE CHANCE TO ACTUALLY BE A PART OF A CREW INSTEAD OF THE TIGHTLY-LACED COURTESAN WHO'S BARELY TOLERATED AND NEVER INVITED ALONG FOR THE FUN.
YOU AND I COULD GET ALONG IF YOU'D JUST STOP HATING ME FOR BEING EXACTLY WHAT I AM.
AND WHAT'S THAT?

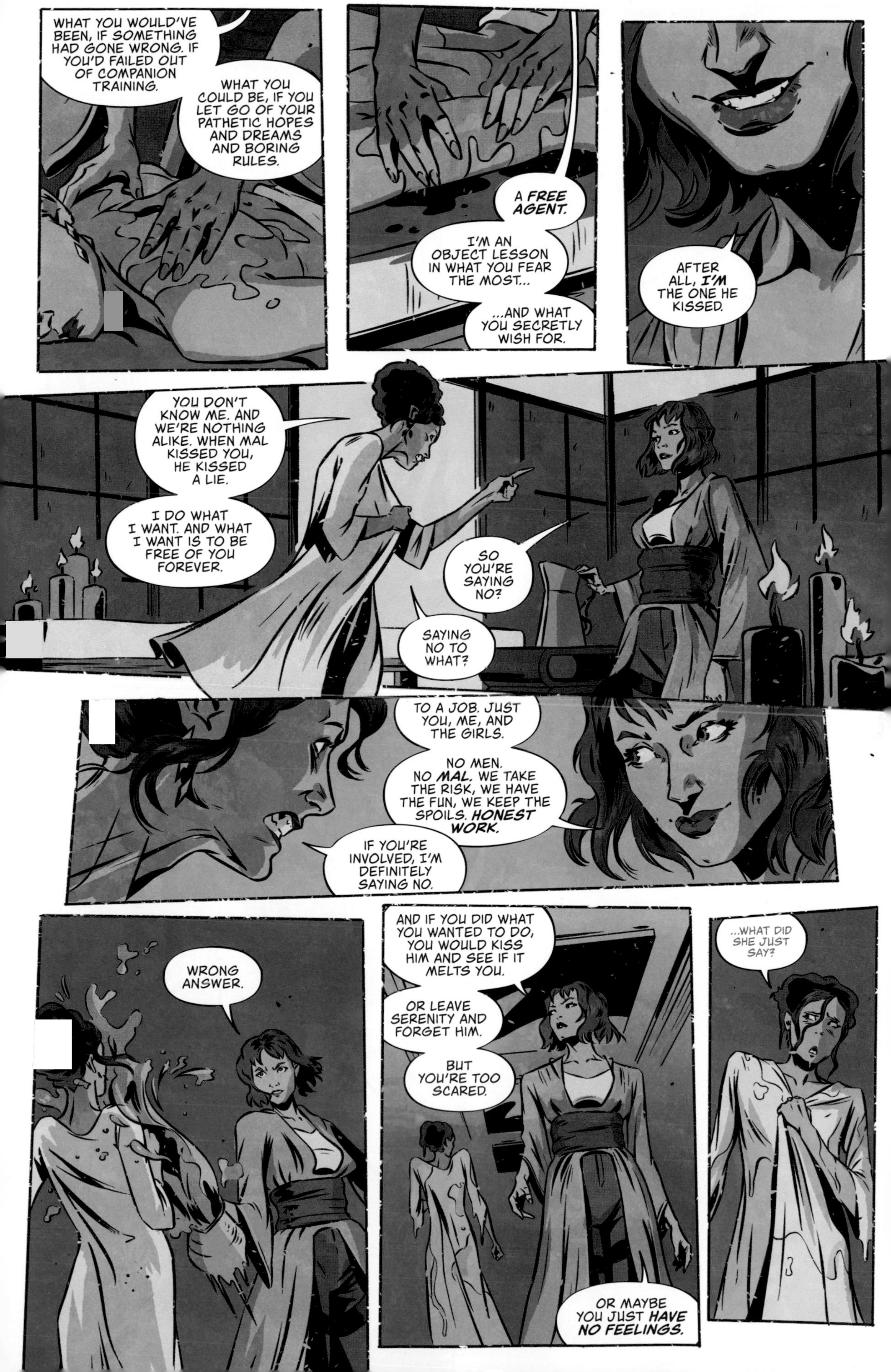

WHAT YOU WOULD'VE BEEN, IF SOMETHING HAD GONE WRONG. IF YOU'D FAILED OUT OF COMPANION TRAINING.
WHAT YOU COULD BE, IF YOU LET GO OF YOUR PATHETIC HOPES AND DREAMS AND BORING RULES.
A FREE AGENT.
I'M AN OBJECT LESSON IN WHAT YOU FEAR THE MOST...
...AND WHAT YOU SECRETLY WISH FOR.
AFTER ALL, I'M THE ONE HE KISSED.
YOU DON'T KNOW ME. AND WE'RE NOTHING ALIKE. WHEN MAL KISSED YOU, HE KISSED A LIE.
I DO WHAT I WANT. AND WHAT I WANT IS TO BE FREE OF YOU FOREVER.
SO YOU'RE SAYING NO?
SAYING NO TO WHAT?
TO A JOB. JUST YOU, ME, AND THE GIRLS.
NO MEN. NO MAL. WE TAKE THE RISK, WE HAVE THE FUN, WE KEEP THE SPOILS. HONEST WORK.
IF YOU'RE INVOLVED, I'M DEFINITELY SAYING NO.
WRONG ANSWER.
AND IF YOU DID WHAT YOU WANTED TO DO, YOU WOULD KISS HIM AND SEE IF IT MELTS YOU.
OR LEAVE SERENITY AND FORGET HIM.
BUT YOU'RE TOO SCARED.
OR MAYBE YOU JUST HAVE NO FEELINGS.
...WHAT DID SHE JUST SAY?

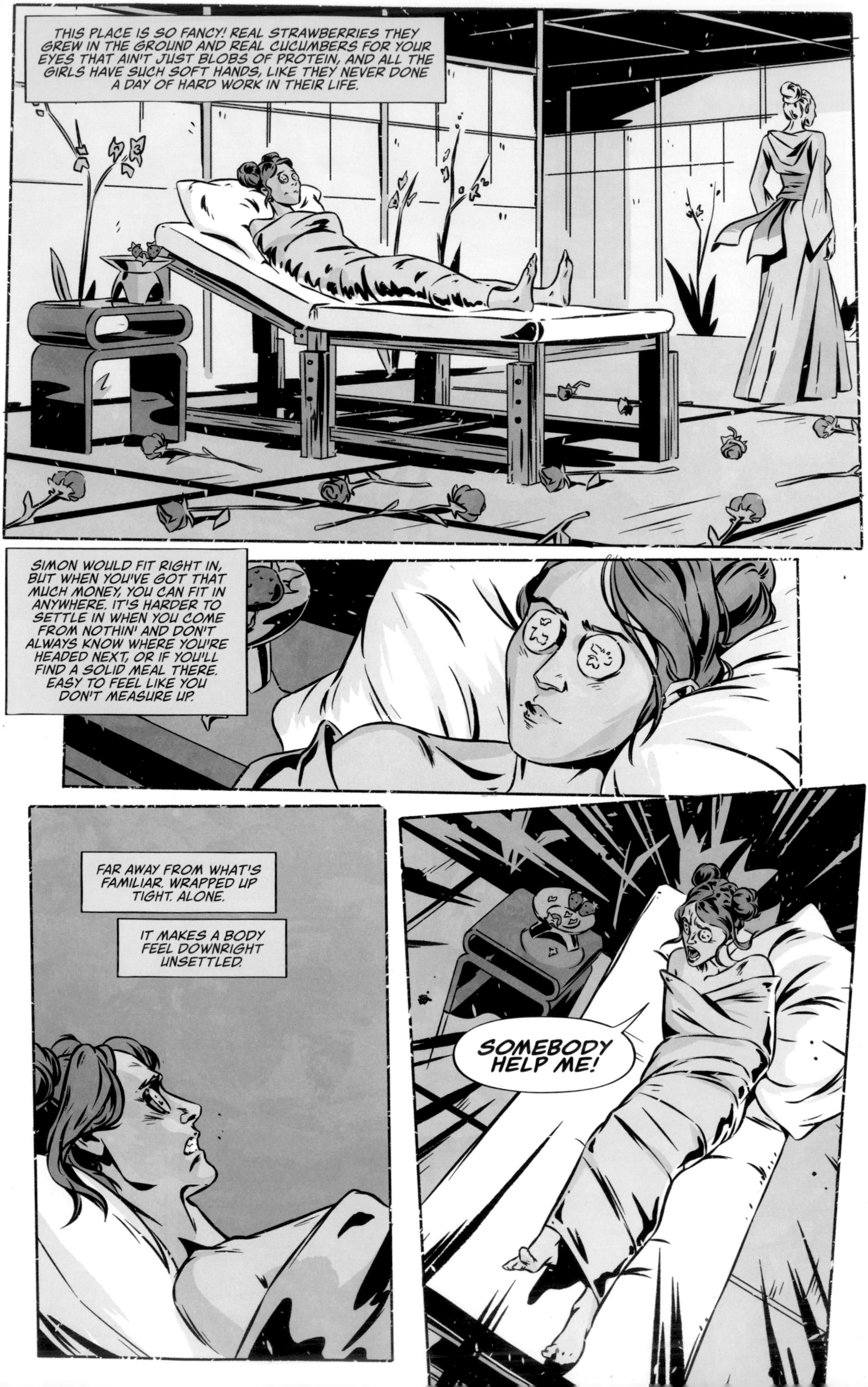
THIS PLACE IS SO FANCY! REAL STRAWBERRIES THEY GREW IN THE GROUND AND REAL CUCUMBERS FOR YOUR EYES THAT AIN'T JUST BLOBS OF PROTEIN, AND ALL THE GIRLS HAVE SUCH SOFT HANDS, LIKE THEY NEVER DONE A DAY OF HARD WORK IN THEIR LIFE.
SIMON WOULD FIT RIGHT IN, BUT WHEN YOU'VE GOT THAT MUCH MONEY, YOU CAN FIT IN ANYWHERE. IT'S HARDER TO SETTLE IN WHEN YOU COME FROM NOTHIN' AND DON'T ALWAYS KNOW WHERE YOU'RE HEADED NEXT, OR IF YOU'LL FIND A SOLID MEAL THERE. EASY TO FEEL LIKE YOU DON'T MEASURE UP.
FAR AWAY FROM WHAT'S FAMILIAR. WRAPPED UP TIGHT. ALONE.
IT MAKES A BODY FEEL DOWNRIGHT UNSETTLED.
SOMEBODY HELP ME!

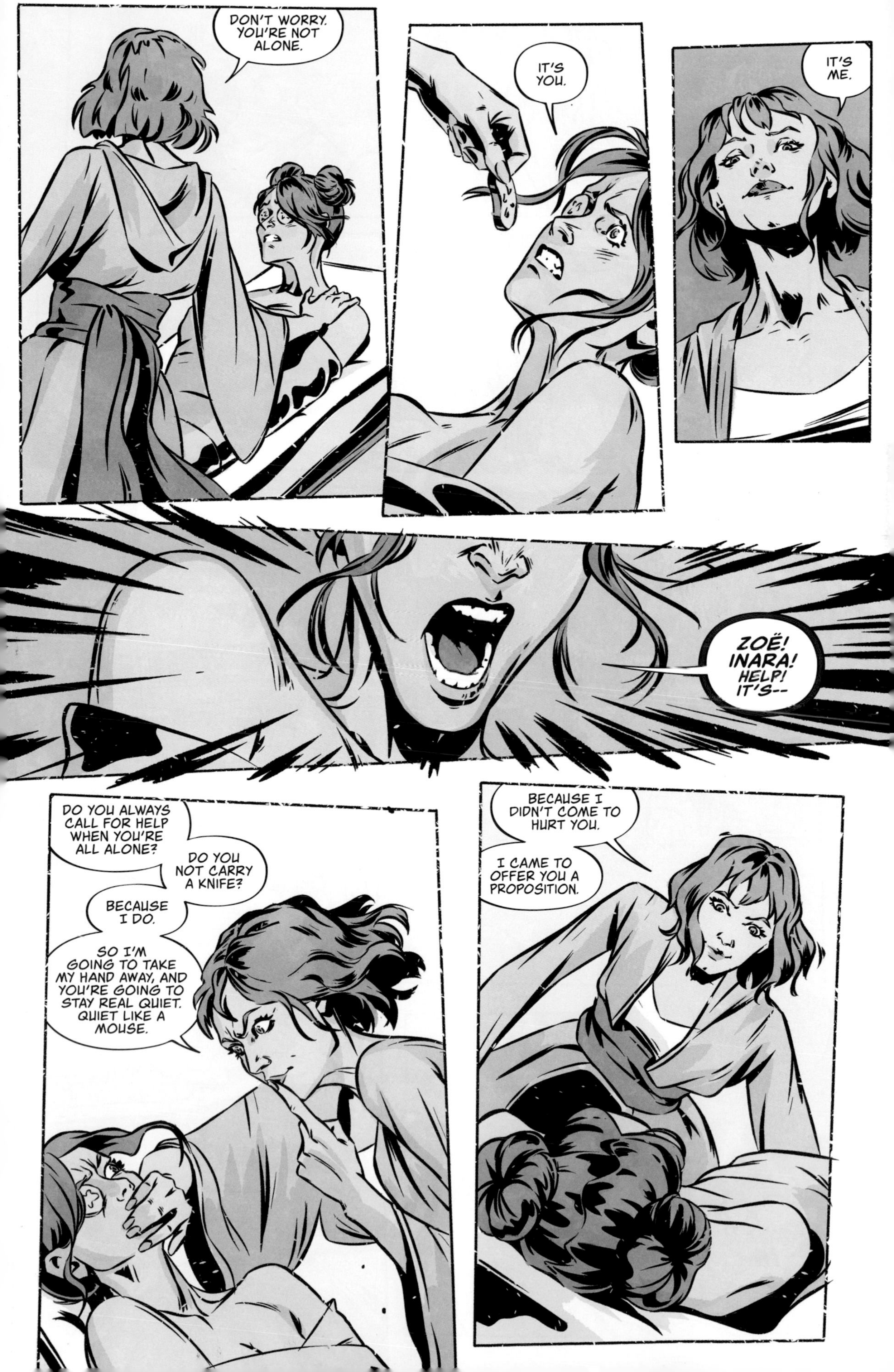
DON'T WORRY. YOU'RE NOT ALONE.
IT'S YOU.
IT'S ME.
ZOË! INARA! HELP! IT'S--
DO YOU ALWAYS CALL FOR HELP WHEN YOU'RE ALL ALONE?
DO YOU NOT CARRY A KNIFE?
BECAUSE I DO.
SO I'M GOING TO TAKE MY HAND AWAY, AND YOU'RE GOING TO STAY REAL QUIET. QUIET LIKE A MOUSE.
BECAUSE I DIDN'T COME TO HURT YOU.
I CAME TO OFFER YOU A PROPOSITION.

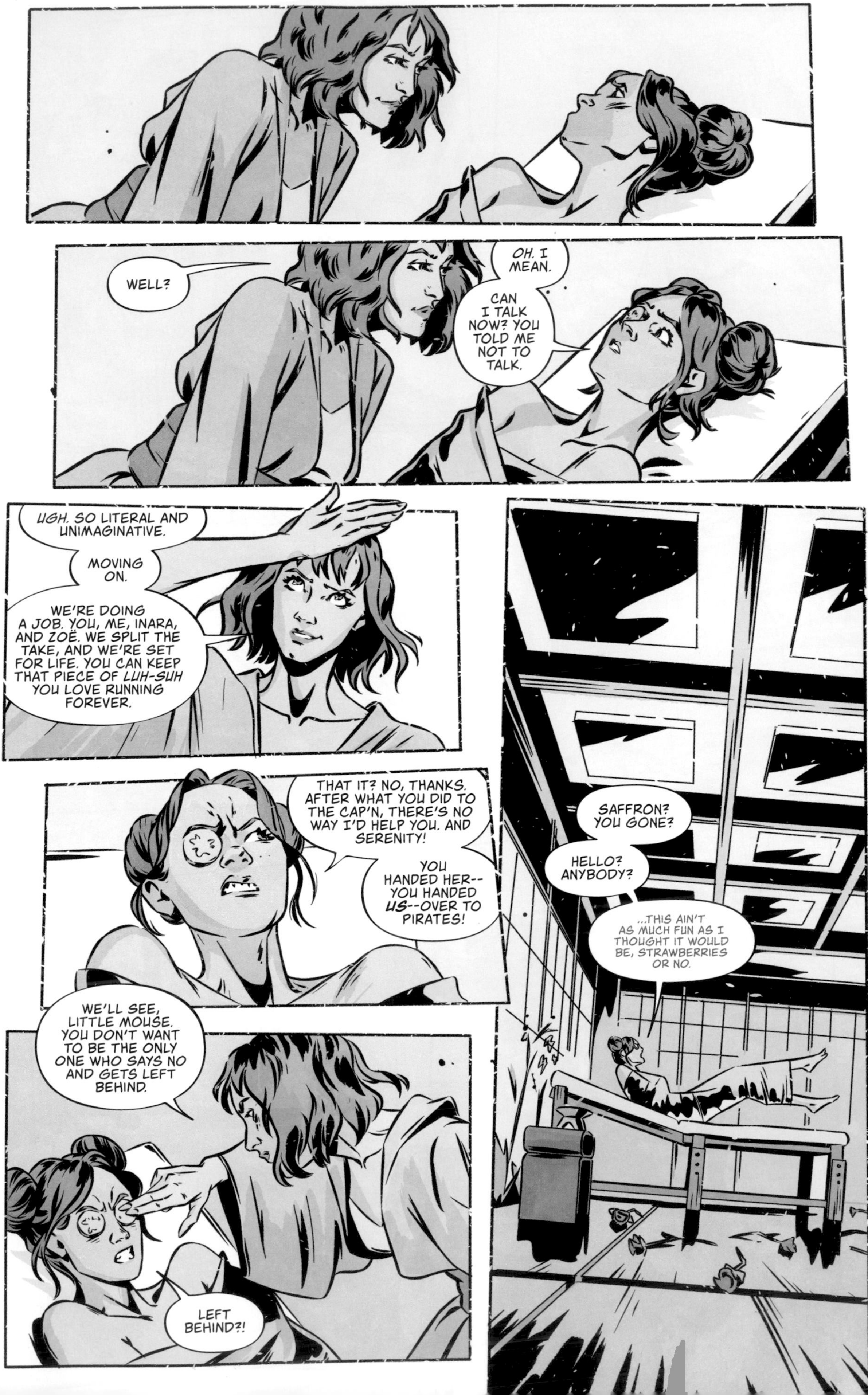
WELL?
OH. I MEAN.
CAN I TALK NOW? YOU TOLD ME NOT TO TALK.
UGH. SO LITERAL AND UNIMAGINATIVE.
MOVING ON.
WE'RE DOING A JOB. YOU, ME, INARA, AND ZOË. WE SPLIT THE TAKE, AND WE'RE SET FOR LIFE. YOU CAN KEEP THAT PIECE OF LUH-SUH YOU LOVE RUNNING FOREVER.
THAT IT? NO, THANKS. AFTER WHAT YOU DID TO THE CAP'N, THERE'S NO WAY I'D HELP YOU. AND SERENITY!
YOU HANDED HER--YOU HANDED US--OVER TO PIRATES!
WE'LL SEE, LITTLE MOUSE. YOU DON'T WANT TO BE THE ONLY ONE WHO SAYS NO AND GETS LEFT BEHIND.
LEFT BEHIND?!
SAFFRON? YOU GONE?
HELLO? ANYBODY?
...THIS AIN'T AS MUCH FUN AS I THOUGHT IT WOULD BE, STRAWBERRIES OR NO.

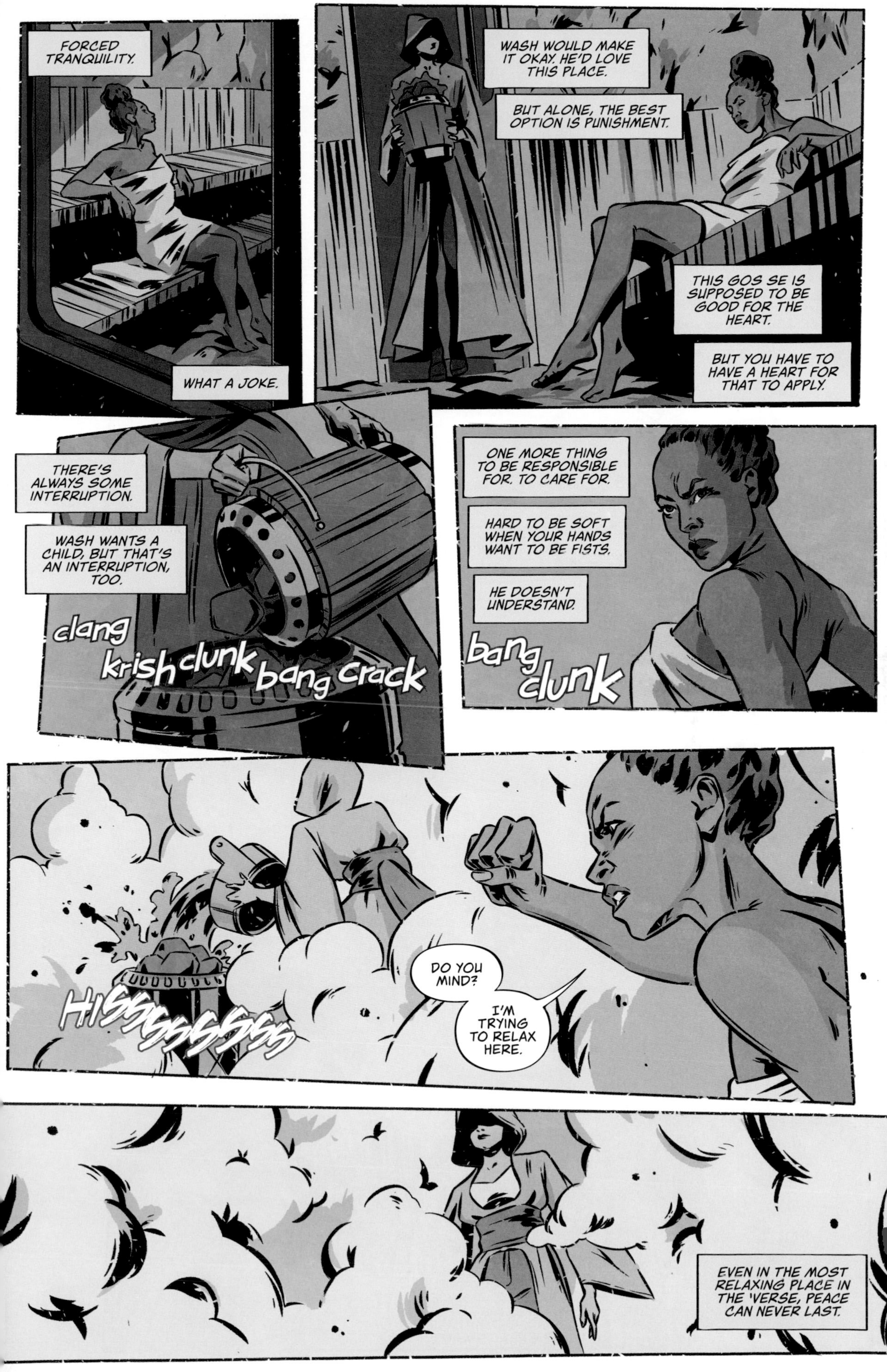
FORCED TRANQUILITY.
WHAT A JOKE.
WASH WOULD MAKE IT OKAY. HE'D LOVE THIS PLACE.
BUT ALONE, THE BEST OPTION IS PUNISHMENT.
THIS GOS SE IS SUPPOSED TO BE GOOD FOR THE HEART.
BUT YOU HAVE TO HAVE A HEART FOR THAT TO APPLY.
THERE'S ALWAYS SOME INTERRUPTION.
WASH WANTS A CHILD, BUT THAT'S AN INTERRUPTION, TOO.
clang
krish clunk bang crack
ONE MORE THING TO BE RESPONSIBLE FOR. TO CARE FOR.
HARD TO BE SOFT WHEN YOUR HANDS WANT TO BE FISTS.
HE DOESN'T UNDERSTAND.
bang
clunk
HISSSSSSSS
DO YOU MIND?
I'M TRYING TO RELAX HERE.
EVEN IN THE MOST RELAXING PLACE IN THE 'VERSE, PEACE CAN NEVER LAST.

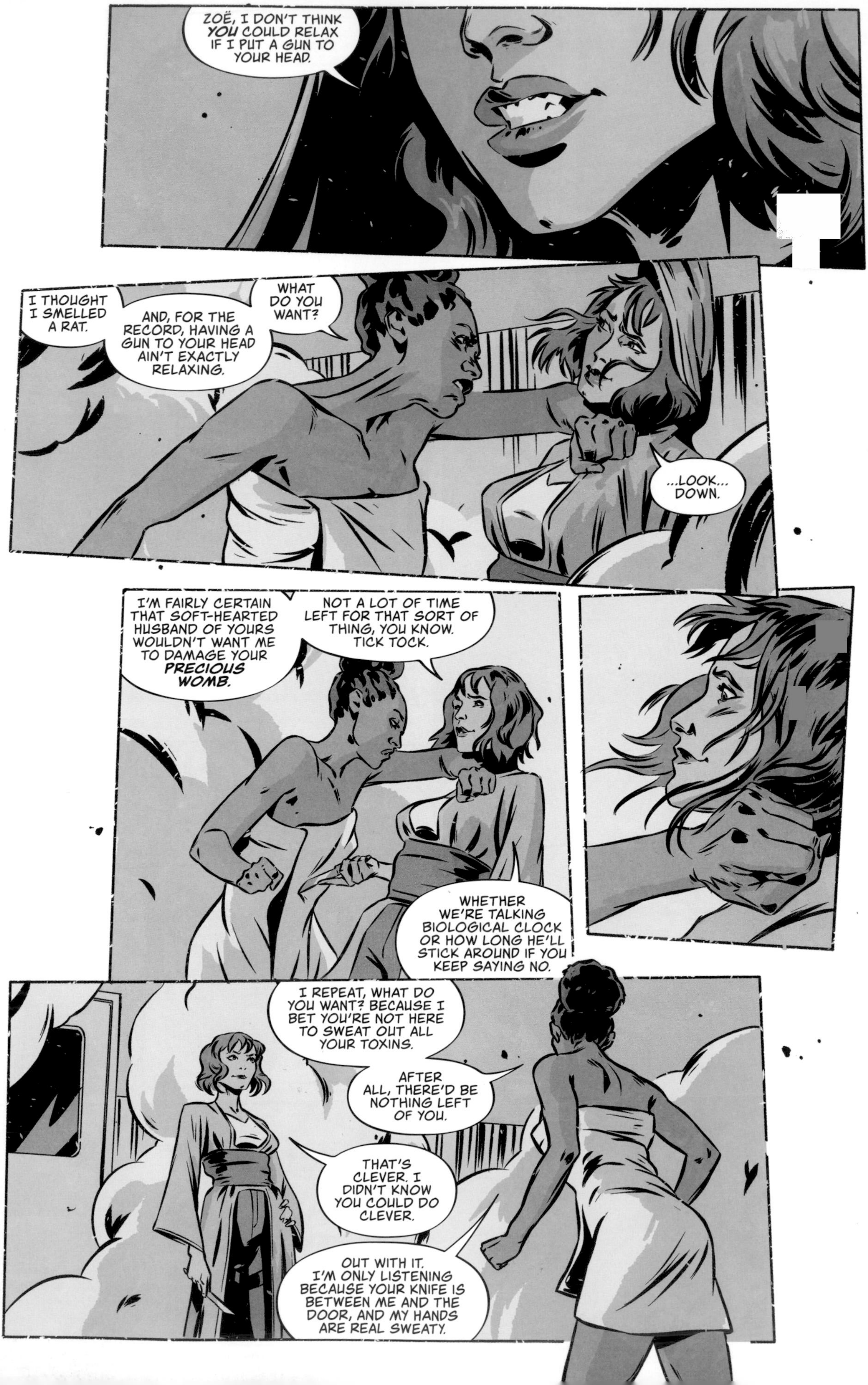
ZOË, I DON'T THINK YOU COULD RELAX IF I PUT A GUN TO YOUR HEAD.
I THOUGHT I SMELLED A RAT.
AND, FOR THE RECORD, HAVING A GUN TO YOUR HEAD AIN'T EXACTLY RELAXING.
WHAT DO YOU WANT?
...LOOK... DOWN.
I'M FAIRLY CERTAIN THAT SOFT-HEARTED HUSBAND OF YOURS WOULDN'T WANT ME TO DAMAGE YOUR PRECIOUS WOMB.
NOT A LOT OF TIME LEFT FOR THAT SORT OF THING, YOU KNOW. TICK TOCK.
WHETHER WE'RE TALKING BIOLOGICAL CLOCK OR HOW LONG HE'LL STICK AROUND IF YOU KEEP SAYING NO.
I REPEAT, WHAT DO YOU WANT? BECAUSE I BET YOU'RE NOT HERE TO SWEAT OUT ALL YOUR TOXINS.
AFTER ALL, THERE'D BE NOTHING LEFT OF YOU.
THAT'S CLEVER. I DIDN'T KNOW YOU COULD DO CLEVER.
OUT WITH IT. I'M ONLY LISTENING BECAUSE YOUR KNIFE IS BETWEEN ME AND THE DOOR, AND MY HANDS ARE REAL SWEATY.

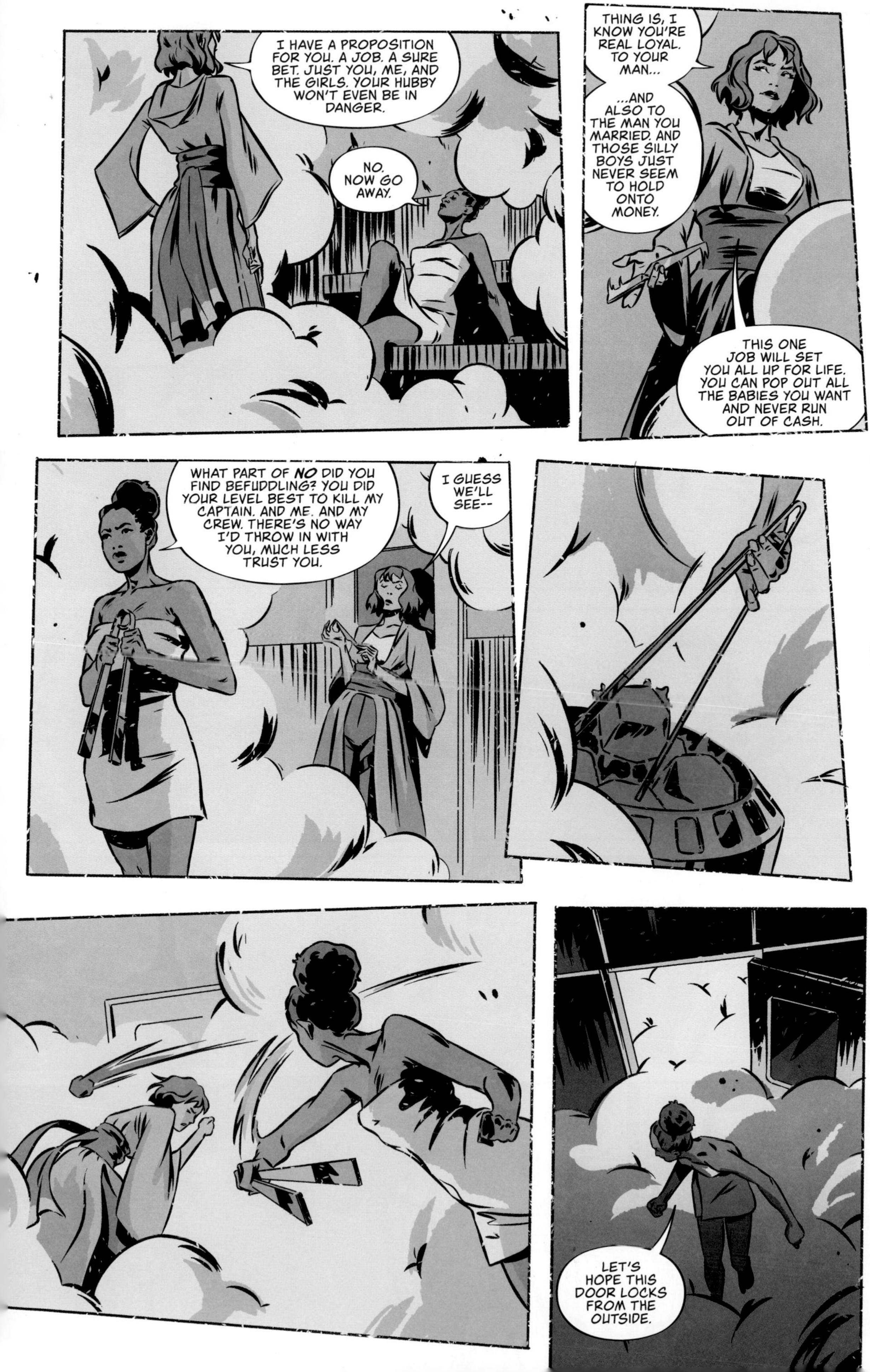
I HAVE A PROPOSITION FOR YOU. A JOB. A SURE BET. JUST YOU, ME, AND THE GIRLS. YOUR HUBBY WON'T EVEN BE IN DANGER.
NO. NOW GO AWAY.
THING IS, I KNOW YOU'RE REAL LOYAL. TO YOUR MAN...
...AND ALSO TO THE MAN YOU MARRIED. AND THOSE SILLY BOYS JUST NEVER SEEM TO HOLD ONTO MONEY.
THIS ONE JOB WILL SET YOU ALL UP FOR LIFE. YOU CAN POP OUT ALL THE BABIES YOU WANT AND NEVER RUN OUT OF CASH.
WHAT PART OF **NO** DID YOU FIND BEFUDDLING? YOU DID YOUR LEVEL BEST TO KILL MY CAPTAIN. AND ME. AND MY CREW. THERE'S NO WAY I'D THROW IN WITH YOU, MUCH LESS TRUST YOU.
I GUESS WE'LL SEE--
LET'S HOPE THIS DOOR LOCKS FROM THE OUTSIDE.

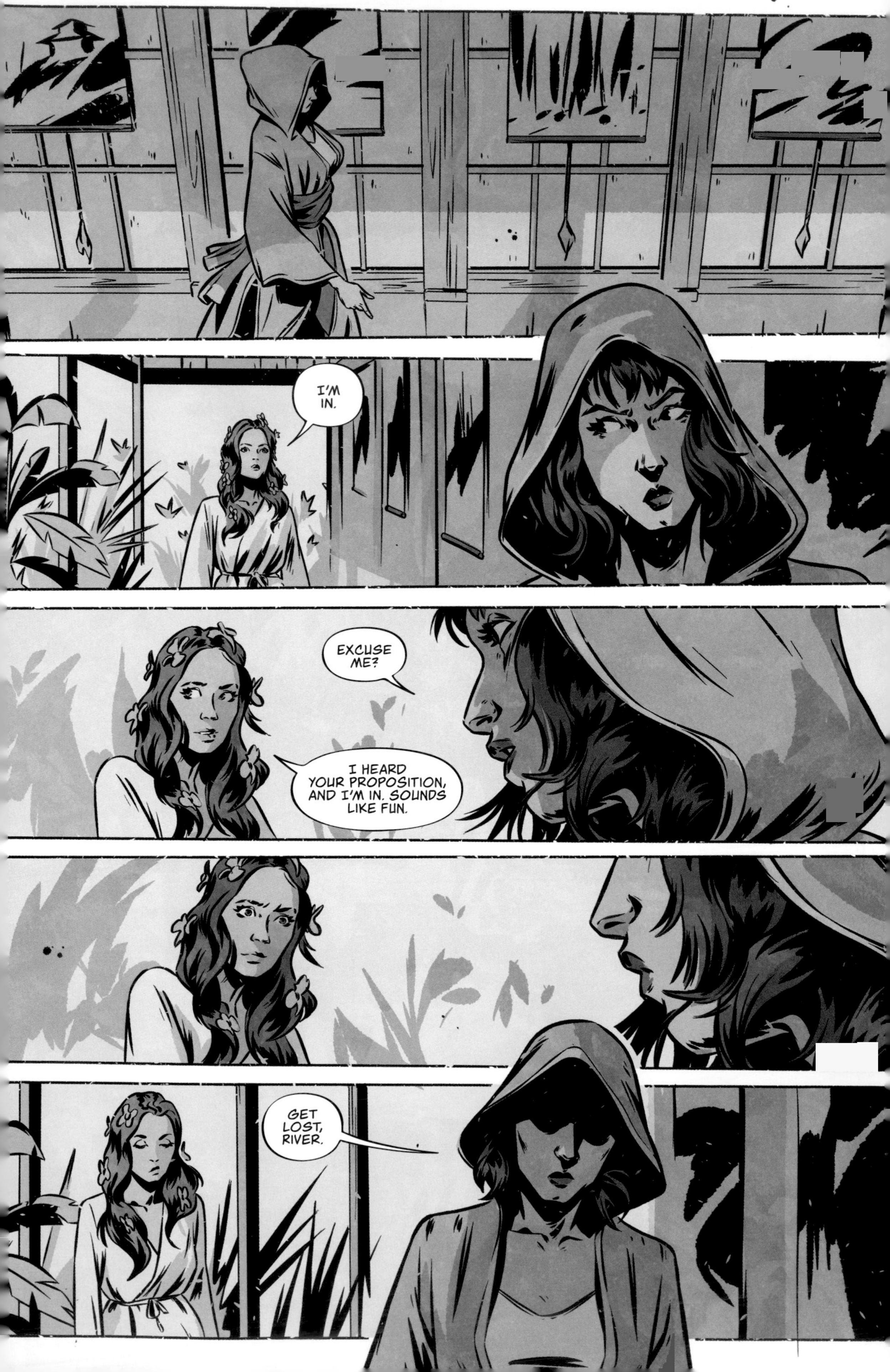
I'M IN.
EXCUSE ME?
I HEARD YOUR PROPOSITION, AND I'M IN. SOUNDS LIKE FUN.
GET LOST, RIVER.

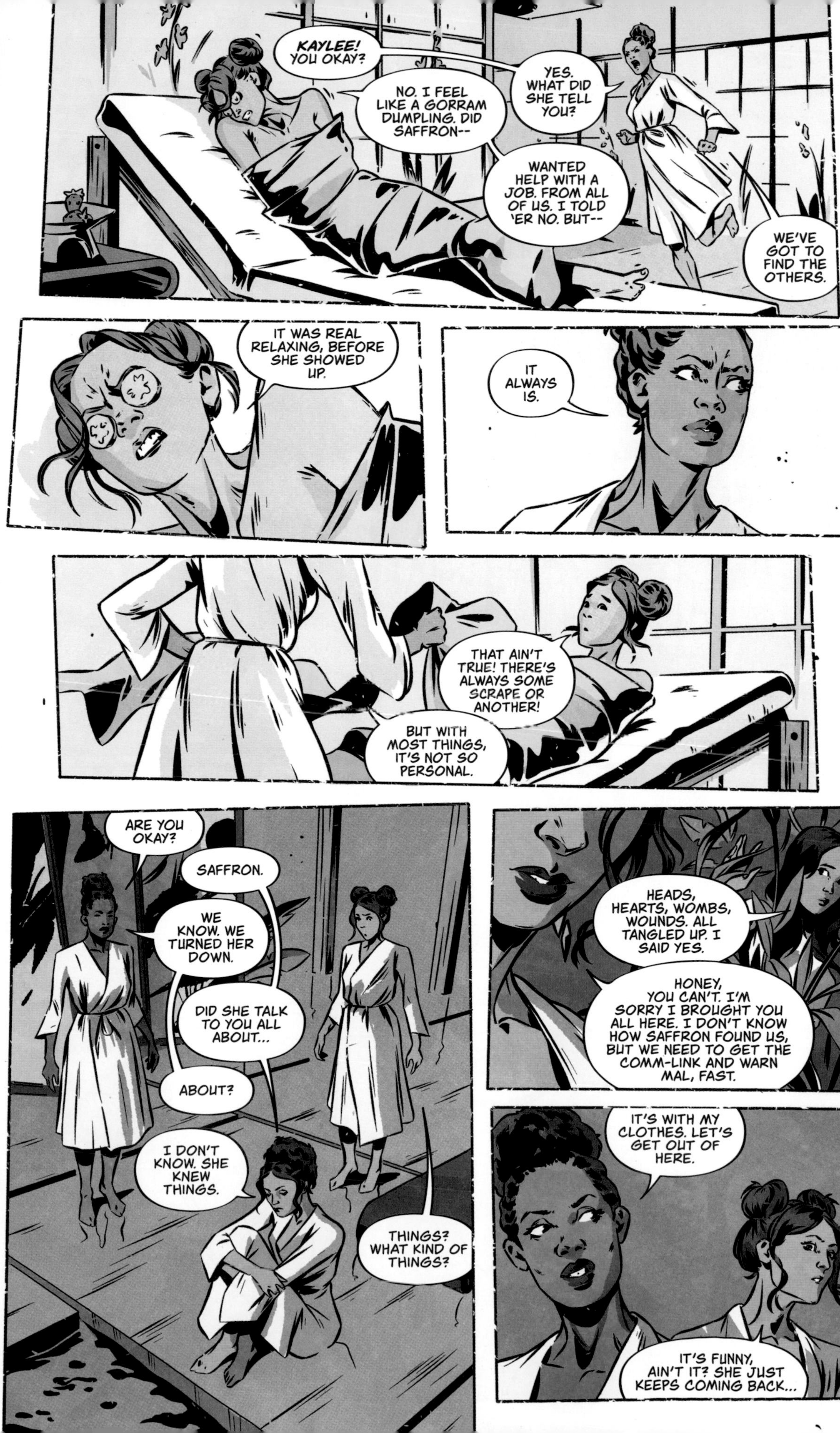
KAYLEE! YOU OKAY?
NO. I FEEL LIKE A GORRAM DUMPLING. DID SAFFRON--
YES. WHAT DID SHE TELL YOU?
WANTED HELP WITH A JOB. FROM ALL OF US. I TOLD 'ER NO. BUT--
WE'VE GOT TO FIND THE OTHERS.
IT WAS REAL RELAXING, BEFORE SHE SHOWED UP.
IT ALWAYS IS.
THAT AIN'T TRUE! THERE'S ALWAYS SOME SCRAPE OR ANOTHER!
BUT WITH MOST THINGS, IT'S NOT SO PERSONAL.
ARE YOU OKAY?
SAFFRON.
WE KNOW. WE TURNED HER DOWN.
DID SHE TALK TO YOU ALL ABOUT...
ABOUT?
I DON'T KNOW. SHE KNEW THINGS.
THINGS? WHAT KIND OF THINGS?
HEADS, HEARTS, WOMBS, WOUNDS. ALL TANGLED UP. I SAID YES.
HONEY, YOU CAN'T. I'M SORRY I BROUGHT YOU ALL HERE. I DON'T KNOW HOW SAFFRON FOUND US, BUT WE NEED TO GET THE COMM-LINK AND WARN MAL, FAST.
IT'S WITH MY CLOTHES. LET'S GET OUT OF HERE.
IT'S FUNNY, AIN'T IT? SHE JUST KEEPS COMING BACK...

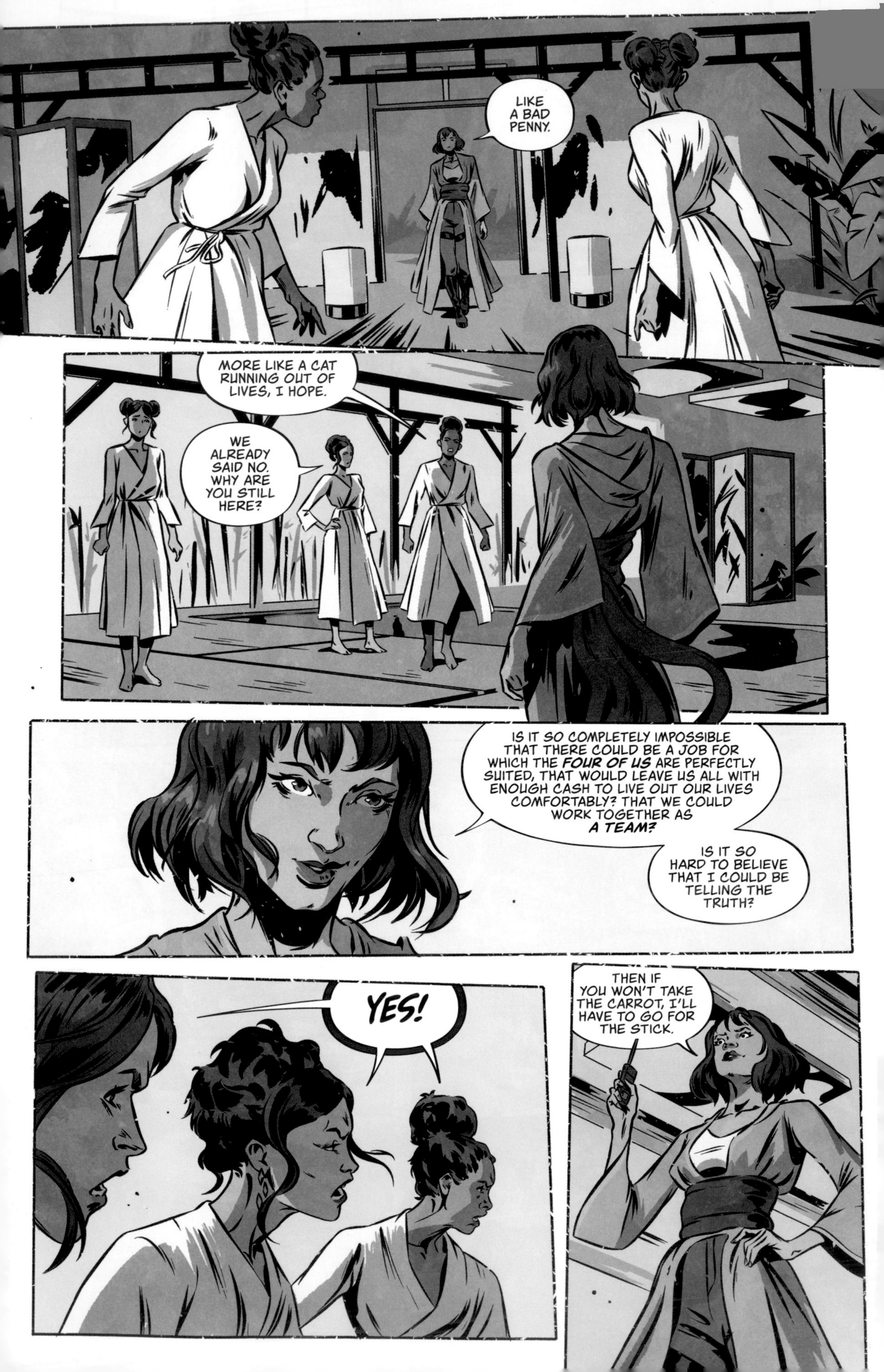
LIKE A BAD PENNY.
MORE LIKE A CAT RUNNING OUT OF LIVES, I HOPE.
WE ALREADY SAID NO. WHY ARE YOU STILL HERE?
IS IT SO COMPLETELY IMPOSSIBLE THAT THERE COULD BE A JOB FOR WHICH THE *FOUR OF US* ARE PERFECTLY SUITED, THAT WOULD LEAVE US ALL WITH ENOUGH CASH TO LIVE OUT OUR LIVES COMFORTABLY? THAT WE COULD WORK TOGETHER AS *A TEAM?*
IS IT SO HARD TO BELIEVE THAT I COULD BE TELLING THE TRUTH?
YES!
THEN IF YOU WON'T TAKE THE CARROT, I'LL HAVE TO GO FOR THE STICK.

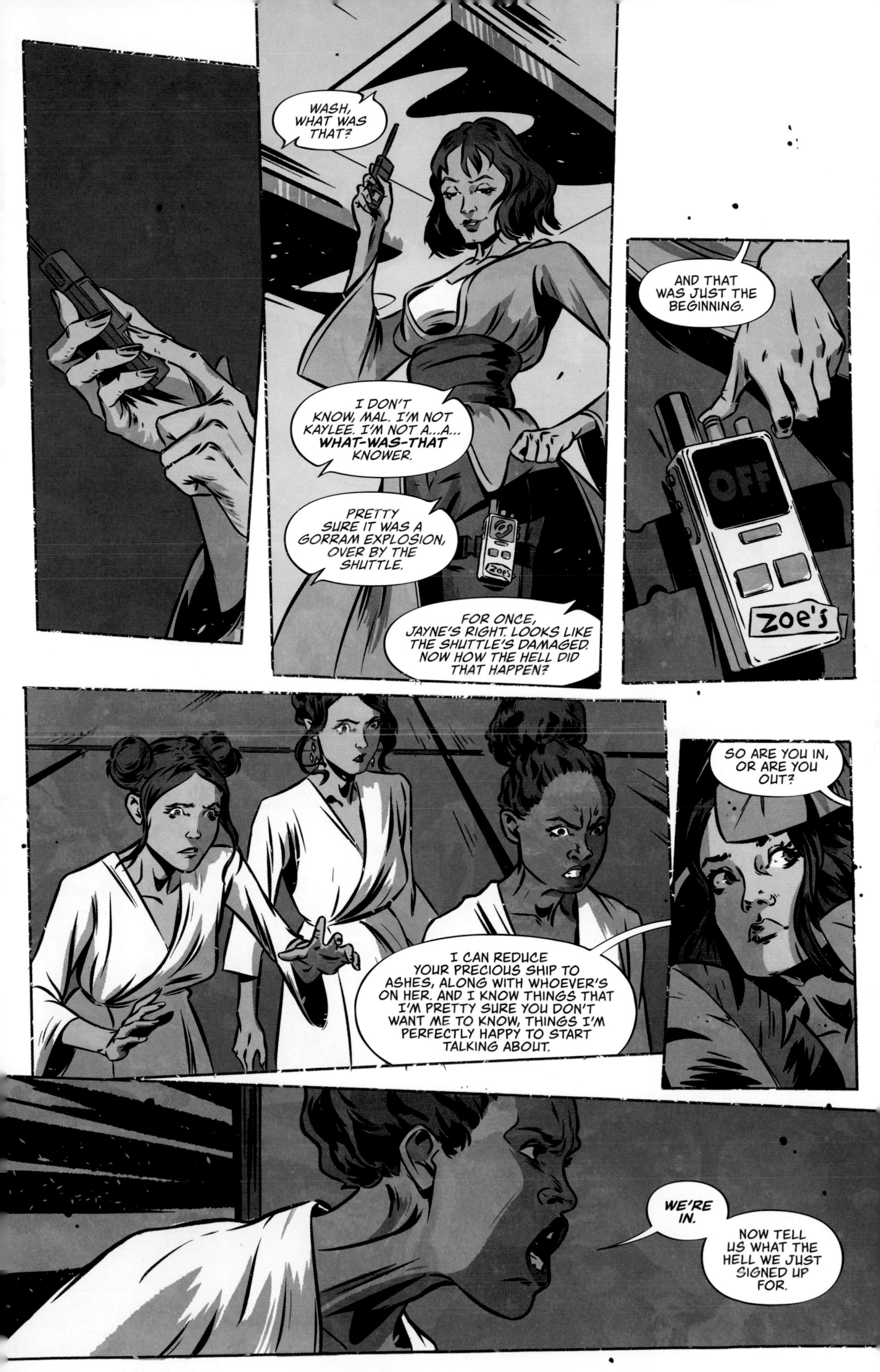
WASH, WHAT WAS THAT?
I DON'T KNOW, MAL. I'M NOT KAYLEE. I'M NOT A...A... **WHAT-WAS-THAT** KNOWER.
PRETTY SURE IT WAS A GORRAM EXPLOSION, OVER BY THE SHUTTLE.
FOR ONCE, JAYNE'S RIGHT. LOOKS LIKE THE SHUTTLE'S DAMAGED. NOW HOW THE HELL DID THAT HAPPEN?
AND THAT WAS JUST THE BEGINNING.
OFF
ZOE'S
SO ARE YOU IN, OR ARE YOU OUT?
I CAN REDUCE YOUR PRECIOUS SHIP TO ASHES, ALONG WITH WHOEVER'S ON HER. AND I KNOW THINGS THAT I'M PRETTY SURE YOU DON'T WANT ME TO KNOW, THINGS I'M PERFECTLY HAPPY TO START TALKING ABOUT.
WE'RE IN.
NOW TELL US WHAT THE HELL WE JUST SIGNED UP FOR.

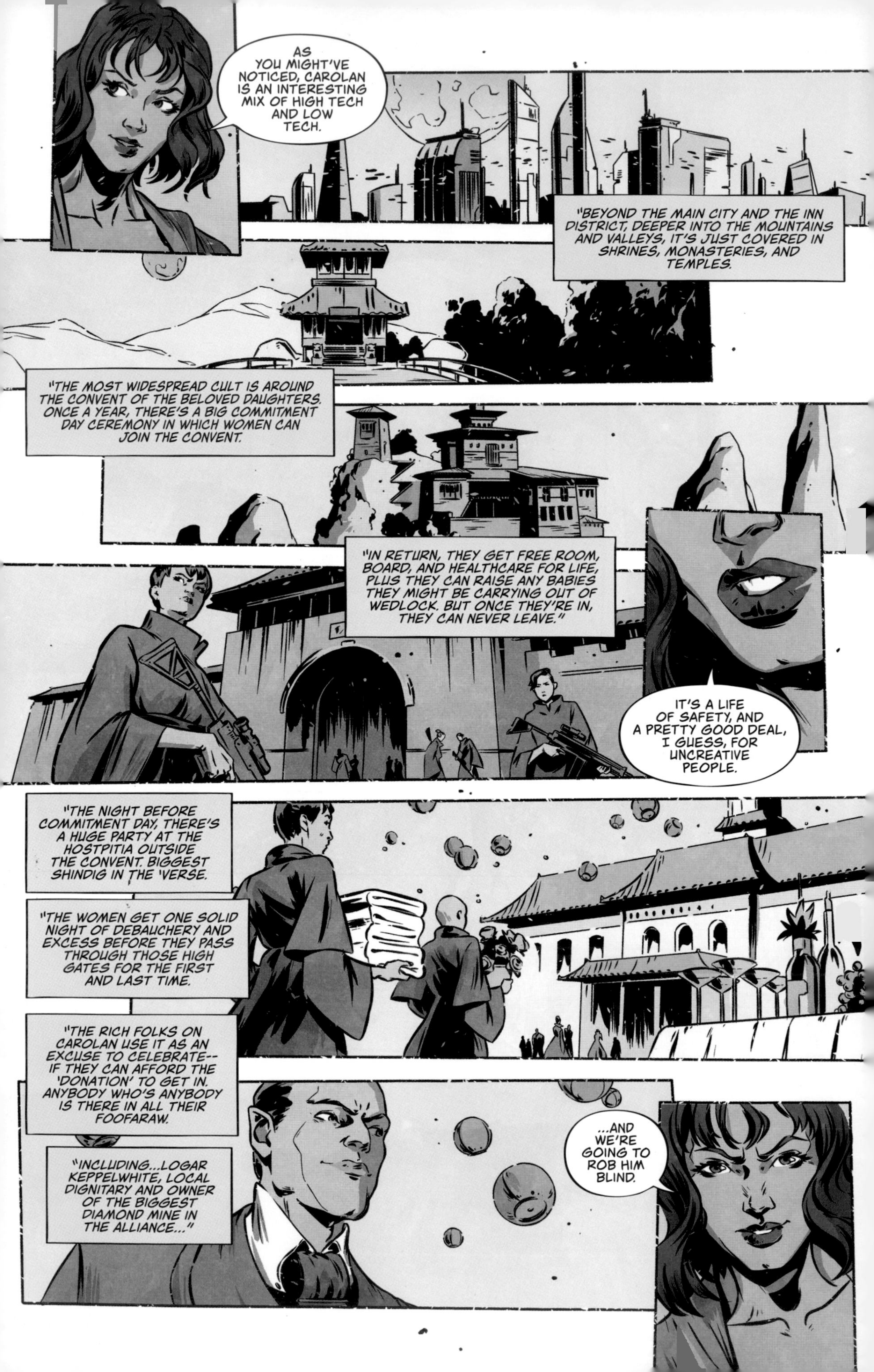

AS YOU MIGHT'VE NOTICED, CAROLAN IS AN INTERESTING MIX OF HIGH TECH AND LOW TECH.
"BEYOND THE MAIN CITY AND THE INN DISTRICT, DEEPER INTO THE MOUNTAINS AND VALLEYS, IT'S JUST COVERED IN SHRINES, MONASTERIES, AND TEMPLES.
"THE MOST WIDESPREAD CULT IS AROUND THE CONVENT OF THE BELOVED DAUGHTERS. ONCE A YEAR, THERE'S A BIG COMMITMENT DAY CEREMONY IN WHICH WOMEN CAN JOIN THE CONVENT.
"IN RETURN, THEY GET FREE ROOM, BOARD, AND HEALTHCARE FOR LIFE, PLUS THEY CAN RAISE ANY BABIES THEY MIGHT BE CARRYING OUT OF WEDLOCK. BUT ONCE THEY'RE IN, THEY CAN NEVER LEAVE."
IT'S A LIFE OF SAFETY, AND A PRETTY GOOD DEAL, I GUESS, FOR UNCREATIVE PEOPLE.
"THE NIGHT BEFORE COMMITMENT DAY, THERE'S A HUGE PARTY AT THE HOSTPITIA OUTSIDE THE CONVENT. BIGGEST SHINDIG IN THE 'VERSE.
"THE WOMEN GET ONE SOLID NIGHT OF DEBAUCHERY AND EXCESS BEFORE THEY PASS THROUGH THOSE HIGH GATES FOR THE FIRST AND LAST TIME.
"THE RICH FOLKS ON CAROLAN USE IT AS AN EXCUSE TO CELEBRATE-- IF THEY CAN AFFORD THE 'DONATION' TO GET IN. ANYBODY WHO'S ANYBODY IS THERE IN ALL THEIR FOOFARAW.
"INCLUDING...LOGAR KEPPELWHITE, LOCAL DIGNITARY AND OWNER OF THE BIGGEST DIAMOND MINE IN THE ALLIANCE..."
...AND WE'RE GOING TO ROB HIM BLIND.

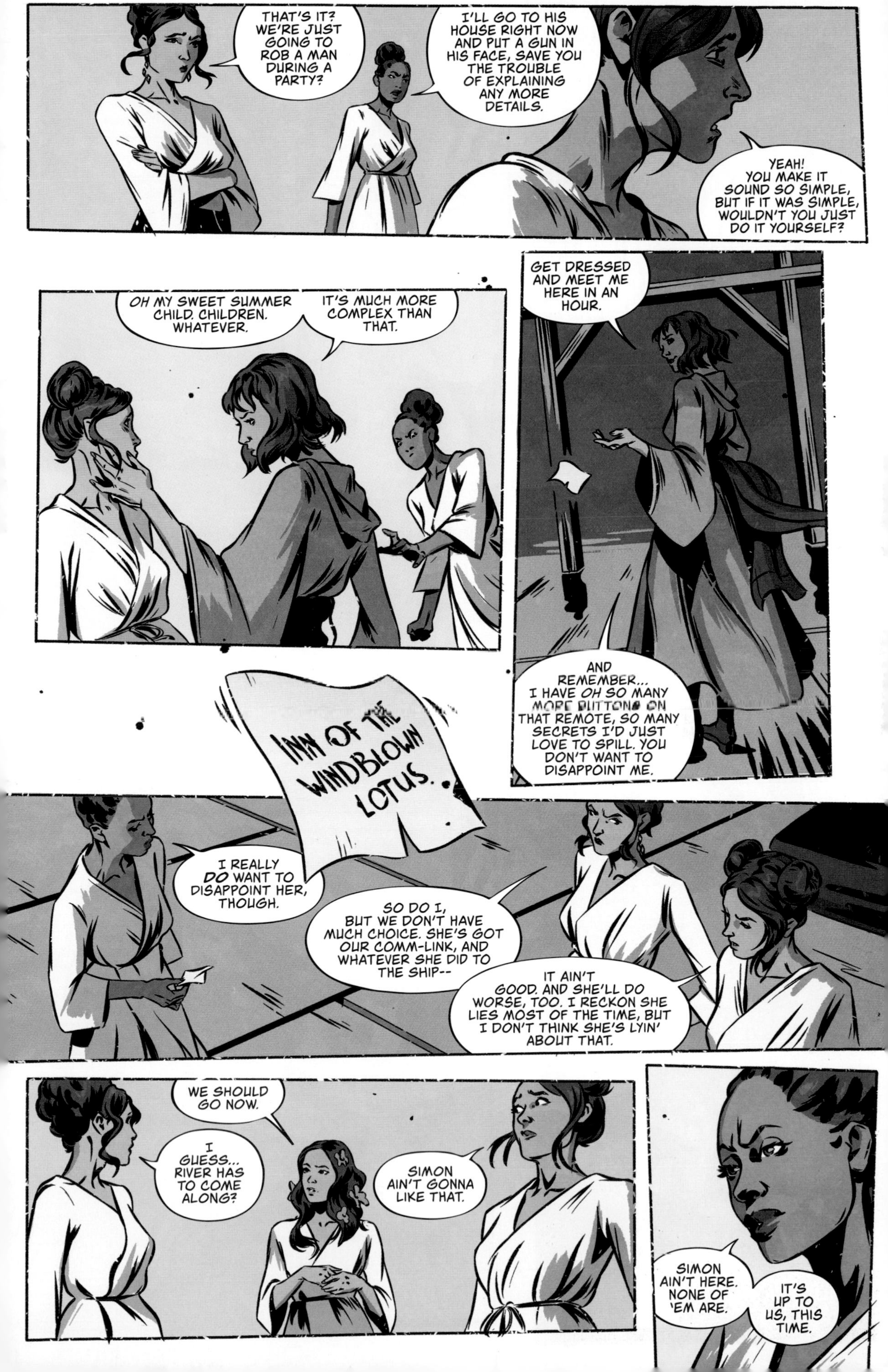

THAT'S IT? WE'RE JUST GOING TO ROB A MAN DURING A PARTY?
I'LL GO TO HIS HOUSE RIGHT NOW AND PUT A GUN IN HIS FACE, SAVE YOU THE TROUBLE OF EXPLAINING ANY MORE DETAILS.
YEAH! YOU MAKE IT SOUND SO SIMPLE, BUT IF IT WAS SIMPLE, WOULDN'T YOU JUST DO IT YOURSELF?
OH MY SWEET SUMMER CHILD. CHILDREN. WHATEVER.
IT'S MUCH MORE COMPLEX THAN THAT.
GET DRESSED AND MEET ME HERE IN AN HOUR.
AND REMEMBER... I HAVE OH SO MANY MORE BUTTONS ON THAT REMOTE, SO MANY SECRETS I'D JUST LOVE TO SPILL. YOU DON'T WANT TO DISAPPOINT ME.
INN OF THE WINDBLOWN LOTUS.
I REALLY DO WANT TO DISAPPOINT HER, THOUGH.
SO DO I, BUT WE DON'T HAVE MUCH CHOICE. SHE'S GOT OUR COMM-LINK, AND WHATEVER SHE DID TO THE SHIP--
IT AIN'T GOOD. AND SHE'LL DO WORSE, TOO. I RECKON SHE LIES MOST OF THE TIME, BUT I DON'T THINK SHE'S LYIN' ABOUT THAT.
WE SHOULD GO NOW.
I GUESS... RIVER HAS TO COME ALONG?
SIMON AIN'T GONNA LIKE THAT.
SIMON AIN'T HERE. NONE OF 'EM ARE.
IT'S UP TO US, THIS TIME.

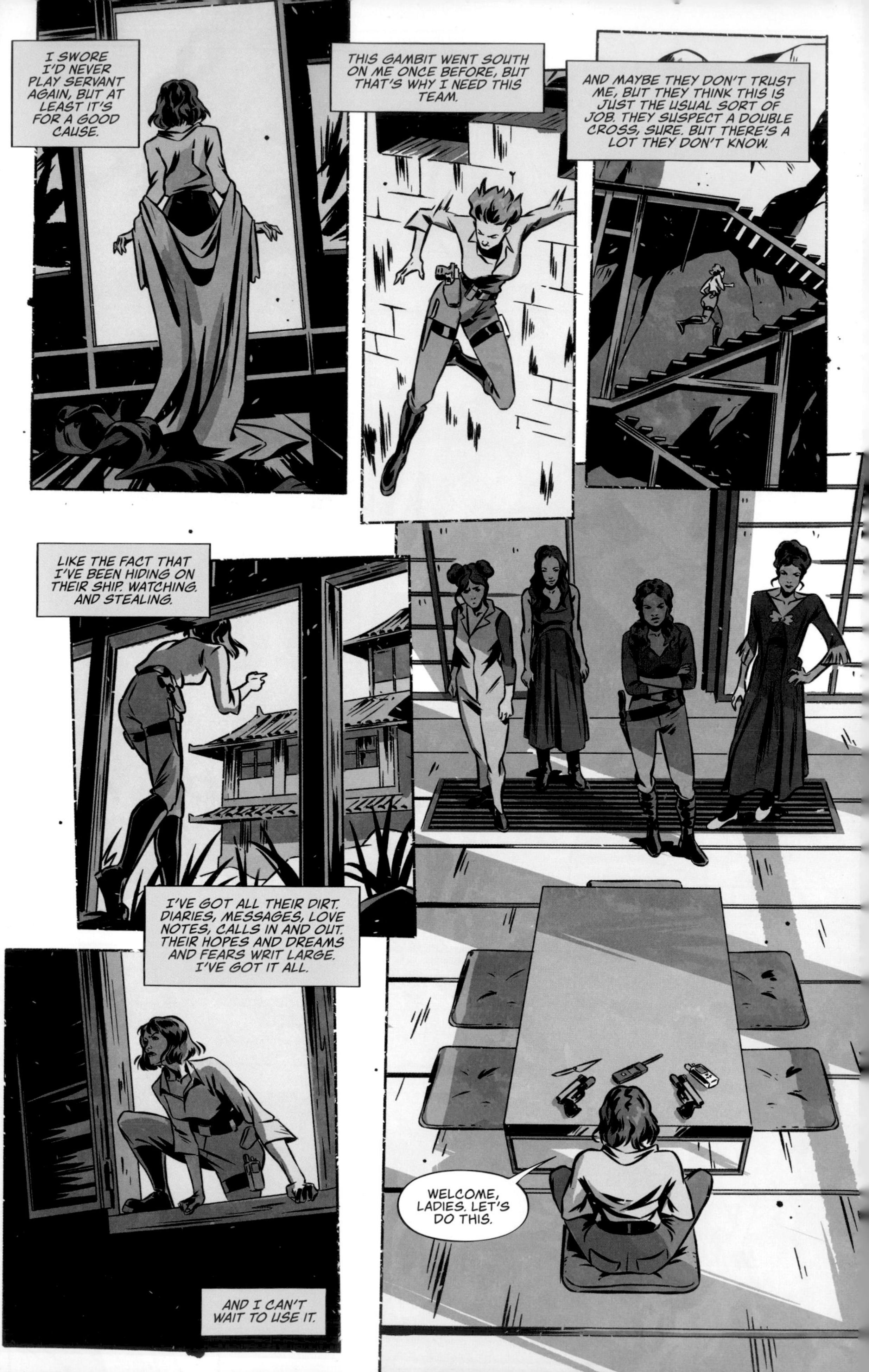

I SWORE I'D NEVER PLAY SERVANT AGAIN, BUT AT LEAST IT'S FOR A GOOD CAUSE.
THIS GAMBIT WENT SOUTH ON ME ONCE BEFORE, BUT THAT'S WHY I NEED THIS TEAM.
AND MAYBE THEY DON'T TRUST ME, BUT THEY THINK THIS IS JUST THE USUAL SORT OF JOB. THEY SUSPECT A DOUBLE CROSS, SURE. BUT THERE'S A LOT THEY DON'T KNOW.
LIKE THE FACT THAT I'VE BEEN HIDING ON THEIR SHIP. WATCHING. AND STEALING.
I'VE GOT ALL THEIR DIRT. DIARIES, MESSAGES, LOVE NOTES, CALLS IN AND OUT. THEIR HOPES AND DREAMS AND FEARS WRIT LARGE. I'VE GOT IT ALL.
AND I CAN'T WAIT TO USE IT.
WELCOME, LADIES. LET'S DO THIS.

FIVE WOMEN. NO MEN.
ONE BIG GORRAM DIAMOND.

CREATED BY **JOSS WHEDON**   WRITTEN BY **DELILAH S. DAWSON**

firefly
STING
the

PIUS BAK

SERG ACUÑA

RICHARD ORTIZ

RODRIGO LORENZO

HYEONJIN KIM

BOOM!

JOSS WHEDON

FIREFLY THE STING

DAWSON · BAK · ACUÑA · ORTIZ · KIM · LORENZO

AVAILABLE IN STORES NOW
Cover by **Marco D'Alfonso**

ABOUT THE AUTHOR

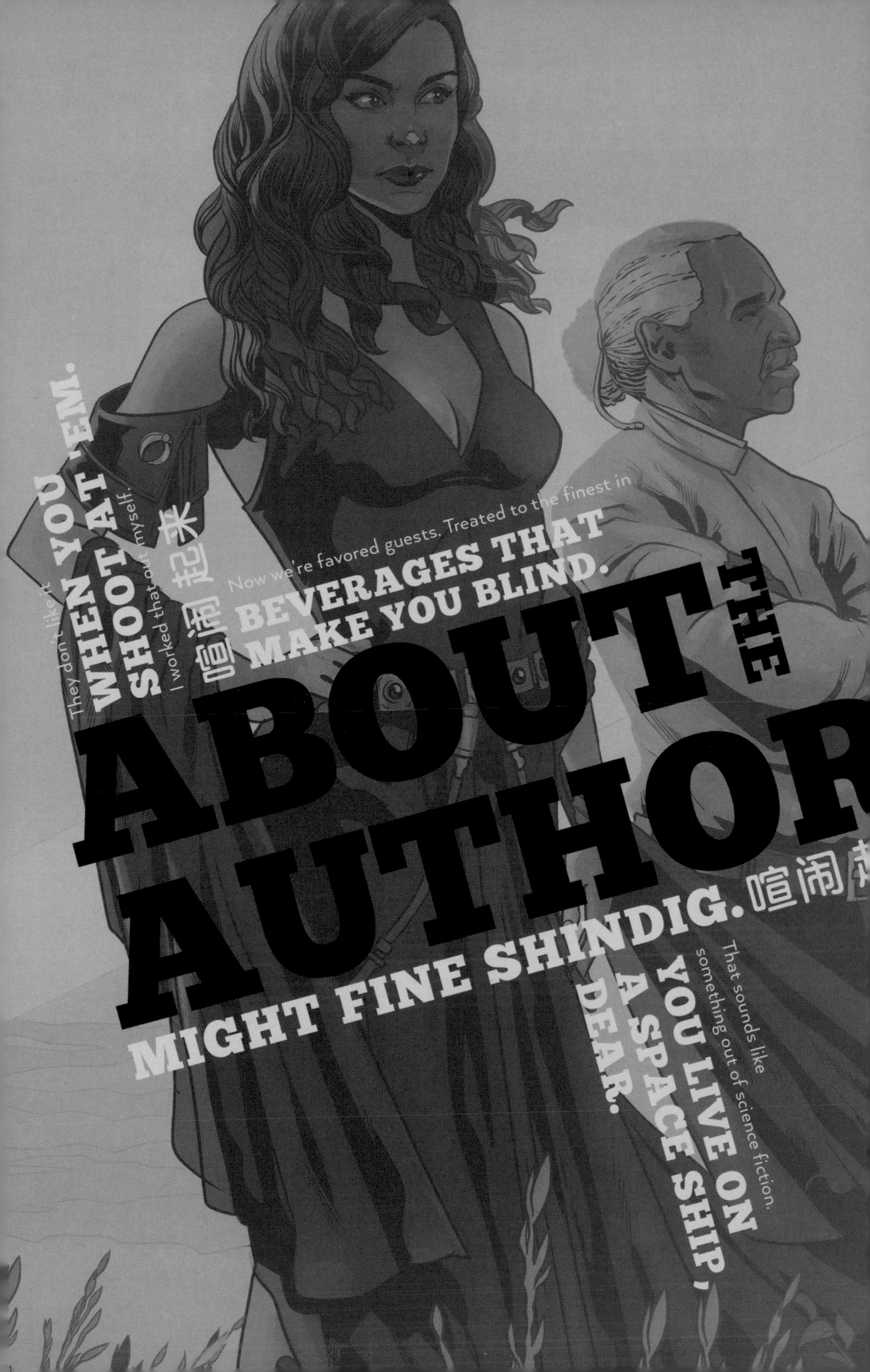
They don't like it
WHEN YOU
SHOOT AT 'EM.
I worked that out myself.
喧闹起来
Now we're favored guests. Treated to the finest in
BEVERAGES THAT
MAKE YOU BLIND.
MIGHT FINE SHINDIG. 喧闹
That sounds like
something out of science fiction.
YOU LIVE ON
A SPACE SHIP,
DEAR.

Joss Whedon is one of Hollywood's top creators, scripting several hit films including Marvel's *The Avengers*, which was a breakout success and became one of the highest grossing films of all time, and its sequel *Avengers: Age of Ultron*, and creating one of television's most critically praised shows, *Buffy the Vampire Slayer*. In 2000, Whedon garnered his first Emmy nomination in the category of Outstanding Writing for a Drama Series for his groundbreaking episode entitled "Hush," and he earned an Academy Award nomination for Best Screenplay with Disney's box-office smash *Toy Story*. Originally hailing from New York, Whedon is a third-generation television writer. His grandfather and father were both successful sitcom writers on shows such as *The Donna Reed Show*, *Leave It to Beaver* and *The Golden Girls*.

Greg Pak is a Korean American filmmaker and comic book writer best known for his award-winning feature film *Robot Stories*, his blockbuster comic book series like Marvel Comics' *Planet Hulk* and *World War Hulk*, and his record-breaking Kickstarter publishing projects with Jonathan Coulton, *Code Monkey Save World* and *The Princess Who Saved Herself*. His other projects at BOOM! Studios include the award-winning creator-owned *Mech Cadet Yu* and *Ronin Island*.

Dan McDaid is a British comics artist and writer with a lustrous head of black hair and a full, healthy beard. After breaking into comics with the UK's *Doctor Who Magazine*, he went on to co-create *Jersey Gods* for Image Comics and *Time Share* for Oni Press, as well as drawing cult favorites *Big Trouble in Little China* and *Dawn of the Planet of the Apes*. Following a well-regarded run on IDW's *Judge Dredd*, he launched his own webcomic, *DEGA*, and is currently drawing the new adventures of the Serenity crew in BOOM! Studios' *Firefly*. He lives in Scotland with his partner Deborah and a large gray cat whose name means "Dark Stranger".

Vincenzo Federici is an Italian comic book artist from Naples. After his Classical Arts studies, he started to work in comics for French publishers, like Soleil Éditions and on a creator owned project for the Italian publisher Noise Press, called *The Kabuki Fight*. He then moved to American publishers, working with IDW Publishing, Zenescope Entertainment, Dynamite Entertainment, BOOM! Studios and more, on series like *Army of Darkness/Bubba Ho-Tep*, *M. A. S. K.*, *Star Trek*, *Firefly*, *Go Go Power Rangers* and more. He also is a teacher in different Italian Comic Art schools.

Marcelo Costa is a comics artist and colorist. As a colorist, he's best known for his work on *Power Rangers: Shattered Grid* and *Power Rangers: Soul of the Dragon*, and *Planet of the Apes Visionaries*. As an artist, he's worked on Zenoscope's *Grimm Fairy Tales*, Action Lab's *Season 3*, and the episode "Star Trip", from the Society of Virtue YouTube Channel. Currently, Marcelo is also working on *Self/Made* and *Teenage Mutant Ninja Turtles: Shredder in Hell*, in a partnership with Matheus Santolouco.

Joana Lafuente is a self-taught illustrator that has a Master's degree in computer engineering, but gave up on programming to follow her dream as an artist as soon as she could. She has been mostly working in comics, but not exclusively, having also worked for game and advertising companies.

Jim Campbell has been lettering comics professionally for almost a decade, before which he worked in newspaper and magazine publishing for even longer. He knows more about print production than mortal man was meant to know and has also scanned more images than you've had hot dinners. Unless you're ninety years old. If you're very unlucky, he might start talking to you about ligatures.

CAN'T STOP THE SIGNAL...

FIREFLY

LEGACY EDITION BOOK ONE

"...has everything *Firefly* fans would expect from the House of Whedon.

—AIN'T IT COOL NEWS"

Legacy Edition Book One Cover by
Nimit Malavia

BOOK ONE COLLECTS

Serenity Volume 1: Those Left Behind
Serenity Volume 2: Better Days
Serenity: The Shepherd's Tale OGN

From Joss Whedon (creator of *Buffy the Vampire Slayer*), Serenity rides again, in these official sequels to the critically acclaimed show *Firefly*, collected for the first time under one cover!

Featuring stories by Joss Whedon, Emmy Award-winning comedian Patton Oswalt, and Eisner Award-winning artist Chris Samnee, buried histories and secret identities are revealed, along with all the heist-takin', authority-dodgin', death-defyin' space-cowboyin' you've been missing from your life, as this ragtag crew of mercenaries, outlaws, and fugitives travel the stars in search of their next adventure.

Legacy Editions collect every issue of the most popular BOOM! Studios series in chronological order and in a newly designed, value priced format for the very first time.

AVAILABLE IN STORES NOW

BOOK TWO ALSO AVAILABLE NOW

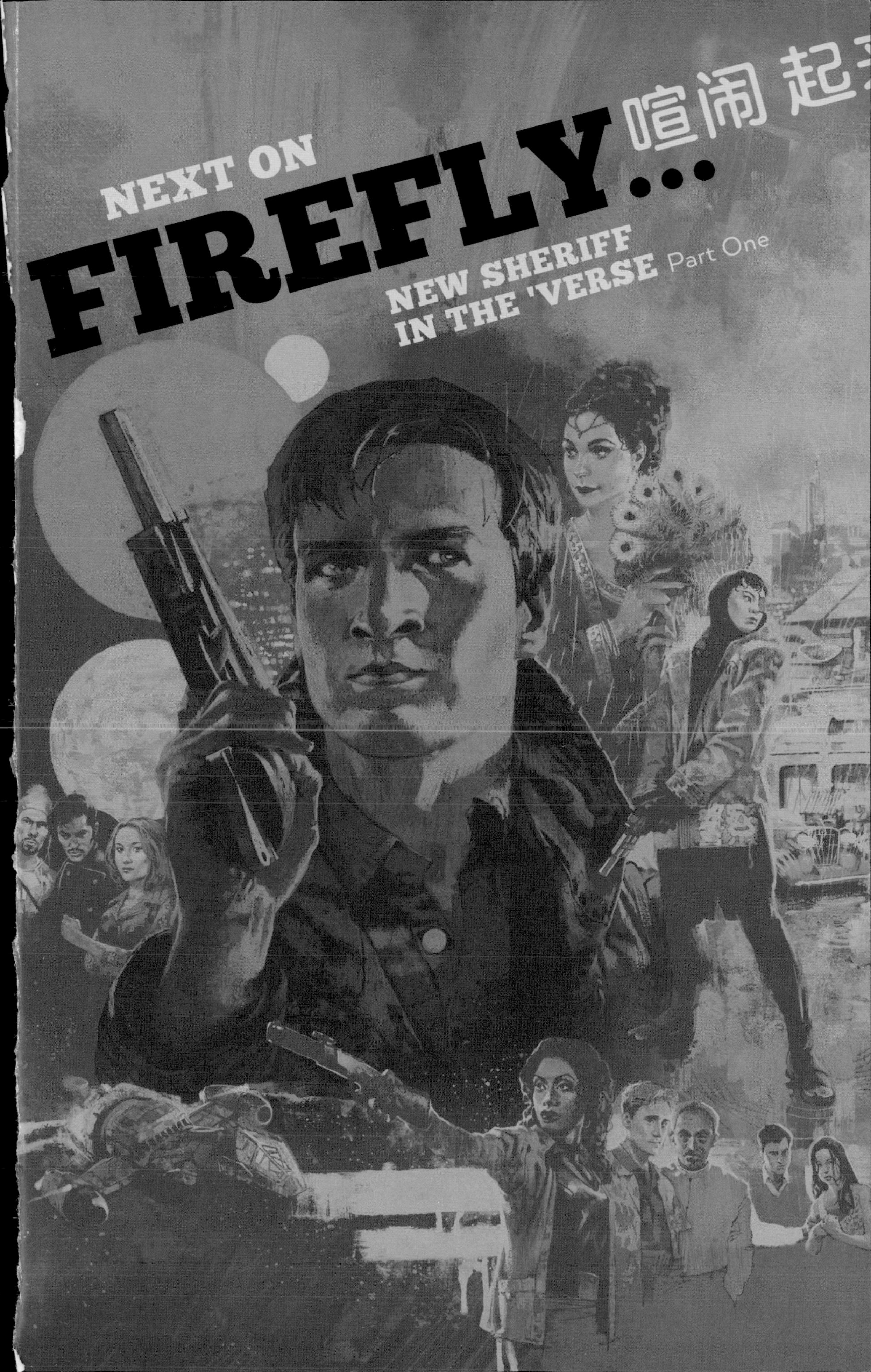
NEXT ON
FIREFLY...
喧闹起来
NEW SHERIFF
IN THE 'VERSE Part One

DISCOVER
VISIONARY CREATORS

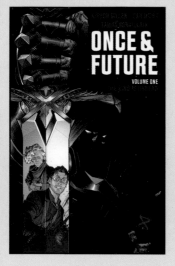

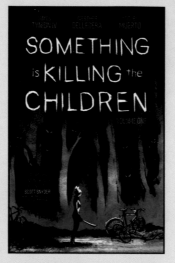

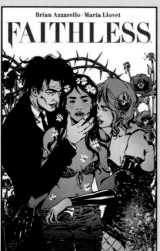

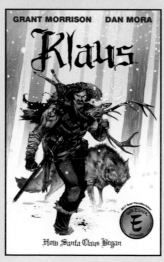

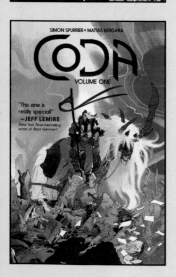

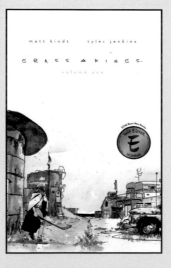

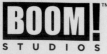

ONCE &
FUTURE
VOLUME ONE

SOMETHING is KILLING the CHILDREN

Brian Azzarello · Maria Llovet
FAITHLESS

GRANT MORRISON DAN MORA
Klaus
How Santa Claus Began

SIMON SPURRIER × MATÍAS BERGARA
CODA
VOLUME ONE
"This one is really special!" —JEFF LEMIRE
New York Times bestselling writer of Black Hammer

matt kindt tyler jenkins
GRASS KINGS

AVAILABLE AT YOUR LOCAL COMICS SHOP AND BOOKSTORE

To find a comics shop in your area, visit www.comicshoplocator.com

WWW.**BOOM-STUDIOS**.COM

Once & Future
Kieron Gillen, Dan Mora
Volume 1
ISBN: 978-1-68415-491-3 | $16.99 US

Something is Killing the Children
James Tynion IV, Werther Dell'Edera
Volume 1
ISBN: 978-1-68415-558-3 | $14.99 US

Faithless
Brian Azzarello, Maria Llovet
ISBN: 978-1-68415-432-6 | $17.99 US

Klaus
Grant Morrison, Dan Mora
Klaus: How Santa Claus Began SC
ISBN: 978-1-68415-393-0 | $15.99 US
Klaus: The New Adventures of Santa Claus HC
ISBN: 978-1-68415-666-5 | $17.99 US

Coda
Simon Spurrier, Matias Bergara
Volume 1
ISBN: 978-1-68415-321-3 | $14.99 US
Volume 2
ISBN: 978-1-68415-369-5 | $14.99 US
Volume 3
ISBN: 978-1-68415-429-6 | $14.99 US

Grass Kings
Matt Kindt, Tyler Jenkins
Volume 1
ISBN: 978-1-64144-362-3 | $17.99 US
Volume 2
ISBN: 978-1-64144-557-3 | $17.99 US
Volume 3
ISBN: 978-1-64144-650-1 | $17.99 US

Bone Parish
Cullen Bunn, Jonas Scharf
Volume 1
ISBN: 978-1-64144-337-1 | $14.99 US
Volume 2
ISBN: 978-1-64144-542-9 | $14.99 US
Volume 3
ISBN: 978-1-64144-543-6 | $14.99 US

Ronin Island
Greg Pak, Giannis Milonogiannis
Volume 1
ISBN: 978-1-64144-576-4 | $14.99 US
Volume 2
ISBN: 978-1-64144-723-2 | $14.99 US
Volume 3
ISBN: 978-1-64668-035-1 | $14.99 US

Victor LaValle's Destroyer
Victor LaValle, Dietrich Smith
ISBN: 978-1-61398-732-2 | $19.99 US